Studies in Autobiography

Studies
in Autobiography

Edited by
JAMES OLNEY

New York   Oxford
OXFORD UNIVERSITY PRESS
1988

Oxford University Press

Oxford   New York   Toronto
Dellhi   Bombay   Calcutta   Madras   Karachi
Petaling Jaya   Singapore   Hong Kong   Tokyo
Nairobi   Dar es Salaam   Cape Town
Melbourne   Auckland

and associated companies in
Berlin   Ibadan

Library of Congress Cataloging-in-Publication Data
Studies in autobiography/edited by James Olney.
p.   cm.
Essays from the International Symposium on Autobiography and
Autobiography Studies, held at Louisiana State University in Mar.
1985.
Includes index.
ISBN 0–19–505131–9
1. American prose literature—History and criticism—Congresses.
2. Autobiography—Congresses.   3. English prose literature—History
and criticism—Congresses.   I. Olney, James.   II. International
Symposium on Autobiography and Autobiography Studies (1985:
Louisiana State University)
PS366.A88S84 1988
809–dc19   87–35010
                                                           CIP

24.95

2 4 6 8 9 7 5 3 1

Printed in the United States of America
on acid-free paper

Acknowledgments

Thanks are due the following for the parts they played in the International Symposium on Autobiography and Autobiography Studies and in publication of the present volume:

The National Endowment for the Humanities, the Exxon Education Foundation, and the LSU College of Arts and Sciences and Department of English for sponsorship and funding.

LSU Graduate Students in English: Lucinda Cole and J. T. Ellenberger, who initiated the idea of the symposium; Calvin Thomas, who assisted with submissions; Donna Perreault, who helped prepare papers for publication and compiled the index; and, most particularly, Martha Regalis, who assisted with submissions, corresponded with participants, and coordinated the entire symposium and all of its various activities from beginning to end.

Lewis P. Simpson, Daniel Littlefield, J. Gerald Kennedy, Jefferson Humphries, and Adelaide Russo, all of the LSU faculty, who chaired the different sessions of the symposium.

Alfred Hornung, of the University of Würzburg, Lucinda MacKethan, of North Carolina State University, Frederick Keener, of Hofstra University, and John Halperin, of Vanderbilt University, who responded to papers at the four daytime sessions.

Marion Osmun and Mimi Melek, who guided the manuscript through the editorial process at Oxford University Press, and Sarah S. East, who read proofs.

Baton Rouge, La.   J.O.
October 1987

Contents

AUTOBIOGRAPHY AS CULTURAL EXPRESSION

WOMEN'S AUTOBIOGRAPHY

Contributors

William L. Andrews is Professor of English at the University of Wisconsin-Madison. He is the author of *To Tell a Free Story: The First Century of Afro-American Autobiography, 1760–1865* (1986), as well as the editor of *Sisters of the Spirit: Three Black Women's Autobiographies of the Nineteenth Century* (1986) and Frederick Douglass's *My Bondage and My Freedom* (1987). He is also the general editor of a series of books on American autobiography published by the University of Wisconsin Press.

Germaine Brʹ the *doyenne* of French letters in America, was born in France and has li . in the United States since 1931. She has taught at Bryn Mawr, New York University, and the University of Wisconsin and is Kenan Professor Emeritus in the Humanities, Department of Romance Languages, at Wake Forest University. She is a past president of the Modern Language Association and is the author of numerous books, including *Albert Camus, The World of Marcel Proust, Marcel Proust and Deliverance from Time, Camus and Sartre, Women Writers in France*, and *Twentieth-Century French Literature*.

Suzanne L. Bunkers is Professor of English at Mankato State University, Mankato, Minnesota. She has received fellowships from the National Endowment for the Humanities, the Fulbright Commission, and the American Council of Learned Societies. Her publications include many articles on women's autobiography, Midwestern authors, and women's humor. Her edition of *The Civil War Diary of Caroline Seabury* is forthcoming from the University of Wisconsin Press. At present she is completing a book-length critical study of the diaries and journals of nineteenth-century Midwestern American women.

G. Thomas Couser, Associate Professor of English at Hofstra University, is the author of *American Autobiography: The Prophetic Mode* (University of Massachusetts Press, 1979).

James M. Cox, Professor of English at Dartmouth, is the author of *Mark Twain: The Fate of Humor* (Princeton, 1966). A collection of his essays on American autobiography entitled *Recovering Literature's Lost Ground* will be published by the Louisiana State University Press.

Paul John Eakin's most recent book is *Fictions in Autobiography: Studies in the Art of Self-Invention* (1985). He has just completed an edition of the essays of Philippe Lejeune, *On Autobiography*, which is to be published by the University of Minnesota Press, and he is now at work on a new book on autobiography as a referential art.

Wallace Fowlie is James B. Duke Professor of Romance Languages at Duke University. Although he retired in 1978, he still teaches three of his favorite courses at Duke: Dante, Proust, and the French symbolist poets. His most recent books, published by Duke University Press, are three volumes of autobiography: *Journal of Rehearsals*, *Aubade: A Teacher's Notebook*, and *Sites: A Third Memoir*.

Henry Louis Gates, Jr., Professor of English, Africana Studies, and Comparative Literature at Cornell University, is the author of *Figures in Black* and *The Signifying Monkey*, and the editor of *The Slave's Narrative* and *In the House of Osugbo*, all published by Oxford University Press. He is also General Editor of Oxford's 1988 set, The Schomburg Library of Nineteenth-Century Black Women Writers.

Georges Gusdorf, Professor Emeritus of Philosophy at the University of Strasbourg, has published twelve volumes of *Les Sciences humaines et la pensée Occidentale*, a project of more than twenty years' duration. His essay in this collection is a translation of a portion of *Ecritures du Moi*, and a new book on autobiography, *Auto-Bio-Graphie*, is forthcoming.

Geoffrey Galt Harpham has written numerous articles on modern fiction and literary theory and is the author of *On the Grotesque: Strategies of Contradiction in Art and Literature* and *The Ascetic Imperative in Culture and Criticism*. He teaches in the English Department at Tulane University.

Ira B. Nadel, Professor of English, University of British Columbia, has published *Biography: Fiction, Fact & Form* (1984), as well as essays on nineteenth-century fiction and nonfiction. His study, *Joyce and the Jews: Culture and Texts*, will appear in 1988.

Felicity A. Nussbaum, Professor of English at Syracuse University, recently held a Rockefeller Humanist-in-Residence Fellowship at the Institute for Research on Women at Rutgers University to complete a forthcoming book on eighteenth-century autobiography, gender, and ideology. She is also the author of *The Brink of All We Hate: English Satires on Women, 1660–1750* and coeditor (with Laura Brown) of *The New Eighteenth Century: Theory/Politics/English Literature* (Methuen, 1987).

James Olney, Voorhies Professor of English and French and Italian at Louisiana State University, has published numerous books and essays on autobiography.

Metaphors of Self: The Meaning of Autobiography and *Tell Me Africa: An Approach to African Literature*, both from Princeton University Press, are his major books on the subject. He also edited *Autobiography: Essays Theoretical and Critical* (Princeton, 1980) and is currently editor of *The Southern Review*.

Linda H. Peterson is Associate Professor of English and Director of the Bass Writing Program at Yale. Her recent book, *Victorian Autobiography: The Tradition of Self-Interpretation* (1986), traces the development of the spiritual autobiography from Bunyan's *Grace Abounding* through the major nineteenth-century exemplars of the genre: Carlyle, Ruskin, Newman, Martineau, and Gosse. Her current work-in-progress, *Reclaiming the Genre*, focuses on Victorian women's forms of self-writing.

Charles J. Rzepka specializes in English Romanticism, with particular emphasis on the problem of personal identity and on the psychological and phenomenological theories of self-representation and individuation. He is the author of numerous articles on the English romantic poets and of a recent book, *The Self as Mind*, a study of disembodiment and encounter in the work of Wordsworth, Coleridge, and Keats. Professor Rzepka currently teaches at Boston University.

John Sekora is Professor of English at North Carolina Central University. He has written *Luxury* (1978), edited *The Art of Slave Narrative* (1983), and is completing a book on the genre of the slave narrative. He has written about thirty articles on Afro-American literature, most of them on nineteenth-century writers. He has received grants from Fulbright, the National Endowment for the Humanities, and the National Humanities Center.

Thomas R. Smith has taught at Rutgers University and the University of Georgia and is currently Assistant Professor at Pennsylvania State University, Schuylkill Campus. He has written on autobiography in *The Hudson Review*, *The Southern Review*, and *A/B: Auto/biography Studies*. He is completing a study of late nineteenth- and early twentieth-century English literary autobiography.

Julia Watson is interested in the theory and practice of women's autobiography. She has organized several conference sessions on the topic and given papers on aspects of women's autobiographical practice. Her current project is an edited collection of essays on nontraditional women's autobiography. She has also written on self-reflection in Montaigne's *Essais*, in Rilke, and in New German film, and has published translations from German literature. She is presently an Associate Professor of English at Elizabethtown College.

Introduction

James Olney

This volume of essays on autobiography and the literary study of autobiography is one outcome (there were others, such as the founding of the journal *A/B*) of a conference convened at Louisiana State University in March 1985 under the rubric "International Symposium on Autobiography and Autobiography Studies." That symposium, generously supported by the National Endowment for the Humanities, the Exxon Education Foundation, and the LSU College of Arts and Sciences and Department of English, was very successful and was particularly distinguished by its spirit of cooperative collegiality and an atmosphere of eager participation in advancing autobiography studies. The gathering in Baton Rouge came at a time when there seemed both the need and an opportunity to survey the work on autobiography produced in recent years, to take stock of what had been done and was being done, and to consider directions that such work might profitably take in the future. The moment was propitious and the participants, both those who gave formal papers and those who came to join in the discussions, were more than equal to the occasion.

The moment was propitious. . . . To have proposed a national or international symposium on autobiography and the state of autobiography studies twenty-five or thirty years earlier would have made very little sense and would have been virtually impossible to justify or bring to a successful conclusion; to propose such a symposium in 1985, however, was merely to recognize the thoroughgoing changes that have occurred in our understanding both of the autobiographical act and of the place of autobiography in newly designed, differently oriented university curricula. Prior to the mid-1950s autobiography was seen as little more than a special variety of biography and as a kind of stepchild of history and literature, with neither of those disciplines granting it full recognition as a respectable subject for study in itself. Likewise, other disciplines—psychology, anthropology, sociology, and religion, for example—made their own uses of autobiography but always as an ancillary matter, a kind of service literature, never taking it as a mode of writing with an interest of its own and demanding the sort of philosophical, rhetorical, and linguistic scrutiny that would be given to any other variety of literature. This situation has been radically altered: Autobiography's time has come and with it, in 1985, had come the proper moment for a symposium and now the proper moment for publication of the proceedings of that symposium.

There are no doubt a number of reasons why autobiography suffered critical neglect for so long until the recent change in its fortunes, but without question the primary reason that this state of affairs has been so dramatically altered and that autobiography has received so much attention in the past few years is that literary historians and theorists have come to see autobiography as a distinct and distinguishable mode of literature with all sorts of complex ties to other, more traditional literary genres and with much to teach theorists concerned with both literary genres and literary history. The vastly increased interest in autobiography as a matter for literary scrutiny can be most conveniently seen in two bibliographical studies published at the beginning of this decade: the twenty-five page introductory essay, supplemented by an actual bibliography of ten pages, "Autobiography and the Cultural Moment: A Thematic, Historical and Bibliographical Introduction," in *Autobiography: Essays Theoretical and Critical* (1980), edited by James Olney; and the seventy-five page "Bibliographical Essay" at the end of William Spengemann's *The Forms of Autobiography* (1980). Almost all the items in both of these bibliographical studies are post-1955 in date and the great majority of them, perhaps eighty or ninety percent, adopt an approach to autobiography that could best be described as literary in nature. The increased interest in autobiography can also be seen in the number of major books on the subject published since these two bibliographical studies and even more, perhaps, in the number of books in preparation or in press. Similarly, several literary journals (*Genre, Georgia Review, Modern Language Notes, New Literary History, Revue d'histoire littéraire de la France, Sewanee Review, Southern Review, Granta, Prose Studies*, et al.) have devoted special numbers to autobiography in the past ten years or so.

In the academic world of the previous decade there has been a concerted effort to reconstruct American literature (and other literatures as well, of course) and to redefine the canon that determines who and what will be admitted to serious literary study. Not only have previously excluded groups of writers—women, blacks, other minorities—been given entry into the canon, but also various writing modes, in particular autobiography, are recognized as having claims equal to those of more traditional literary genres. And these two aspects of the redefinition of the literary canon are not unrelated since women and Afro-Americans especially among previously slighted groups have always been strongly drawn to creation of a distinct identity through autobiographical expression. Thus, the number of courses on autobiography, in one or another of its literary guises, has increased dramatically in the past quarter of a century and the various "studies" that have arisen in university curricula—Women's Studies, American Studies, Afro-American Studies—are often organized around autobiographical writings. Sessions on autobiography have become commonplace in the convention programs of professional organizations ranging from the Modern Language Association and American Studies Association to all the regional MLAs and such local groups as the Philological Association of the Carolinas. Autobiography (joined to biography) has recently been elevated to the status of a discussion-group subject by the MLA Program Committee and so will enjoy a guaranteed, continuing presence on the program of the annual MLA convention. It could reasonably be said that in the past twenty years autobiography has proved itself capable of providing a curricular and organizational center for a broad range of humanistic and interdiscipilinary studies.

All this can be taken as a fair indication of the intense interest in autobiography as a literary and humanistic study and the intense activity that surrounds it at the present time. Despite all this interest and activity, however, no national or international meeting had been called prior to 1985 to unify, focus, and coordinate all the work of recent years. At other meetings, the focus of the whole group lay elsewhere (on "American Studies," for example, at ASA meetings) or given sessions only treated a single, specific aspect of autobiography ("Autobiography and Modernism" at MLA, for example). The need sensed by those who convened the Baton Rouge symposium was to bring together people working on autobiography from various different perspectives—the theory of autobiography, women's autobiography, Afro-American autobiography, national autobiography (American, French, English, Japanese, et al.), period autobiography (eighteenth century, modern, etc.)—and to invite a number of different disciplines (history, anthropology, philosophy, psychology, religion) to join with critics, theorists, and historians of literature in a common effort to view autobiography and autobiography studies from all sides and, as it were, in the round. That the call for articles that preceded the symposium was more successful in eliciting essays from people who might be said to adopt a literary orientation toward the act of autobiography than in bringing forth essays from people working in other disciplines will be evident from the Contents; whether this was the result of such extrinsic factors as the nature of the journals in which the call for articles was published or whether it is to be explained by the intrinsic nature of autobiography itself and the corresponding interest that thinkers are today showing toward the subject is unclear. It may be that the larger symposium that would bring historians, anthropologists, philosophers (the Baton Rouge symposium did have its philosopher in Georges Gusdorf), psychologists, and students of religion together with critics, theorists, and historians of literature is yet awaiting its moment.

What distinguishes the present volume from other collections on the subject of autobiography is its commemoration of a particular occasion, its marking of an event located in a specific place and in a dense moment of time. This coming together, with the sense generally shared by all participants that it was an epochal event, made for proceedings and for a publication different in kind from (for example) the volume edited in 1980 for Princeton University Press by the present editor. The intention in 1980, as the prefatory note to that volume (*Autobiography: Essays Theoretical and Critical*) says, was "to provide a forum for as many different voices as possible . . . ʾvith a minimum of repetition or overlap." While the symposium, and therefore this book, did not seek to reduce the number of different voices, nor—obviously—did it seek the maximum of repetition or overlap, it did attempt to draw articles together into more or less loose groupings that would form individual sessions of the colloquium, so that each essay should resonate with its fellows and thus suggest, as indeed seemed to be the case, that various people around this country and in Europe were working along similar lines and to common ends. The makeup of the present volume is intended to reflect and repeat the symposium occasion or event as faithfully and as completely as possible. The symposium was composed of four half-day sessions (plus an after-dinner talk by Wallace Fowlie, "On Writing Autobiography") with a principal speaker for each session, followed by three articles more or less closely related to the approach taken to autobiography by the principal essay. The four individual sessions were designated as "The Interpretation of Autobiography," "Ethnic and Minority Autobiography," "Autobiography as Cultural Expression," and "Women's Autobiography," as indicated in the Contents. The principal essays by James M. Cox, Henry Louis Gates, Jr., Georges Gusdorf, Wallace Fowlie, and Germaine Brée were all invited; the twelve remaining articles were chosen from about one hundred submissions in response to the call for articles. The groupings were to a certain extent arbitrary and certainly other groupings, along quite different lines and perhaps with different essays, would have been possible, but the general feeling of those in attendance was that the articles—and perhaps even more the people presenting them—came together to an astonishing degree and in a very short period of time formed a communality with regard to thought about and study of autobiography. One can see the pattern of the symposium evolving in the way in which the principal essays establish large, general positions that are then filled out or revised or responded to by the three articles that follow in the particular session; and the process of filling out, revising, responding to also occurs across the session lines so that the essays grouped together under "Ethnic and Minority Autobiography," for example, have ties back to those included under "The Interpretation of Autobiography" and forward to articles included in sessions devoted to "Autobiography as Cultural Expression" and "Women's Autobiography." Of course, a good part of the exchange of ideas about autobiography and related subjects took place outside the official parameters of the symposium—in hallways, lounges, and offices at LSU, around the campus and the city of Baton Rouge, in motel rooms and bars and night-spots. The editor of this volume recalls with pleasure a late night excursion to Catfish Town with Skip Gates to eat alligator stew, a walk on the levee along the Mississippi and a subsequent day in New Orleans with Simone and Georges Gusdorf, an argument (for which the editor is no doubt the better, though he didn't think so at the time) far into the night with Jim Cox in his room at the LSU Faculty Club, and a host of other memories that, together with the essays presented and the discussions surrounding them, add up for him to the complex, rich, and splendid experience of the Baton Rouge/ LSU International Symposium on Autobiography and Autobiography Studies. It cannot all be represented here, but at least the official, replicable part of the symposium is preserved both for those who were and those who were not able to be present for the occasion.

Studies in Autobiography

1

The Memoirs of Henry James: Self-Interest as Autobiography

James M. Cox

I have remarked elsewhere that the convention of autobiography offers descent from form into "life" for the professional writer at the same time it offers ascent from life into form for the "amateur" writer. Of course I know there is no way for the artist to leave his form any more than there is a way for the man of action to leave his life—save by the broad though difficult avenue of death. And of course I also know that the medium—or shall we say the current?—of autobiography is language, and so amateurs as well as artists are condemned to that current the moment they embark on writing their lives. Still and all, the artist of language—the student, if not the master, of forms—perforce views the great gaping convention of autobiography as an opportunity for experiment, a chance to expose the very rigidity of the convention to the pressure of craft, artifice, and experiment; whereas the man of action views it as the sturdy convention for chronicling his life. The one writer would follow Henry James's contention to H. G. Wells that art makes life; the other would, with a naïveté far exceeding that of Wells, believe that life made art.

Because James is, by the whole conscious devotion of his life to art, the consummate artist, I have always wanted to pursue his autobiography. For a writer of James's particular and very conscious identity, autobiography presented a particular problem. After all, James's whole creative project rested on the premise that his art *was* his life, and, after completing his prefaces for and revisions of the works he selected for

This chapter appeared in *The Southern Review*, 22, no. 2 (1986): 231–51. Copyright © 1986 by James M. Cox. Reprinted by permission of the author.

the magisterial New York edition of his works, he had, perhaps more than he could afford to know, completed his life and could have, following his friend Henry Adams, contended that whatever life remained to him would be posthumous. But James was not Henry Adams. As long as the artist in him remained alive, that active, creative principle would make life. Since that principle was insatiable, he turned, after the death of his brother, William James, to the task—or the pleasure—of making the unlived life, which is to say the life before he became an artist, into the life of art.

Thus, in a very proper sense, not merely for James but for the critic of James's autobiography, James's fiction *is* his life; and, if it is, why isn't it, properly speaking, the true autobiography? I don't wish to say that it isn't, yet James—by whom I mean the author of the novels—would be most resistant to such a critical contention or strategy for the simple reason that his art, his truest life, was cast or rather made by the novel, the term as well as the form which made the life. And if James was sure of anything—he, who was so sure of many things—he was sure that the novel was *not* autobiography. For he could see, and all his truest life was bent on seeing, that if the novels were seen as autobiography, then the critic would perforce become the biographer—which is to say the critic would become Leon Edel, writing a magisterial biography to translate the novels, which made the life, into the life which expressed itself through the novels.

That is not all. James did not merely accept conventions; he believed in them, and genres *were* conventions, which is to say that they were at once the social forms and categories of written experience. Thus there were conventions of literature—there were poems, plays, travel books, essays, and prose fiction—and in prose fiction there were short stories, nouvelles, and novels. These forms constituted not so much the socialization as the society of literature. They were the ground or the inheritance of the writer, and inheritance the writer was not to defy but to take possession of. And James saw himself as having taken possession of the novel and, in that possession, as having lifted it from the status of bourgeois or middle-class art into high art. Such elevation gave the novel classic form, in effect finished it, which is to say gave it the full finish of consciousness and living design.

To see so much is to begin to see the meaning of the action, the form, and even the title of James's New York edition. The fiction James chose for inclusion in the edition was preponderantly international in scope, and the considerable amount of fiction that was not international was exclusively European in setting and repeatedly dealt with the life of art and artists. Thus James excluded from the New York edition such estimable work as *The Bostonians* and *Washington Square*, indicating that, inclusive as the twenty-four volumes of the New York edition clearly were, they nonetheless represented, on the part of their author, an act of deliberate choice in relation to the entire body of his work. Moreover, the terms of the international theme are fairly clear, involving as they do the American in Europe. The American, leaving an essentially formless, unfurnished world from which he had accumulated—whether through inheritance, enterprise, or speculation—sufficient monetary wealth, embarks for Europe, the embodiment of history, social forms, and finished society. This American spirit—innocent, morally confident, intelligent, and essentially good natured as it rides on the money it has inherited, made, or won—returns to Europe to experience the world from which it had originally separated itself. The European spirit, seeing the American and recognizing the wealth, the good nature, and the innocence of social forms, nonetheless holds hard to the conventions, the society, the discriminations and time of life against the inrushing, returning spirit. The inrush and the resistance to it constitute the romance of the James international novel—a romance usually built on a melodramatic substructure. But James's scene of Europe with its forms, its exclusions, its discriminations, its art, its history, constitutes not only the setting but the layered world of manners that literally socializes, or, we might say, realizes, the melodrama of the idealistic American's quest for love in the darkened world of experience. James's resolution of the international theme may seem to many irresolute, since the American spirit discovers in the face of European form sufficient resistance to discover that its impulse toward freedom and possibility had more possessiveness at its root than its outsetting consciousness has taken into account. Similarly, the European counterpart discovers that its receptiveness to the impulse toward renewal is nonetheless bounded by form and authority that have become increasingly rigid and conventional in the face of a determination to be free. Put another way, the American spirit finds, in going to the romance of Europe, that it is at the threshold of wanting possession of its old home, thereby losing the America of free good nature that had originally drawn it forth from Europe; whereas the European spirit is always threatened with the suffocating realization of why it had never left Europe in the first place.

In the resistance of the relationship, James as writer tends to relinquish authorial omniscience in favor of the point of view of the questing American. That point of view, beginning from innocence and freedom of impulse with the confident moral assurance that accompanies such illusory spiritual well-being, confronts in the resistant form and scene of Europe a disillusionment that the point of view can only overcome by allowing its intelligence to displace its moral rigidity with an acquisition of impressions. Such displacement and such acquisition are at once the readiness and the responsibility of the American hero or heroine. The relation between America and Europe is thus not realized in the opposition or even the reconciliation of the melodramatic substructure, but by a conversion of the conflict into growth of awareness and realization of the limits of the originally innocent, abstract spirit.

I realize of course this summary—an extreme abstraction of James's authorizing themes and action—may seem like a constructed straitjacket to impose on whatever I shall say about the autobiography. But James *was* such a writer who had, through the most heroic and devoted concentration, lived such a life through the form of his writing; and, with the completion of *The Golden Bowl*, he had consciously completed his long fictional life in the international novel.

It is significant, I think, that on completing *The Golden Bowl* he returned to America, after a more than twenty-year residence in England, to devote himself to facing what he was to call *The American Scene*. Indeed, it would be possible to say that the most significant works he produced after *The Golden Bowl* were, with the impressive exception of "The Jolly Corner," not only nonfictional but also prominently autobiographical. First there was *The American Scene*, in which James faced the bare and, to him, often barren scene from which he had launched his fictional American expeditionary force into Europe. Then there was the New York edition of his work, which he not only selected and revised but for which he also provided prefaces. In addition to affording an occasion for the artist to review, criticize, and define the nature of fictive art, the prefaces put James directly in touch with the memory—which is to say the experience—of creating those works. As he repeatedly announced, he was, in describing the way the separate fictions took seed in his mind, "remounting the stream of composition." Finally, there were the three relatively direct autobiographical works— *A Small Boy and Others*, *Notes of a Son and Brother*, and the posthumous fragment *The Middle Years*—in which James, ostensibly setting out to provide a memoir of his recently dead brother, William James, all but immediately displaced the declared subject with his remembered—or is it his creating?—consciousness of himself as a small boy experiencing his relations to his family and his world.

Now if we look at *The American Scene*, the prefaces to the New York edition, and the relatively direct autobiography, certain salient facts come to the fore. First of all, these works are decisively in James's late style, that style which represents the height of Jamesian elaboration and refinement, the style in which objects are circumlocuted or displaced with emotional states, a style not so much involuted as interpolated—the interpolations extending and multiplying a process of qualification. This continuous process of qualification puts the quality of persons or things prior to their objective reality; it also places consciousness prior to action to such an extent that consciousness itself becomes the action. Surveying the upper-class world of James, a world of leisure, refinement, and possessions, we are truly seeing what Huck Finn would have called the Quality. For James, this quality consists essentially of taste achieved through intelligent discrimination. Quality is, in other words, the end process of aestheticizing experience.

The basic model for the process is the world of capitalism in which James had his being, a world of trade, greed, aggression, and acquisitiveness that qualified taste can only deplore as vulgar. A great part of James's genius lay in his capacity to commit himself to an aesthetic world of high art and exclusive society that would yet disclose through a highly wrought and elaborated style the primitive, ruthless, and vulgar activities that were not repressed so much as discreetly—oh, *so* discreetly!— operating in the very sanctuary of aesthetic contemplation. The very terms that James employs for defining the aestheticism he seeks disclose how conscious he is of his capitalistic base of operations. There is, for example, the idea of moral principle, which James constantly imagines as resting on a moneyed base—true principal. Similarly, the freedom to imagine—or at least the freedom to realize projects of the imagination—requires a free inheritance, as in the instance of Isabel Archer, or a free spirit of enterprise to "make" money, as in the instance of Christopher Newman, or freedom of speculation to win money, as in the instance of Adam Verver. Money is thus the minted material refinement of nature at the base of the American's *good* nature. It provides the ground for the investment of that good nature into the aesthetic operation—the action of *appreciating* the objects, landscapes, persons, and places of Europe. Such appreciation requires time and takes money. Thus history and society on the one hand are forms and conventions that are the resulting accumulations of time; on the other, they are the embodiment of experience, their very existence being a seal of their capacity to endure through time. These are the properties of the Old World that actively generate an accompanying system of manners or propriety to protect as well as sustain them.

Such a world is at once exclusive and powerful, which is to say pos-

sessed and attractive—attractive enough to excite acquisitive desire on
the part of an outsider with means. Vulgar use of those means is mere
purchase, seizure of the object without being possessed by it. Desire
invested through time, resistance, and risk brings acquisition not of the
object but of consciousness of the object, so that the life of the object
(whether it be a thing or a person or a place) literally comes to life with
its experience, its endurance, its genuinely appreciated value. Here is
true appreciation, an exchange resulting in added value, an acquisition
of consciousness superior to conscience, since conscience rests too easily
on original principle and has a correspondingly fixed and exclusive vision
of goodness. The aestheticizing of capitalism is thus toward acquisition
not of money or things but of consciousness, the very act of which will
be the *interest* of life and the novel. For the artist, whose act is the
imagination and invention, the form of the invention is the novel—
which is at once an art "object" that yet has life within it both waiting
and yearning for the investing consciousness of the reader to meet and
bring out. The final result of this aestheticism is to convert the original
principle of freedom and good nature into growth of consciousness that
takes generous account of others and at the same time discovers the
implications of its own actions. Such a consciousness constitutes the
generosity, the responsibility, and the beauty of action. This aestheticizing of conscience into consciousness, of realism and romance into a
very particular act of impressionism, of art into life, of still life into still
life—this was the James novel as act of life; this was the finished form
and the achieved style that James brought from Europe to America as
the monumental New York edition.

And if *The American Scene* was his strongest attempt to confront
America with that style, his autobiographical effort was to reinvest that
style and consciousness into his own relatively unconscious life *before*
he became an artist. Thus in *A Small Boy and Others* he literally lavishes
the finished style on his relatively impoverished American life before
art. His Small Boy is envisioned as the delicate, sensitive, dawdling,
and gaping consciousness—a consciousness literally overwrought with
the finished style of the achieved life. It is just here that I think grave
problems emerge for James, problems that had initially and all but fatally
emerged in *The American Scene*. In his international novels, largely
abjuring American landscape, James had played his American character
of good fortune and good nature against the European scene of culture
and genuine social experience—a true dialectic situation providing the
ground for an extended dramatic action, and, in James's repeated returns
to the situation, an ever-emerging style of increasing refinement.

But when James brought the achieved style of *The American Scene* and his autobiography to what he wanted to believe was the simplicity of his and America's past, the style lacked sufficient ground to justify itself. Rather than emerging out of a conflicting relation, it is more and more applied to the American scene and the American past. Now the late James style has always been subject to charges of snobbery, obfuscation, and overripe mannerism, but in *The Golden Bowl* it achieves a clear reflection of sensitive characters responding to each other. The tightness of the plot holds the complicated language in fine suspension. But in *The American Scene*, when James attempts to use it as an instrument of cultural analysis, it tends to caress what is familiar and reject what seems foreign. What seems foreign is simply all but the whole of America that had grown up in James's twenty-year absence. Where there was once simplicity of community there is now the simplicity of violent energy sending up skyscrapers; where was once good old inherited money, there is now the vulgar acquisitiveness and accumulation of mere trade. It isn't that James isn't aware of his problem. Casting himself as restless analyst, he from time to time has the architecture or the streets or the throngs, of which the cultivation of his style has to disapprove, talk back to him in comic dialogue. And it isn't that James isn't sensitive and intelligent about America. He sees that the cult of the common man reduces the individual's power for discrimination; he on occasion sharply selects polarizing details that raise haunting questions. Thus, in Philadelphia, he finds himself setting the prison famous for first putting criminals in solitary cells against the ideal architecture and ideal of Independence Hall that had housed the possibility of individual rights.

Yet the cumulative effect of *The American Scene* is more disappointing, tending toward retreat from difficulty rather than persistent encounter with it. To be sure, the analyst's intelligence recognizes in the very lack of discrimination and loss of "beauty," consequent on American insensitivity to history, an energy of rising expectation to be seen in the parents' confident belief in children and the children's belief in themselves. Yet the consciousness of the restless analyst—his determination to see the possibilities of that energy—is prone to stop precisely at the point of the raised question, choosing to move comfortably, even complacently, to another place in the itinerary.

This movement is nowhere more evident than in the Newport chapter. Faced with the huge mansions of the newly rich that have come to dominate the Newport scene, James can only verbally caress the old remembered Newport in which he spent such happy times. In the old

Newport there was a "circle," to use James's figure for the exclusionary principle that, he feels, was not based on the principle of mere money but on a broader culture, sufficiently European in quality and discrimination to be detached and isolated from the essentially barren and egalitarian impulses of an America that, even in the old days of a finer simplicity, threatened it. True culture in James's terminology is synonymous with leisure, and in the old days the leisure could be purchased with a minimum of means—say the *interest* that the James family enjoyed from the bequest of the redoubtable Billy James of Albany, who had amassed a fortune of three million dollars at his death in 1832, which was parcelled out in twelve partitions to his heirs. As one of those heirs, the elder Henry James determined, as far as we can say, to live as freely as he could on his interest, content to let principal rest free from business. Not that such interest, and the freedom it provided, wasn't itself a principle of enormous value. And not that the fortunes that produced the vulgarizations of Newport after the Civil War didn't represent a decline of the culture James nostalgically holds so dear. Yet James, for all that he casts himself in the role of the restless analyst, doesn't try to analyze the space, or the time, between the new money and the old. That time was, of course, the Civil War itself, the precise time that the James family returned from years in Europe to Newport at the outbreak of hostilities.

Of course, in *The American Scene*, as the very title suggests, James isn't dealing, or would like to think he isn't dealing, with history. He can thus contend that he is looking at the present face of a nation that can do no better than name its towns Jackson, New Hampshire, or Jacksonville, Florida. Why such a name is deplorable and why the old name, Radley's, of the Adelphi Hotel in Liverpool is charming, James never makes clear, remaining supremely and, I like to think, comically content on dismaying us with the arbitrary evaluation available to the genuinely cultured traveler. I can't help somewhat liking these abrupt sallies of cultural authority with their power to anger readers holding to a democratic ethos and to discomfit those committed to an upward cultural mobility.

Yet the fact remains that James is dealing with history when, seeing the present Newport, he can only fall back on the past. Beyond that, the moral attitudes James perforce has to exploit in relation to the Civil War are of course northern, which is to say, whether in 1904 or 1865, American. Thus when James revisits Cambridge and sees the electric and jumbled architecture of the expanding and confident Harvard of 1904, though he regrets the loss of the old simple Harvard (in which he had attended law school during the Civil War), he nonetheless finds Memorial Hall, erected to commemorate the northern sons of Harvard who died in the war, a hushed and almost sacred place. Similarly, he finds Saint-Gaudens' bronze relief of Robert Shaw leading his Negro regiment, unveiled in 1897, a monumental achievement precisely by virtue of its capacity to evoke personal memories of a heroism devoted to an ideal cause that James shows no sign of disapproving. Yet the heroism and the cause that James approves are surely related, and related economically, to the displacement of the fine old Newport society by the vulgar new one. James, in giving himself up to the extravagances of metaphor afforded by the late style, likens Newport to a delicate and secluded haunt that

> had simply lain there like a little, bare, white, open hand, with slightly-parted fingers for the observer with a presumed sense for hands to take or leave. The observer with a real sense never failed to pay this image the tribute of quite tenderly grasping the hand, and even of raising it, delicately, to his lips; having no less, at the same time, the instinct of not shaking it too hard, and that above all of never putting it to any rough work.

Extending the analogy for two or three pages, James proceeds to indulgently approve the remembered Newport scene and the society that had a sufficient aesthetic sense of the place to build nothing more than modest "cottages" to escape the summer heat of cities. Such modest structures had the good taste not to dominate or obscure the scene; rather they harmonized with it in just the way to keep the place a small white hand.

The extended analogy of the hand is precisely what displaces the process of change that has overtaken Newport. Sustaining that image involves James in retrospectively and courteously kissing the hand that was, at the consummation of which he retreats from what he calls the white elephants—the huge vulgar houses—that have intruded themselves on the tasteful scale of Old Newport. This violent intrusion is not, of course, to be attributed solely to the Civil War and its consequent release of capitalistic energy, yet clearly it is related—and the violence of this history was going on at precisely the time of James's evocative kiss of the delicate hand of the past. Here again, I am not requiring James to have dealt with the history—the process—of the white hand being displaced by white elephants, but pointing out how the elaboration of the aesthetic style circumvents that space with a transfiguring image.

Such circumvention is at the very heart of James's mobility in America, exposing a motive of retreat in his relatively arbitrary itinerary. Departing from Newport, he enters Boston, where once again deplorable urban energy has risen, not merely to crowd out but literally tear down the houses and structures of his personal past in the same way that New York energy has demolished the house in which he was born. From Boston, he pursues his itinerary south to Philadelphia, Baltimore, and Washington, where, in the monosyllabic utterance of the Washington Monument and the polished public buildings, he faces the architectural constitution of "the brazen face of history and . . . the printless pavements of the State."

This is the America of the present state, from which the restless analyst, though he cannot deny its power, nonetheless recoils. But his recoil leads him directly to Richmond, and here he sees the specter of the ruin on whose demise the printless pavements were built. Yet here again, James eschews the relation of that ruin to the power and energy he finds so disconcerting. All that he can see is the futility of a region having recourse only to the worthless relics of its past, relics that, in their very poverty, merely affirm the hopelessness and lostness of the cause that has left such unappreciable articles for posterity. In arriving at the judgment, James, though he does not advance it in moral terms, is clearly relying on the moral capital of the war against slavery. Conversing with a southerner who is living on the approval of the deeds of his countrymen who fought the hated Yankees, James indulgently allows him the romance of his memories and his contention that he would like to fight the Yankees again, yet cannot forbear observing that the very impotence of the contention might be but an index of the violence such a man might do to a Negro.

That is not all. Looking at the pathetic unreality of the Confederate museums, James reflects that the real aesthetic force of the past would surely reside in the battlefields. Yet he does not go to the battlefields; he does not even regret, beyond the sentence of his observation, not going. The battlefields are, however, the *land*, and James's not going to them reflects more than the mere constriction of his itinerary. He is not really interested in the land at any point in his visitations, since he sees land only as landscape, as cultured scene, not as agricultural life. Instead of going to land to contemplate its power—whether on a battlefield or in a cornfield—James goes instead to what he calls a "castle of enchantment" in North Carolina—actually the great Vanderbilt monstrosity of a chateau above Asheville—before going on to Charleston and Florida. The circumlocution of a style that can call the Vanderbilt mansion a castle of enchantment (James actually deplored it, and I like to think that the attack of gout he suffered there was a punishment for having taken shelter in such a white elephant) is surely related to his evasion of the land, which, he concludes, is simply flat, vast, and vacant. The reader who recognizes how the late style effaces nature almost as much as it displaces history will begin to see that the fierce process by which land becomes scene, nature becomes culture, and money becomes beauty is what is largely left out of James's encounter with and rejection of the American Scene.

This missing struggle James must have wanted to come to terms with once he undertook his account of his unlived life in his autobiographies. There are two key points, one in each of the two completed volumes, that reveal his wish. One is the nightmare—the dream of the Louvre—in *A Small Boy and Others*; the other is the account of the obscure wound suffered at the time of the Civil War in *Notes of a Son and Brother*. It strikes me as far from accidental that these two incidents have constantly struck appreciators of Henry James as the primary narrative capital of James's autobiography.

Both incidents constitute "negative" revelations in otherwise largely positive and approving accounts of his past. For in both books James, lavishing his late style on his unlived life, clearly intended to provide a varnish or finish that would give his fresh portrait of his early years something of the fine tone of an old portrait. The portrait in each volume was, of course, quite new, since James, even in remembering the past, was freshly painting it. And just as James at the outset of his career concealed his youth by adopting, in his earliest book reviews, the style of a confident, authoritative, experienced, and mature critic, so in his age he brought to the painting of his youth a style of the utmost urbanity characterized by the ultimate refinement of taste. He says at the outset of *A Small Boy and Others*—a volume to be devoted to memorializing the life of the recently dead William James—that it was to "memory" that his "appeal" to the past had to be made in order to "recover anything like the full treasure of the scattered, wasted circumstances" and so "live over the spent experience itself, so deep and rich and rare." There would be, he says, "sadder and sorer intensities even with whatever poorer and thinner passages, after the manner of everyone's experience" that would cause him

> to find discrimination among the parts of my subject again and again difficult—so inescapable and beautifully they seemed to hang together and the comprehensive case to decline mutilation or refuse to be treated otherwise than handsomely. This meant that aspects began to multiply and images to swarm, so far at least as they showed, to appreciation, as

true terms and happy values; and that I might positively and exceedingly rejoice in my relation to most of them, using it for all that, as the phrase is, it should be worth. To knock at the door of the past was in a word to see it open to me quite wide—to see the world within begin to "compose" with a grace of its own round the primary figure, see it people itself vividly and insistently. Such then is the circle of my commemoration and so much these free and copious notes a labour of love and loyalty.

I quote the passage at such length to show the presence and intention of James's style. It is accomplished style, easily and socially elaborating itself through a confident and articulate expansiveness and abundance equal to the abundant treasures it is already receiving from its knock on the door of the past. It is thus a recovery of the treasures that are the wasted or spent experience that the recovering memory—working through the rich, mature style—will bring together in an accumulated unity that will in turn all but conceal the fragmentation into which their spentness has scattered them. The terms of the style, as Richard Hocks in his discussion of the late style has pointed out, assume a decency, a world of refined social relations in which the expansion and qualification disclose that the process of consciousness is more important than any fixed position. Thus the style immediately discloses that the process of recovering the treasures is as important as the treasures themselves (which couldn't even be treasures without the process), just as the process of composition is as important as the things being composed. Moreover, the tone is deeply set—the composition is one of freedom and abundance coupled with love and loyalty.

And indeed that declaration of intent prevails throughout *A Small Boy and Others*—prevails, if anything, too much. But that is not all. By the time James reaches his reference to the primary figure of the commemoration—the figure clearly and irrevocably being William James— the figure has already been thrown into dubiety by the very description of the process of commemoration. Thus at the very outset of the volume, the figure to be commemorated is already being crowded out by the mental process of the commemorator. How quickly and how fatally this is all done. And how completely it is done is attested by the whole book itself. It is James the author in league with the gaping, dawdling, small boy he sees himself as having been—these joint components of the compositional process—who crowd out William James throughout the entire volume. Thus William James becomes one of the Others, a presence to be sure, but seen through the glow of commemorative consciousness as an able older brother whose very confidence and competence originally threatened the small boy now being reinvested as the primary figure of commemorating autobiographical consciousness.

It is just in this larger context of the whole act of composition and commemoration that the famous nightmare scene takes on a special illumination. In the nightmare, which the composer, introducing near the end of the volume—in the twenty-fifth of twenty-nine chapters— says happened to him much later in life, but which "applies" to the passage of life that is presently coming through the wide open door on which memory has knocked, a passage recounting the small boy's grow- ing love of, yet inadequacy to, the art in which brother William is already advancing—in this nightmare, the dreamer envisions himself trapped in a room into which a threatening figure is attempting to make its way. Suddenly turning the tables, the cowering dreamer forces the door out- ward and drives the "awful agent, creature, or presence" down a long corridor which, in the lurid light of thunder and lightning, is revealed to be none other than the Galerie d'Apollon of the Louvre, which the memorializing autobiographer has just been describing as the place of his nascent artistic ambition.

This "appalling and admirable" nightmare—to use the autobiogra- pher's terminology—has naturally inspired interpretation precisely be- cause it is uncharacteristic in the encomiastic narrative. For F. W. Dupee it is the nightmare within the dream of the past that signals the "growth of relative moral servitude to relative moral freedom." For Leon Edel it is doubly focused, reflecting on the one hand James's disclosure of his having literally displaced his brother in the realm of art, and on the other acting for the aging autobiographer, who has suffered a breakdown when the New York edition failed, as a kind of therapeutic vision, a promise of a return of his suspended creative powers. Paul John Eakin, in a fine essay on James as autobiographer, follows Edel's biographical interpretation, but goes on to show that the nightmare, in a condensed symbolic act, discloses James's autobiographical art itself, the housing of an ambitious artistic self in a work of art. Eakin feels that the dream is a double prophecy—on the one hand forecasting for the remembering autobiographer, the true future of the small boy whose consciousness he is pursuing; on the other promising for the autobiographer his own artistic triumph awaiting him in the second volume of the autobiography, the triumph over his obscure wounds suffered in the Civil War.

I do not wish to take issue with these interpretations. They are trials of a dramatic textual moment offering almost undecidable possibilities. Indeed, that moment is at once the most dramatic and undecidable in

the entire book. Without trying to determine the meaning of the nightmare univocally, I nonetheless think that a more negative reading might
be wrought from it, though it would have to be somewhat hurled in the
face of the positive reading James himself wants to give it. But then
James's commitment to everything in the book *is* positive; that is both
his tone and his determination. Even so, this *is* a nightmare, the only
one in this consciously positive and commemorative book. Yet, significantly, we are brought to a door not altogether unlike the "door of the
past" on which the autobiographer's memory knocked at the outset.
That door opened wide. This one is being assaulted by an agent, a
creature, a presence, and a terrified self within suddenly thrusts the door
outward and appalls the apparition. James has throughout this rather
oversweet book been presenting the small boy as timid with nothing to
show. Yet here the cowering consciousness reveals aggression sufficiently frightening to terrify the "presence." Wouldn't, or couldn't, the
"presence" be a nightmare sense of the *present* autobiographer prying
into the past, wishing to fondle the timid, frightened, retiring past spirit
of himself, only to be routed by the true image of himself as fierce
aggressor and usurper—who, whether or not he usurped William James's
past place in the house of art, has certainly usurped his place in the
present book? This nightmare, like Spencer Brydon's in "The Jolly
Corner," surely reveals the two halves of the self in an admirable and
appalling light—and in a nightmare form that the autobiographer's "labour of love and loyalty" has actually aroused rather than repressed.

I suggest such a reading not as an attempt to displace past readings
but as an antidote to the positive readings that have formed an overlay
on James's own largely positive reading of his hoarded treasures. Here,
in the form of a true nightmare—and admirable because somehow true
even as it is appalling in its figuration—a revelation breaks out of the
overrich style that is somehow offending truth with its loyalty. Small
wonder that, as *A Small Boy and Others* ends, there is a loss of consciousness, again similar to the loss of consciousness in "The Jolly Corner." In that story the loss of consciousness first occurs in the space
between the time Spencer Brydon pursues and corners the ghost of what
he would have been and his subsequent confrontation with the mutilated
presence that stands at the front door of the loved house of his childhood;
and it occurs again after he has seen that overwhelming presence block-
ing his escape. This time the loss of consciousness occurs when James
reaches a moment of crisis in Boulogne as he remembers a tutor he had
there—a M. Ansiot—who was kind, sweet natured, and a representative
of the vieux temps, but "too helpless and unaggressive, too smothered

in his poor facts of person and circumstance, of overgrown time of life alone to incur with justness the harshness of classification." Something in M. Ansiot's weak tutorings begins to seem sufficiently immense to the Small Boy to bring on a sickness that puts him to bed, where, alone and helpless, he feels momentous change into "something queer" coming over him—a change so immense that in a kind of fright he tries to get up, but the "strong sick whirl of everything" about him causes him to fall into the "lapse of consciousness" that ends the volume. Here again, without insisting on my interpretation, there nonetheless seems to me a relation between the sweet, unaggressive old tutor living in the dear old past—a past that was producing reflexive "three-volume bad novels"—and the act of the solitary old autobiographer knocking on the door of the past to welcome the throng of impressions that come flooding out in such sweet abundance. That abundance that "swarmed in images" turns into a swirl and loss of consciousness at the end of the book.

Be that as it may, as Hawthorne was so fond of saying, the lapse of consciousness ends the first volume with what James calls "a considerable gap." That gap is the space of discontinuity between the first and second volumes, since the autobiographer never refers back to it as he takes up his narrative again. Equally important, the form of the second volume reflects a marked discontinuity with that of the first volume. It is much more conventional in form, following as it does the life-in-letters model that sons or relatives of prominent figures were prone to adopt in memorializing their subjects at the end of the nineteenth and the beginning of the twentieth centuries. Such a convention enables James to include the direct presence of the Others who could only appear as *impressions* of the richly invested consciousness of the Small Boy.

This direct presence of the others takes the form of *texts* of letters by three members of the James family—Henry James the elder, William James, and Garth Wilkinson James, a younger brother—as well as a correspondence between a dying cousin, Mary Temple, and an "admirable friend" (actually John Chapman Gray). The commemorative text of the autobiographer is devoted to elaborately glossing these texts in an effort to register the life of the correspondents, all of whom are dead at the time of his writing. The letters, vividly possessed of enough life in and of themselves, justify the autobiographer's ruminations, and so the "past" in the form of these life-giving texts has sufficient body to feed the autobiographical consciousness that fleshes out its own narrative of the years 1855–70 in which James was finding his vocation. I do not use this analogy lightly, though I would want to retain an element of lightheartedness in using it. For James, in caressing the past with his labor of love and loyalty, is nonetheless pleasurably feeding on it. The letters, the visible remains of the dead, thus provide the solid body of text out of which James peoples his narrating consciousness as he struggles to convert the death of the past into the life of art.

But the texts of the dead, while they provide something of a spine for James's narrative, are by no means the only body of the work. There is the continuing narrative, in which the autobiographer pursues his "unlived" life through the years when he was all but paralyzed as to what to do with a life that, according to the old autobiographer, had nothing to show until he determined on the vocation of writing. Time after time, even in *A Small Boy*, and particularly in *Notes of a Son and Brother*, James alludes to cousins and acquaintances cut off in the bloom of life by typhoid or tuberculosis—a strain of the book culminating in the long last segment recording the death of Minnie Temple.

The prime killer of that earlier time, however, was the Civil War. From the moment James knocks on the door of the past, he is not only moving toward his choice of vocation, which would be his life, but also toward the war. These two actions—the one personal, the other historic—converge as James confronts, almost at the outset of his autobiographical project, the fact that many of the friends and kinsmen of his youth are slated for death during the very time James is to discover his life. There is, for example, his cousin Gus Barker, whose mother had died at his birth and whose fine military quality and authority of youth led only to stopping a Confederate bullet in 1863; there was Vernon King, who, the epitome of ideal youth and education, "laid down before Petersburg a young life of understanding and pain"; there was Cabot Russell, nephew of James Russell Lowell, who had been in Robert Shaw's regiment and had fallen at Fort Wagner. His father, searching vainly for him on the battlefield, found instead Henry's badly wounded brother Wilky and accompanied him home. Those ghostly presences, appearing unforgettably to the autobiographer's memory, are a measure of the inevitable burden the narrative at once carries and forecasts as it makes its way toward 1861. They are intimately related to the James family either by blood or action. Thus, Cabot Russell, though not a blood relation, is a relation of the poet Lowell that James idealizes. As brother Wilky's closest friend, he brings Wilky's own fate to the front of the narrative. Wilky, who James says was the most vivid, frank, and friendly of all the brothers and dedicated to a life of action, never did get over his wounds. Though James does not detail Wilky's essentially defeated life after the war, the incident of his being brought back north by Cabot Russell's father provides the gateway through which James, significantly in the ninth chapter of his Augustinian thirteen-chapter second volume, enters the obscure and difficult narrative of the obscure wound accompanying his birth as an artist. That narrative, taking place in what had been the little, bare, white hand of Newport, constitutes the most treacherous terrain in James's autobiography. For in confronting the multitudinous death out of which his life as an artist took shape, James faced the deepest necessities of his narrative—the point at which what had been the private life of a campaign that failed was to be converted into the public art of a newborn life in literature that succeeded. The elaborateness of the conversion is sufficient to exceed the resources of the celebrated later style. For although the obscurity of the wound is made to order for the style, there is more convergence of forces than the style can negotiate. The auto-biographer begins the dificult campaign by insisting that the wound occurred at the time of Fort Sumter. Biographically considered, it didn't happen then, but in the fall of 1861. Without wishing to take away all the biographical freedom from James, the critic of autobiography can at least see the strategy of the artist realizing the determination of the narrative. James has already set up the relation between the artist and soldier only pages before the difficult personal campaign begins, first by referring to Wilky's war wound and then, in a preliminary diversion from rigid chronological sequence, by remarking his meeting Dickens in 1867 at the Shady Hill home of Charles Eliot Norton. In the brief moment of being formally introduced to that towering literary figure, James felt himself exposed to what he calls "a merciless *military* eye," as if the recognition by the senior author of the outsetting artist were being framed in terms of a military challenge.

Such preliminary deployments are the simplifications, even the ma-nipulations, designed to bridge the treacherous passage of narrative James is determined to negotiate. He begins the sequence of his private civil war with his decision to enter Harvard Law School in 1862, a decision that he still has trouble accounting for. He wasn't interested in law, but going to Cambridge gave him retirement from the public eye and the opportunity more easily to pursue the vocation he had rather hesitantly begun to "want to want"—the vocation of being "just *liter-ary*." Reflection on the law school decision leads him back to the obscure hurt he had suffered, according to the autobiographer's calendar of events, more than a year earlier at the time of Fort Sumter. The later James style refuses to get more specific, just as it refuses to call the

elder Henry James's loss of a leg anything more than an "accident" he
had suffered in youth. Here is how the late James style at once en-
counters and screens the event:

> Jammed into the acute angle between two high fences, where the rhythmic
> play of my arms in tune with that of several other pairs, but at a dire
> disadvantage of position, induced a rural, a rusty, a quasiextemporised
> old engine to work and a saving stream to flow, I had done myself, in
> face of shabby conflagration, a horrid even if an obscure hurt; and what
> was interesting from the first was my not doubting in the least its dura-
> tion—though what seemed equally clear was that I needn't as a matter
> of course adopt and appropriate it, so to speak, or place it for increase
> of interest on exhibition. The interest of it, I very presently knew, would
> certainly be of the greatest, would even in conditions kept as simple as I
> might make them become little less than than absorbing. The shortest
> account of what was to follow for a long time after is therefore to plead
> that the interest never did fail. It was naturally what is called a painful
> one, but it consistently declined, as an influence at play, to drop for a
> single instant. Circumstances, by a wonderful chance, overwhelmingly
> favoured it—*as* an interest, and inexhaustible, I mean; since I also felt in
> the whole enveloping tonic atmosphere a force promoting its growth.
> Interest, the interest of life and death, of our national existence, of the
> fate of those, the vastly numerous, whom it closely concerned, the interest
> of the extending War, in fine, the hurrying troops, the transfigured scene,
> formed a cover for every sort of intensity, made tension itself in fact
> contagious—so that almost any tension would do, would serve for one's
> share.

There it is. The insistent repetition of that word *interest* tells us much
about how the later style both labors in the war encounter and at the
same time capitalizes on it. The interest is, of course, primarily self-
interest. At the same time, the obscuring of the wound gives the style
the latitude for an elaborate relation of the wound not only to private
pain and family injury but to the wound the body politic of the entire
nation experienced at the time. To make that relation clear, James tells
first of going with his father to a famous Boston surgeon after suffering
more than a year from the unhealing hurt, only to be pooh-poohed, all
of which left him in an even more troubled relation to the tides of war.
For the visit complicated the troubled family privacy of his condition
by exposing it to an evaluation at once public and professional, at the
same time making the law school decision more possible, since James
could scarcely remain at home in the face of the surgeon's clean bill of
health.

What resolution could there be for this young man entering a law school having no interest for him even as he suffered from an isolating private wound made all but imaginary by virtue of a professional evaluation? James finds his way out of the dilemma by telling of a visit to the war wounded at Portsmouth Grove in the late summer of 1862, and asserting that this war experience, unlike those involving his accounts of Wilky's wound and the handsome Cabot Russell's death that merely accentuated his own absence and isolation from the fields of decision and action, gave him, with his highly complicated sense of inner hurt and depression, a tragic fellowship with the mutilated, fragile, and depressed soldiers returning from the summer of their war. He goes so far as to contend that his felt sense of community with the wounded actually anticipated Walt Whitman's ministrations to and imaginative comprehension of the wounds of war.

Paul John Eakin, in what is unquestionably the finest account of James's narrative of his obscure hurt, is the first interpreter to give sufficient weight to the Portsmouth Grove experience. Along with James himself, he sees it as the autobiographer's resolution, in the fullest sense of the word, to face and answer his difficult passage through war to vocation. Fully facing the difficulties of James's account—his tortured style, his transfer of the Portsmouth Grove episode from its biographical happening in 1861 to its autobiographical location in 1862, and his general evasiveness even in efforts at precision—Eakin follows James in concluding that the experience at Portsmouth Grove successfully integrates James's sense of separation between himself and American life into the resolved unity of the life of art.

Yet granting James both the courage of his determination to face the Civil War and to recover—or is it to discover?—his choice of vocation in terms of a reexperienced, reconstructed, and refought Civil War campaign, I find an alarming treachery in James's vision of himself as the forerunner of the poet he calls "dear old Walt" on one occasion and "the good Walt" on another. For the fact is that James reviewed Whitman's *Drum Taps* for the *Nation* in 1865 and found Whitman a fraud of a poet, a poet whose blatant assertion of ego deserved the righteous judgment of a stern and war-tried people. James was young and bold when he wrote that review, surely one of the best negative reviews of Whitman ever written. Indeed, I find it much more penetrating and decisive than the old autobiographer's rather fulsome account of having anticipated the "good Walt" in feeling the wounds of the soldiers even though he didn't "come armed like him with oranges and peppermints."

When one thinks of how much more Whitman came armed with than the oranges and peppermints he so touchingly did bring to the hospitals, of how genuinely he had prepared himself in the 1855 *Leaves of Grass* to speak through the faint red roofs of the mouths of the dead, and of how, facing the amputated arms and legs at Fredericksburg, he spoke through the wounds of the body politic and wrote letters home for soldiers, southern as well as northern, who did not know how to write— when one thinks about all this, what *is* one to say of James's claimed anticipation of such an achievement? It isn't that James should have confessed to his youthful attack on dear old Walt; it's that his elaborated self-interest, no matter how literary, prevents him from recognizing the value of Whitman's achievement. Thus, although James may have won his own campaign, or persuaded himself that he had won it, his victory does not result in genuine literary vision.

Nor does it result in enhanced political vision. Once out of his passage on the war, James can do no more than make the easiest, the most utterly complacent and conventional judgments on national politics. Lincoln of course gets accolades for having a "commanding Style," with his "mould-smashing mask," whereas Andrew Johnson is merely "common," a national catastrophe, a product of a nation unable to mount the stairs where the world could be viewed from the high window of "esthetic sense." Yet surely, if anything is sure, it was just such a high window that would have precluded a vision of Lincoln in 1861 as anything more than common. It is hardly surprising that James has nothing to say of the *living* Lincoln. Only in death does he assume the exquisite figure whose "unrelated head had itself revealed a type—as if by the very fact that what made in it for roughness of kind looked out only less than what made in it for splendid final stamp."

Content to see the figure of Andrew Johnson as little more than a monstrosity sufficient to cause people of exquisite sensibility to express a sense of national guilt about what had been done, James shows, in 1913, no sign of having moved a jot forward from the complacent reconstruction politics of 1866. About all we can say is that though the style is rich, the vision is impoverished. Small wonder that James was totally unprepared for World War I, writing that it had burst catastrophically upon the unsuspecting decent civilization in which he had lived. Small wonder too that, turning back to the commemorative style, he concluded his second volume with an affectionate and sensitive commentary on the brightly vivid letters of the dying Minnie Temple. Small wonder, finally, that, after beginning a third volume of autobiography that quickly degenerated into an account of meeting great authors of the dying Victorian period, he simply quit his autobiography, for he was doing no more than converting the period in which he had genuinely lived into a memorial to its death. Surely he must have known that his title for that third volume, "The Middle Years," had a chilling personal irony. Dencombe, the dying author in James's great story of the same title, yearned for a second chance enabling him to exceed what he had previously done, only to discover at the moment of death that such a vision was itself the delusion:

> There never was but one. We work in the dark—we do what we can— we give what we have. Our doubt is our passion and our passion is our task. The rest is the madness of art.

James had indeed given what he had out of his doubt and his passion and his madness to make the life of art. In his autobiography he must have felt himself increasingly submerged in the illusion of the second chance where his doubt was being stifled by belief and his criticism was being suffocated by his determination to praise. He had lived long enough. What remained for him in the terror of World War I was to try to nurse the wounded as Whitman had done before him, and finally to leave the America that he had bravely left so long before.

2

The Biographer's Secret

Ira B. Nadel

> The only portraits in which one believes are portraits where there
> is very little of the sitter, and a very great deal of the artist.
>
> OSCAR WILDE, *"The Decay of Lying"*

Modern biographers, like their Victorian forebears, have become the
victims of fact. Substituting research and detail for the Victorian habit
of documentary quotation, the modern biographer creates lives that
expand to enormous proportions. Irvin Ehrenpreis's three-volume life
of Swift requires 2142 pages to complete; Leslie Marchand's three-
volume life of Byron runs to 1500 pages; Michael Holroyd's life of Lytton
Strachey (who lived only 52 years) stretches to two volumes and 1229
pages; Frederick Karl's account of Joseph Conrad, limiting itself to one
volume, contains 1008 pages, while Richard Ellmann's revised life of
Joyce remains a hefty 887 pages. European writers are not excluded
from such massive lives: George Painter's two-volume narrative of
Proust is 775 pages, while Michael Scammell's recent life of Solzhenitsyn
(still alive of course) is a hearty 1051 pages. The reason for this expansion
is neatly summed up by Matthew Bruccoli in his recent biography of F.
Scott Fitzgerald. Bruccoli's laconic answer to the question why publish
another biography of Fitzgerald is the direct, "More facts."[1]

Biographers, however, seem increasingly aware of the distortions implicit in the so-called facts, in the linguistic and narrative transformations
that occur in the retelling of a life. But this doubt of fact, an ironic
product of what Leon Edel has called the age of the archive, does not
prevent readers of biographies from believing that the accounts they
read, by their sheer size, are complete and definitive. Philosophic concepts of knowledge, however, outlined by Karl Popper and others, un-

dercut such naive faith in facts and call attention to epistemological problems and narrative alterations that inevitably change fact and its presentation. "The trade of clothing facts in words," the Italian autobiographer Primo Levi has written, "is bound by its very nature to fail."[2] No fact, we now understand, is without its fiction.

Biographers know this and it is their secret. They understand that facts cannot tell all, that they are sometimes manipulated, altered or forgotten in the telling of a life. As Oscar Wilde once quipped, facts may be "entirely excluded, on the general ground of dullness." Or they may be entirely eliminated because they do not coincide with the biographer's conception of his or her subject. The biographer's defense, however, is to prevent the reader from knowing this, which is done through the strenuous assertion of the accuracy and reliability of what the biographer *has* researched. Hence, Boswell's declaration of his assiduous searching out of correct dates and facts concerning Johnson that often meant running "half over London . . . [which] would obtain me no praise, though a failure would have been to my discredit."[3] Or, the more likely substitution of autobiographical elements by the biographer that consciously form part of the narrative, deflecting the reader from the inadequacies of the facts or lack of comprehensiveness. The biographer, to cover up his secret, then places himself in the foreground of the narrative, as Boswell so skillfully and amusingly demonstrates. Such a development both enhances and distorts the life, providing the reader with a more immediate and engrossing persona, that of the author, to focus the reader's attention.

The autobiographical dimension of biography, generated by the author as a defense against the charge of incompleteness or expressed through his strenuous assertion of detail, establishes an identity between biographer and subject. This becomes not only the sympathy and admiration of Johnson that Boswell repeatedly demonstrates but the very appearance of Boswell as a character in the life and its creation. A. J. A. Symons' 1934 biography *The Quest for Corvo* or Andrew Field's 1977 work *Nabokov: His Life in Part* are dramatic, modern illustrations of this development. But whatever role the biographer consciously chooses, his or her presence in the text is inescapable through the tropes, narrative style, and language of the work. And this reveals the essential secret of the enterprise: that the biography is fundamentally self-reflexive, as Harold Nicolson summarized in 1956: "biography is always a collaboration between the author and his subject . . . the reflection of one temperament in the mirror of another." To paraphrase Proust, if "in reality each reader reads only what is already within himself," each biographer writes only what he perceives about himself in the life of another.[4]

The self-identity of the biographer with his subject, the interaction between the biographer and the biographee, occurs on several levels. One is the historical where the biographer actually knew the subject and cannot avoid including himself in the account, as Boswell illustrates. The danger of course is competition with the primary subject, as many have noted in Boswell's frequent overshadowing of his protagonist. A similar charge was brought against John Forster in his life of Dickens (1872–74), unsympathetically referred to by various readers as Forster's life by Dickens. This question of identity may be handled more sophisticatedly, however, through psychological means as in Margaret Drabble's limited intrusion in her life of Arnold Bennett, citing parallels between her own life and writing and that of Bennett. The ego of the biographer generally knows no historical limitations, and although he may have never met his subject, the biographer may nonetheless establish his relation to his subject as the central theme of the biography. A classic example of this form of biography is A. J. A. Symons's narrative of his life of Frederick Rolfe, Baron Corvo.

Written in 1934, *The Quest for Corvo* is a work that poses more questions than answers, focusing on method more than fact. Composed by the gourmand, bibliophile, and historian A. J. A. Symons, the opening sentence immediately introduces us to the personal style that will shape the entire pattern of the biography: "My quest for Corvo was started by accident one summer afternoon in 1925, in the company of Christopher Millard."[5] Ignorance of Corvo by the narrator leads to his pursuit as curiosity rather than admiration of the subject propels him and the reader onward. Direct addresses to the reader become common as does the disruption of chronology for the sake of pattern or personality. But simultaneously, the narrator's personality emerges as he shares with the reader his inquisitiveness, disappointments, and surprises. The tone of the entire biography takes its keynote from the character of the narrator who occasionally withholds information, confesses his pleasures or conveys his dilemmas to the reader. Inconsistencies, which other biographers might suppress, do not surprise Symons who notes that "reactions to Rolfe of those who met him depended less on what he did and was than on the temperament of the observor" (p. 82). And nowhere do we find a more explicit declaration of the biographer's secret than in Symons's assertion that documents and facts "*sometimes make it possible, when the material has been collated and sifted, to write with certainty*" (p. 116). But without that information, the biographer needs a more flexible form to permit what he did discover to be conveyed without *"abandoning the framework of my Quest"* (p. 116). The narrator of the *Quest for Corvo* does not impinge on the story of his subject; he becomes it.

An intrusive narrator, however, is often necessary to complete as well as tell the story. An example of this procedure is the massive life of Faulkner by Joseph Blotner where in the second volume, after 1636 pages, the author enters the story (which still has 200 pages to go) to finish the life through his personal involvement.[6] But not all biographers permit themselves to intrude and when they cannot often a breakdown of the narrative occurs. Unable to synthesize the documents he collected for his life of D. H. Lawrence, Edward H. Nehls had no choice but to publish his extensive materials in three volumes as *D. H. Lawrence: A Composite Biography*. Virginia Woolf, stymied by the conflict between what she knew of Roger Fry's personality and private life and the facts presented to her by others and by her research, wrote a wooden account, lacking the vivid personality of Fry she could capture only in her letters and journals. "How can one cut loose from facts when there they are, contradicting my theories?" Woolf asked while composing the biography, trapped by the mass of letters and other details that prevented her from creating the life. The literalness of the life continually hindered her until she succumbed, producing a work generally recognized as limited and lifeless.[7]

At this point, several questions might focus the issues I have been examining: Does the recognition of the inadequacies of fact and necessity for creative, if not fictional, methods of writing biography mean it is fundamentally an unreliable genre? Does the presence of the biographer in the work undermine its authenticity? Does the discovery of the biographer's secret mean biography is *abinitio* false? The answers, of course, are no; the critic, however, must identify and evaluate the presence of the biographer and understand what he contributes to making the life a work of art rather than a failure. And I would propose that the presence of the biographer in the biography marks a new maturity in biographical form because it shows that biographers recognize the disorderly nature of life and the incompleteness of their literary form. To place themselves in the narrative is to become cognizant of their need to relate to their subjects in immediate ways. And it means that they understand that they possess not a limited, singular perception of their subject but one that is flexible, fluid, and above all honest. That the biographer may ponder, question, or admit ignorance of an aspect of his subject in the text is to realize the limitations of the undertaking while also accepting its fundamentally literary nature. The intrusion of autobiography seemingly disrupts the narrative pattern but it in fact enhances it, making the reader realize how illusory is the narrative construct with its stress on consecutive events and knowledge of the subject, an illusion unlike life. Consequently, George D. Painter in his life of Proust pauses in the narrative to consider the importance of his verdict on Sainte-Beuve and its meaning for the biographer.

Unbalancing the narrative distance between the narrator and the subject, Painter asks, "Can it be that he [Proust] has applied this shallow and falsifying 'method of Sainte-Beuve' to *A la Recherche* itself?"[8] What follows is a declaration of method by the biographer:

> The biographer's task . . . is to trace the formation and relationship of the very two selves which Proust distinguishes [in the essay]. He must discover, beneath the mask of the artist's every-day, objective life, the secret life from which he extracted his work; show how, in the apparently sterile persons and places of that external life, he found the hidden, universal meanings which are the themes of his book; and reveal the drama of the contrast and interaction between his daily existence and his incommensurably deeper life as a creator. (II: 126)

Throughout the life of Proust, Painter's selective interruptions engage the reader through the provocative considerations of biographical method. Choosing not to glide over these genuinely troubling connections between Proust's life and work, Painter shares them with the reader. He interposes himself between his subject and his reader, recording his own personal and often autobiographical involvement with his subject. This may break down the trust or belief of the reader in the completeness and authority of the biography but it also increases the reader's awareness that one is dealing with a written life, a literary artifact relying on fictional and other conventions, not a definitive and absolute record of the subject.

The intrusion of the biographer in the life of his subject not only exposes the essentially literary nature of his enterprise, correcting the false impression of readers that biography is scientific, objective, historical, and comprehensive, but sometimes limits the overidentification of the biographer with his subject. This excessive sympathy between author and subject produces adulatory lives, uncritical and distorted in their presentation of material as Blotner in his life of Faulkner illustrates. His entrance into the narrative as a character unleashes a flurry of autobiographical feelings that subverts any critical distance or narrative detachment. His behavior is exceeded only by Sybille Bedford's orgy of involvement in her life of Aldous Huxley with its erratic narrative voices and confusing perspectives showing that intrusion does not automatically mean criticism.[9] Drabble displays more effective control and presence in her account of Bennett.

Intimacy with the subject may not be a prerequisite for a successful biography. Irony rather than sympathy, as Strachey showed, may produce the most accomplished works in the genre. And self-analysis by the biographer may render a more revealing and complete life of his subject than attempting to hide behind the screen of facts and mass of consulted documents. Although the biographer may declare his position "off stage," through his language and narrative voice as well as structure and organization, he is always present. What the biographer's secret ultimately reveals is a persistent, although often unacknowledged, awareness of audience.

Through his presence in the life, the biographer acts as a surrogate reader posing questions, or confirming attitudes as Carlyle did in his 1851 biography of John Sterling that begins with the question every reader asks: Why write the life of Sterling? His narrative supplies a moral answer: Even from the life of those who have made little impact on society there is something to learn. In the eighteenth and nineteenth centuries, the major biographies were written by people who had at least limited acquaintance with their subjects. Think of Boswell and Johnson, Lockhart and Scott, Gaskell and Charlotte Brontë, Carlyle and Sterling, Froude and Carlyle, Forster and Dickens. In the twentieth century this is frequently not possible and the response has often been to substitute a plethora of facts for the paucity of personal contact. But with his anxiety over facts, the biographer resorts to placing himself more directly in the narrative. Unable to be a historical contemporary of the subject, he nonetheless becomes a narrative equal providing the reader with a guide to understanding the life. His presence marks the persistence of an autobiographical element in the biography that exceeds external similarities such as a parallel background or analogous set of experiences. This identity is psychological and joined to a sense of the audience. It is also, as Coleridge noted, unavoidable: "when a man is attempting to describe another's character he may be right or he may be wrong—but in one thing he will always succeed, in describing himself."[10] This self-referentiality of biography, embedded in the language, narrative, and structure of the work, originates in the biographer's secret, that recognition of the inadequacy of fact. But it finds resolution in those autobiographical passages that are not only self-interrogative, establishing tension and drama within the work, but declarative—declarative of the life of the biographer as well as the subject.

Notes

1. Irvin Ehrenpreis, *Swift: The Man, His Works, The Age* (Cambridge: Harvard Univ. Press, 1962–1983), 3 vols.; Leslie Marchand, *Byron* (New York: Knopf, 1957), 3 vols.; Michael Holroyd, *Lytton Strachey* (New York: Holt, Rinehart & Winston, 1966), 2 vols.; Frederick Karl, *Joseph Conrad: The Three Lives, A Biography* (New York: Farrar, Straus & Giroux, 1979); Richard Ellmann, *James Joyce* rev. ed. (New York: Oxford Univ. Press, 1982); George D. Painter, *Marcel Proust: A Biography* (London: Chatto and Windus, 1965), 2 vols.; Michael Scammell, *Solzhenitsyn: A Biography* (New York: Norton, 1984); Matthew J. Bruccoli, *Some Sort of Epic Grandeur: The Life of Scott Fitzgerald* (New York: Harcourt Brace Jovanovich, 1981), p. xx.

2. Leon Edel, *The Age of the Archive* (Middletown, Conn.: Centre for Advanced Studies, Wesleyan Univ., 1966); Karl Popper, *Conjectures and Refutations: The Growth of Scientific Knowledge*, 2nd ed. (New York: Basic Books, 1965). On p. 46 Popper reminds us that "observation is always selective." Mikhail Bakhtin has written that language is not "a neutral medium that passes freely and easily into the private property of the speaker's intentions; it is populated—over populated—with the intentions of others." *The Dialogical Imagination*, tr. C. Emerson and M. Holquist, ed. M. Holquist (Austin: Univ. of Texas Press, 1981), p. 294; Primo Levi, *The Periodic Table*, tr. Raymond Rosenthal (1975; New York: Schocken Books, 1984), p. 232.

3. Oscar Wilde, "The Decay of Lying," *Intentions* in *The Artist as Critic*, ed. Richard Ellmann (New York: Vintage, 1969), p. 304; James Boswell, *Life of Johnson*, ed. R. W. Chapman, rev. J. D. Fleeman, Introd. Pat Rogers (Oxford: Oxford Univ. Press, 1980), p. 4. Compare Donald Greene's recent attack on Boswell's limitations and distortions in "Samuel Johnson," *The Craft of Literary Biography*, ed. Jeffrey Meyers (London: Macmillan, 1985), pp. 9–32.

4. Harold Nicolson, "The Practice of Biography," *The English Sense of Humor and Other Essays* (London: Constable, 1956), p. 153; Marcel Proust, *The Past Recaptured* in *Remembrance of Things Past*, tr. Frederic A. Blossom (1928; New York: Random House, 1932), II: 1024. Compare the more recent translation by Andreas Mayor: "In reality every reader is, while he is reading, the reader of his own self." *Time Regained* in *Remembrance of Things Past*, tr. C. K. Scott Moncrieff, Terence Kilmartin, Andreas Mayor (New York: Random House, 1981), III: 949.

5. A. J. A. Symons, *The Quest for Corvo: An Experiment in Biography* (1934; Harmondsworth, England: Penguin, 1979), p. 15. All further references are to this edition.

6. Joseph Blotner, *Faulkner: A Biography* (New York: Random House, 1974), II: 1637–1846. Compare Blotner's monumental treatment of Faulkner's life to David Minter's critical biography entitled *William Faulkner: His Life and Work* (Baltimore: Johns Hopkins Univ. Press, 1980), a mere 251 pages of text.

7. Virginia Woolf, *A Writer's Diary*, ed. Leonard Woolf (New York: Harcourt Brace Jovanovich, 1954), p. 281.

8. George D. Painter, *Marcel Proust: A Biography* (London: Chatto and Windus, 1965), II: 126. All further references are to this edition.

9. See Sybille Bedford, *Aldous Huxley: A Biography* (London: Chatto and Windus, 1973), 2 vols.

10. Samuel Taylor Coleridge, *The Notebooks of Samuel Taylor Coleridge*, ed. Kathleen Coburn (London: Routledge & Kegan Paul, 1957), I: 74.

3

Narrative and Chronology as Structures of Reference and the New Model Autobiographer

Paul John Eakin

Although an autobiographical text always refers beyond itself to the putative historical existence of a self with a past, we have become increasingly accustomed to hear its referential content and structures identified as fictions. Paul de Man, for example, in an article on language in autobiography, argues that the illusions of reference we experience as we read such texts is really only a fiction, a kind of rhetorical effect. Our language is, he believes, a language of deprivation, closed in on itself, powerless truly to refer, to effect a penetration into any reality of human experience that might lie beyond it: "to the extent that language is figure . . . it is indeed not the thing itself but the representation, the picture of the thing and, as such, it is silent, mute as pictures are mute" (p. 930).

The deconstructive challenge to reference in autobiography turns, then, on the relation between the experience of the individual ("the thing itself") and its representation in language ("the picture"). Underlying my defense of narrative and chronology as structures of reference in autobiography is a distinctly different view of the relation between self and language: If our inscription, indeed our circumscription, in language is truly as total and comprehensive as de Man suggests, then human experience in language ("the picture") becomes virtually coextensive with "the thing itself," all of human experience that we may know. In this sense, autobiography may well be consubstantial to a significant degree with the deeply linguistic nature of the reality it presumes to incarnate.

I would like to consider here the position of those who, taking a more optimistic view of the possibility of reference in autobiography than de Man does, argue nonetheless that the present language of autobiography is inadequate to "picture" "the thing itself" of life history. Testing their own conception of the nature of biographical experience against the most familiar received model of autobiographical representation, chronological narrative, certain contemporary critics, notably Philippe Lejeune and John Sturrock, have called for a new model of autobiographical discourse that would more truly represent the nature of life as lived.

In his essay "L'ordre du récit dans *les Mots* de Sartre" (1975), Lejeune rightly insists on the referential import of structure in autobiographical narrative, noting that the expression of individual uniqueness is usually regarded instead as a problem of content or of style. When it comes to structure, he suggests that nine out of ten autobiographers either ramble formlessly at the whim of memory, or else settle for the mindless linearity of chronological order borrowed from biography and the novel. Even though Lejeune can advance a number of reasons to account for the prominence of chronology as a structure for life history (its role in the daily commerce of our relations with others, etc.), he argues that any appeal to the order of memory will discredit the notion that chronological order is somehow an intrinsically "natural" representation of human experience. Only Sartre and Michel Leiris, he believes, among modern autobiographers, have invented new narrative structures and, in so doing, new models for the description and explanation of man ("*une nouvelle anthropologie*" [p. 202]).

Unlike Lejeune, who is careful to dissociate his critique of chronological narrative from any implication that there is such a thing as a "natural" narrative structure for autobiography, John Sturrock bases his attack on chronology in "The New Model Autobiographer" (1977) on his belief that he has identified just such a true model of autobiographical narrative, a model that is, in turn, a function of his concept of the true nature of the self. He would liberate autobiography from its bondage to the conventions of biography, for the chronological order of biography falsifies the truth of biographical experience in implying that what follows after follows from. Rejecting the fictive teleology of biography, Sturrock turns to psychoanalysis for an alternative principle of narrative structure, for "the power of association, of bringing into the light mnemonic instead of temporal contiguities, has infinitely more to tell us about our permanent psychic organization than the power of chronology" (p. 59). A mnemonic structure would feature the free play

of language unfolding in the autobiographical act, in which the autobiographer is more likely to confront repressed passages of inner history
that are so easily masked by the regular surface of linear chronology.
Sturrock concludes by pointing to Leiris as the exemplary practitioner
of this model of associative autobiography.

Christine Downing's essay "Re-Visioning Autobiography: The Bequest of Freud and Jung" (1977), which parallels Sturrock's, emphasizes
the connection between the structure of an autobiography and the concept of the self that it enacts, a connection that informs most recent
critiques of so-called "traditional" or "classical" autobiography. Because the unconscious has its own associative version of the self's history,
Downing believes that autobiographers must abandon their traditional
reliance on an historicist approach to life history in favor of a psychoanalytically informed act of *poiesis* that would feature primary process,
dream material, fiction, and myth.

Critiques like these of the traditional narrative model of life history
underline the central role of models in the history of autobiographical
discourse as we now conceive it: the form of an autobiography is increasingly understood as a manifestation of the autobiographer's concept
of self. Thus Karl Weintraub, for example, has argued that the emergence of autobiography toward the end of the eighteenth century is
directly a function of the rise of a new mode of self-conception as unique
and unrepeatable individuality. Pursuing the logic of this correlation
between autobiographical form and concept of self to its radical conclusion, Paul Jay extends the attack of Sturrock and Downing on chronology to narrative itself. Taking up where Weintraub leaves off, he
offers us a view of the history of autobiography from Wordsworth to
Roland Barthes as determined by the rise and fall of the narrative model
of experience, itself a function of the vicissitudes of the belief in the
unified subject. In the autobiographical writing of Valéry and Barthes
he argues that "the fragmented form of each work becomes a conscious
image on the representational plane of the breakdown of an old epis-
temology of the literary and psychological subjects" (p. 179). The ontological status of narrative becomes a touchstone for students of
autobiography in coming to terms with recent assessments of the genre's
past and future. Are we so sure that we stand at the end of an *episteme*
where we can say that the narrative model of experience is obsolete?
Is narrative as a structure of reference to be understood as a period-
specific phenomenon, an outmoded literary convention that is to be
identified as a vestige of a nineteenth-century historicist model of the
subject?

Returning to Sturrock, and setting aside the specifically associative model he proposes, I want to challenge his contention that chronological narrative is to be understood narrowly as a form of literary convention. Conceiving of narrative less as a literary form than as a mode of perception and cognition, Stephen Crites, Barbara Hardy, Hayden White ("Introduction"), and others have explored the possibility that the structures of narrative reflect, and are derived from, the fundamental structures of consciousness. Drawing on recent work by Paul Ricoeur, who develops a "parallel between the generation of narrative in history and literature and the temporal structure of human existence" (p. 476), Avrom Fleishman interprets the persistence of temporal narrative structure in autobiography as a manifestation of the fact that "life . . . is already structured as a narrative" (p. 478). To look at autobiographical structure in this way is to suggest that our evaluation of the received forms of life history may best be interpreted in the broadest anthropological perspective.[1]

The upshot of the thinking of Ricoeur, Fleishman, and Janet Varner Gunn is to posit a phenomenological correlation between the temporal structure of autobiography and what they take to be the essential narrativity of human experience. The activity of organizing into narrative sequence and the recognition and naming of such sequences is itself regarded as a part of experience, and not merely a feature of autobiographical retrospect. The testimony of Sartre in *The Words* supports this view, for he demonstrates how the living of the life he records was already decisively shaped by a consciousness steeped in the teleology of nineteenth-century biography, a teleology that provided him with structures for the emplotment of a life and the creation of an identity. Thus, returning to my initial formulation of the problem of structure in autobiography as a function of the relation between experience and its representation in language, I would want to argue that "the picture" is an intrinsic part of "the thing itself" and cannot be separated out of it. Even if we were to grant the limitations of chronological narrative as a model of life history, we would nevertheless still have to reckon with the extent to which this model was lived by Sartre—and I accept his case as representative—as a personal and cultural reality, as experiential fact.[2]

In the course of these remarks I have moved inevitably from talking specifically about chronological narrative to talking more generally about narrative itself, for chronology and narrativity are closely intertwined, since all narrative, in the experience of its readers as well as its creators, is necessarily deeply implicated in temporal experience of which the successiveness emphasized by chronology is (often) the central feature. Even when autobiographical narrative seems to espouse some alternative to the principle of chronological order, we are likely to find chronology cropping up anyhow, if not calendar chronology then chronology of the unfolding of the autobiographical act (in the case of Sturrock's Leiris) or chronology of an illness (in the case of Lejeune's Sartre). Sartre's *The Words* offers an intensely problematical instance, for even as he argues that the "retrospective illusion" (p. 125ff.) of nineteenth-century historicism is smashed to bits, he enacts it, showing the extent to which his life *malgré lui* was determined by it. We are willy-nilly the creatures of our culture, marked by its paradigms even in the unfolding of our self-consciousness.

The attack on chronological order has focused on its unreflecting arbitrariness, its potential for the evasion of experience, and while I would concede that these are frequently valid criticisms of a chronological narrative, I do not feel that they are intrinsic features of chronology as a structure. To be sure, chronological order in a narrative—autobiographical or other—frequently does represent a failure of imagination, a mindless substitute for the difficult quest for the form and meaning of the individual life, and there are plenty of texts to support Lejeune's mockery of "*le petit bonhomme de calendrier*" (p. 197). As Sturrock would have it, "chronology invites the autobiographer to draw decently back from memories whose potency worries him" (p. 57). Yet autobiographers of any distinction—Henry James and Mary McCarthy come to mind—disprove the truth of this proposition, for they are led to contemplate repressed passages of inner history precisely as the result of their attempt to render chronology as accurately as possible.

What I am getting at is that the attack on chronological order as a structure of reference in autobiography is misguided in its failure to understand chronology as a manifestation of the ineluctable temporality of human experience. No autobiography is merely chronological, for pure chronology is inevitably the symbol not only of order but of dissolution as well, the sheer unredeemed successiveness of ticking time that destroys life and meaning. In this sense we could plausibly argue that chronological structure is not the least but the most truthful of the structures of life history. From this perspective we could say that the final, annalistic section of Benjamin Franklin's autobiography, for example, frequently dismissed as the least successful because least shaped of the three sections posthumously united in a single volume, offers in fact the most truthful "picture" of the "thing itself" of Franklin's experience. Although we may not prefer the third section to the artful narratives of the first and second sections, we should be wary of privileging the truth of an autobiographical structure to the extent that it is other or more than "merely" chronological.[3]

In drawing attention to the narrativity and chronicity of experience, I have intended not so much to present a defense of chronological autobiographical narrative as such but to question the reasoning that would discredit these structures of reference as necessarily predicating the simple models of unitary selfhood that are presumed to be the stuff of traditional autobiography. Let us not forget that many a so-called "traditional" or "classical" autobiography dramatized the problematics inherent in the concept of the self long before the arrival of the recent criticism that has made so much of this issue. The example of twentieth-century autobiographies by Goronwy Rees, Malcolm X, Sartre, Saul Friedländer, and others should remind us that there need not be a correspondence between the presence of narrative and chronology in a text on the one hand and a belief on the other in what Paul Jay has described variously as the "whole" or "unified" self. As I survey the remarkable production of autobiographies in the 1970s, looking for texts that would exemplify the freshness and originality Sturrock calls for in "the new model autobiographer," and setting aside his specific prescription of an associationist form, I cannot say that the titles that seem to me to extend the possibilities of autobiography can be said to demonstrate the obsolescence of either narrative or chronology.

Two examples will have to suffice. First, a critical favorite written, not surprisingly, by a critic: *Roland Barthes* by Roland Barthes, published in 1975. As Jay suggests (p. 175), Barthes' aesthetic governing this fragmentary text represents a deliberate, programmatic effort to prevent the tendency of autobiographical discourse to fall into the sequential, the narrative connectedness that would coalesce into a single structure that would be the model of a coherent self. Barthes writes: "I do not say: 'I am going to describe myself' but: 'I am writing a text, and I call it R. B.' . . . Do I not know that, *in the field of the subject, there is no referent?*" (p. 56). Yet for all the bias against narrative and the suspicion of reference, the fragmented body of the text not only includes many a micronarrative and microchronology of autobiographical retrospect, but it is framed by sections of narrative and chronology invoking the novel (in the opening sequence of photographs) and biography (in the concluding apparatus)—the two forms that Lejeune and Sturrock identify as sources of the historicist paradigm of classical autobiography.[4]

Not only does Barthes himself acknowledge the failure of his strategy

of the fragment to check the tendency of discourse to constitute a coherent selfhood, but I would argue that this making of a textual self
here and elsewhere in Barthes' later work became a central feature of
his biographical experience. In this sense the fictive structure of reference acquires the status of referential fact. We need to remember that
the *constitution* of such a textual self can be perhaps a—or even *the*—
central informing event in the life history of an individual; it is embedded
in temporal process, it has to be. The concept of a self-reflexive textuality
wholly divorced from biography and chronicity is only a wishful fiction
and nothing more.[5]

My other "new model autobiographer" from the 1970s is Maxine
Hong Kingston, and I want to mention *The Woman Warrior* (1976) only
to demonstrate that conviction of the textuality of self, as pronounced
as anything we find in *Roland Barthes*, can find expression in an intensely
narrative structure and practice. Reference in *The Woman Warrior* is,
if anything, much more problematic than Barthes' comparatively
straightforward and conventional performance in this regard. If most
readers are likely to share in the bewilderment and frustration of Maxine's repudiation of her mother's endless "talk-stories" ("You lie with
stories . . . I can't tell what's real and what you make up" [p. 235]), it
was probably inevitable that the child's saturation in the structures of
myth and legend should have determined the autobiographer's decision
to make of the traditional performance of oral narrative an opportunity
to create a revolutionary, iconoclastic model of selfhood. In Kingston's
radical revisioning of the myth of the woman warrior, Fa Mu Lan,
Maxine fashions from language an heroic identity for herself, and the
text of *The Woman Warrior* is to be understood accordingly as an incarnation of her new body in words. To juxtapose the Kingston text
and the Barthes is to suggest that the presence or absence of narrative
in autobiography is not in itself a reliable basis for identifying an author
as "the new model autobiographer" or "the old."

In concluding, I would like to make two points. First, in making a
case for narrative and chronology as structures of reference in autobiography I have not meant to present a brief against non-narrative,
a-chronological models of autobiography. I would like to align myself
in this respect with Barthes' commitment to *le pluriel*, with the exemplary
catholicity of James Olney's study of the multiple forms that a life, a
bios, may take. Second, my guess is that announcements of the death
of the unified subject are premature, although it is certainly true that
our concept of the self has been hugely problematized by Freud, Sartre,
and others, and so I remain unconvinced that narrative is an obsolescent,

retrograde structure in autobiographical discourse. Narrative is the supremely temporal form, and I believe that it is, finally, our life in time and our mortality that generates much of the impulse to write autobiography.[6]

I would postulate two conditions for the obsolescence of narrative and chronology as structures of reference in autobiography. First, the advent of a post-historical consciousness, that would see no value in the irreversibility of individual experience, with the result that diachronic narrative expression of the unfolding of a life would no longer provide a relevant model of self-reference. The second condition would be the decline of the concept of self as a value, for as Elizabeth Bruss has observed, autobiography—new model or old—"could simply become obsolete if its defining features, such as individual identity, cease to be important for a particular culture" (p. 15). To postulate conditions like these is to suggest that we can expect to learn more about the future of autobiography, about the viability of models past and present, from the speculations of cultural anthropology than from literary criticism or linguistics.

Notes

1. This is, I think, what Claude Bremond was after in his essay "La logique des possibles narratifs," when he suggested that a typology of basic narrative structures would reflect the underlying general patterns of human conduct.

2. Similarly, Roland Barthes has argued that our performance as the readers of books is not narrowly literary but broadly cultural, conditioned by our saturation in the narrative formulas of the social matrix into which we are born and move ("Introduction," *S/Z*).

3. In his study of the comparative estimation of annal, chronicle, and modern narrative history, Hayden White identifies a parallel tendency among contemporary historians to privilege the well-made closure of narrativity as the sign of the real, and in so doing to reject the unnarrativized (apparently random) chronicity of the annal as a failure to achieve a truly historical representation of reality ("Value").

4. The original French edition contains a chronology of Barthes' published work, and all the citations in the text refer to it; the citations and the chronology have been omitted in the English edition.

5. In this sense Jay's insistence in the case of Barthes on a distinction between biographical and textual selves (p. 175) is misleading, for the creation of a textual self may become the principal activity of the biographical self, especially in cases where autobiographers have devoted entire periods of their lives to the perfor-

mance of autobiography (I am thinking of Montaigne, Rousseau, Thoreau, Whitman, and Leiris, and others).

6. For important treatments of the motivation to write autobiography, see work by Barrett J. Mandell and Burton Pike.

Works Cited

Barthes, Roland. "An Introduction to the Structural Analysis of Narrative." Trans. Lionel Duisit. *New Literary History* 6 (1974–75): 237–72.

———. *Roland Barthes.* Paris: Seuil, 1975. Trans. Richard Howard. New York: Hill and Wang, 1977.

———. *S/Z*, Trans. Richard Miller. New York: Hill and Wang, 1974.

Bremond, Claude. "La logique des possibles narratifs." *Communications* 8 (1966): 60–76.

Bruss, Elizabeth W. *Autobiographical Acts: The Changing Situation of a Literary Genre.* Baltimore: Johns Hopkins Univ. Press, 1976.

Crites, Stephen. "The Narrative Quality of Experience." *Journal of the American Academy of Religion* 39 (1971): 291–311.

de Man, Paul. "Autobiography as De-facement." *MLN* 94 (1979): 919–30.

Downing, Christine. "Re-Visioning Autobiography: The Bequest of Freud and Jung." *Soundings* 60 (1977): 210–28.

Fleishman, Avrom. *Figures of Autobiography: The Language of Self-Writing.* Berkeley: Univ. of California Press, 1983.

Gunn, Janel Varner. "Autobiography and the Narrative Experience of Temporality as Depth." *Soundings* 60 (1977): 194–209.

Hardy, Barbara. "Towards a Poetics of Fiction: An Approach Through Narrative." *Novel* 2 (1968–69): 5–14.

Jay, Paul. *Being in the Text: Self-Representation from Wordsworth to Roland Barthes.* Ithaca: Cornell Univ. Press. 1984.

Kingston, Maxine Hong. *The Woman Warrior: Memoirs of a Girlhood Among Ghosts.* 1976. New York: Random House, 1977.

Lejeune, Philippe. "L'ordre du récit dans *les Mots* de Sartre." *Le pacte autobiographique.* Paris: Seuil, 1975. 197–243.

Mandell, Barrett J. " 'Basting the Image with a Certain Liquor': Death in Autobiography." *Soundings* 57 (1974): 175–88.

Olney, James. "Some Versions of Memory / Some Versions of *Bios*: The Ontology of Autobiography." *Autobiography: Essays Theoretical and Critical.* Ed. James Olney. Princeton: Princeton Univ. Press, 1980. 236–67.

Pike, Burton. "Time in Autobiography." *Comparative Literature* 28 (1976): 326–42.

Ricoeur, Paul. "Narrative Time." *Critical Inquiry* 7 (1980): 169–90.

Sartre, Jean-Paul. *The Words.* Trans. Bernard Frechtman. Greenwich, Conn.: Fawcett, 1964.

Sturrock, John. "The New Model Autobiographer." *New Literary History* 9 (1977): 51–63.

Weintraub, Karl J. "Autobiography and Historical Consciousness." *Critical Inquiry* 1 (1975): 821–48.

White, Hayden. "Introduction: Tropology, Discourse, and the Modes of Human Consciousness." *Tropics of Discourse: Essays in Cultural Criticism.* Baltimore: Johns Hopkins Univ. Press, 1978. 1–25.

———. "The Value of Narrativity in the Representation of Reality." *Critical Inquiry* 7 (1980): 5–27.

4

Conversion and the Language of Autobiography

Geoffrey Galt Harpham

One of the late Paul de Man's most ingeniously counterintuitive suggestions was that autobiography produces life rather than the other way round; or, in his words, "whatever the writer *does* is in fact governed by the technical demands of self-portraiture and thus determined, in all its aspects, by the resources of his medium" (p. 920). We might translate and normalize de Man's paradox by saying that lives that at some point issue in autobiography are typically lives lived in anticipation of that fact, lived in consciousness of their own narratability. To employ a concept de Man was himself fond of, autobiographers are characteristically men and women of action, as Hannah Arendt uses that term in *The Human Condition*: a mode of being that has as its primary orientation it own eventual conversion into narrative, its own eventual reading by others.

Thus, it is easy to understand why autobiography, the conversion of experience into narrative, should originate with Augustine's *Confessions* within a theology of conversion. For the conversion that organizes the entire narrative around itself, constituting the most famous event in the text, actually complements and anticipates the conversion Arendt speaks of, the conversion of life into textual self-representation. The two conversions, which we may call conversion$_1$ and conversion$_2$, stand in relation to each other as Old Testament to New Testament, prefiguration to configuration, promise to reward. The first conversion is marked by an epistemological certainty that heralds a sense of true self-knowledge; the second confirms or actualizes this certainty in a narrative of the self. They are not different in kind, for both lead away from what Augustine calls "old life," "habit," or "nature's appetites," and toward an arrest, a stabilization that produces a virtually new self. Formally, conversion₁ appears as an exemplary plot-climax, a reversal of a certain way of being and a recognition, an awakening to essential being, to one's truest self. Conversion₁ is a token of literary form experienced as a change in the character of life; conversion₂ is a literary act that takes its character from events in life.

The synchrony between the two forms, or phases, of conversion is borne out by what scholars such as John Freccaro have called the "literary" nature of Augustine's conversion in Book 8. What Freccaro and others have pointed out is that Augustine's conversion has an elaborately mimetic form, which extends well beyond the borders of the sixth chapter of that book in which the conversion actually occurs. Book 8, it will be remembered, begins with Augustine's visit to Simplicianus, who tells him of the conversion of the pagan Victorinus, at which Augustine "began to glow with fervour to imitate him," to give up being "a vendor of words" in order to cleave, or "cling" to God's Word. Later, Ponticianus visits Augustine and the faithful Alypius, and notices a volume of Paul's epistles lying on a table. He tells them of Anthony of Egypt, of whom they had not heard, and of his own first encounter with Athanasius' *Life of Anthony*. In Trier, two friends of Ponticianus' had discovered this text in a house, just as he had discovered Paul's epistles in Augustine's house. One of the friends had read it "and was so fascinated and thrilled by the story that even before he had finished reading he conceived the idea of taking upon himself the same kind of life." Suffering "the pain of the new life that was taking birth in him," the friend had read on until a cry burst from him and he made the decisive commitment. His companion did the same, and they went back and told the women to whom they were engaged, producing the same result in them.

Hearing all this from Ponticianus, Augustine retires to a garden and, after laboring under great internal stress, hears a child's voice chanting, "Take it and read, take it and read." Recalling a similar incident in the life of Anthony, which he had just heard, Augustine rushes back into the house, seizes Paul's epistles, and opens by chance to the words "spend no more thought on nature and nature's appetites." Doubt vanishes: He rises converted and narratable. But the process is not complete. He shows the passage to Alypius, who, adapting his coloration to the prevailing foliage, reads on in the passage (Romans 14:1), applying the words to himself and converting on the spot. This stacking of models continues even beyond this episode, driving conversion₂. Reflecting on his own text, Augustine says he hopes that his confessions will stir other hearts, providing a model for the wayward and direction-

less "so that they no longer lie listless in despair, crying, 'I cannot.' "
Augustine's conversion$_2$ is intended to produce conversion$_1$ in his
readers.

Reading, we may infer from this sequence of events, stabilizes the
wandering subject by proposing a species of imitation with the power
to convert, to bind the life of the reader into its own pattern. Both
conversion to Christianity and the awakening to self-knowledge have a
powerful textual component. One is "converted" when one discovers
that one's life can be made to conform to certain culturally validated
narrative forms; spiritual "conversion" might simply be a strong form
of reading. In a "native" or "innocent" reading of autobiography, an
author who has lived an extraordinary or unique life tells his or her
story so as to make known its uniqueness. But Augustine's account of
his conversion, and his notions about the uses of his own text, force us
to consider a quite different point, that autobiography confirms an understanding of the self as an imitation or repetition of other selves.
Autobiography, then, reflects and produces not self-understanding *per
se*, but rather a particular kind of self-understanding, the kind we achieve
"in dialogue with texts."

This phrase comes from Hans-Georg Gadamer, who insists, in a discussion "On the Problem of Self-Understanding," that textual self-
understanding is the only kind there is; and, further, that all competent
reading produces self-understanding: "To understand a text is to come
to understand oneself in a kind of dialogue . . . . the text yields understanding only when what is said in the text begins to find expression in
the interpreter's own language." According to Gadamer, self-understanding begins neither with self-examination nor with the act of reading,
but only when we respond to a text with our "own language," only
when we codify our knowledge of the text by speaking or writing in
response to it. Writing from a Christian perspective, Gadamer stresses
the "loss of self" entailed by reading and suggests that the entire process
is exemplified by the way in which the scriptural text "calls us to conversion." Now if Scripture is a high-intensity text, calling us to
conversion$_1$, maybe we can say that autobiography is high-intensity interpretation, a response to the call uttered in the interpreter's own language
in conversion$_2$. Memorializing and securing the subject, the autobiographical text is a kind of machine for conversion; it enables one to
achieve stability and self-knowledge, but only at the expense of all those
features that are peculiar, unique, "natural," or "habitual," all those
elements that cannot be converted into language that responds to the
call of the scriptural model.

When we say that autobiography is a discourse of conversion, we seem to have limited and defined autobiography. But when we study conversion itself, this limit expands rather than contracts, and we find ourselves looking at an enlarged category. The basis of autobiography now seems not to reside in a certain set of formal features or thematic concerns but rather in a way of reading in which the reading subject aligns himself in what de Man calls "mutual reflexive substitution" with the subject of a text—in which, in other words, a reader sees himself troped in a text. The writing of an autobiography is an act of imitation in which the writer confirms and enacts his own conversion, away from a sense of the uniqueness of his or her being, and to an awareness of its tropological and imitative—and imitable—nature. Augustine is converted not when he simply reads the Pauline text, which he had already virtually memorized, but when he understands that it is a model for himself; and he understands himself when he grasps that he not only can imitate the example of Anthony and others, but that he has in fact been doing so all along. His ambition for his own text is that it takes its place in the chain of imitable texts, speaking to others as he had been spoken to. He hopes that his text will shatter his readers' self-sufficiency as his had been shattered. Just as conversion leads us to a larger view of autobiography, it also produces a larger and more inclusive view of the self.

I have been treating the two phases of conversion as though they were entirely synchronous, but this might not be the case. Conversion$_1$ may lie in the grip of imitation; but imitation, which seems about to become a principle of universal replicability, is not the whole story of conversion. As Augustine knew, imitation was a "worldly" phenomenon that threatened a kind of deadness, or deafness, to the revitalizing Word. In fact his autobiography gives fitful evidence of a critique of imitation. It is possible, for example, that such a critique informs the second most famous incident in the *Confessions*, the theft of pears in Book 2, in which a sudden outbreak of imitative fever had the effect of "bewitching my mind in an inexplicable way," as Augustine says. He begins his probing into this fascinating event with the presumption that as human beings have no power to "break" the Law, he and his companions must have merely *imitated* one of the Lord's powers "in a perverse and wicked way." Augustine does not decide which power was perverted, nor does he consider the possibility that imitation itself is perverted. Kenneth Burke has taken the hint, however, arguing in *The Rhetoric of Religion* that this imitative act was itself "perverted" and even "homosexual," a parody of the Brotherhood of the Church in the "absolute unfruitfulness" of the act (p. 95). Imitation, Burke concludes, has a double valence for Augustine, as both exemplary humility and parody, a reworking of the origin in contradiction to itself.

This is not a point on which Augustine is entirely articulate, but he does, in Book 13, suddenly open fire on imitation as false conversion:

> We must obey in full the message which you gave to us through your apostle when you said: *Do not fall in with the manners of this world . . .* the next words you spoke were *There must be an inward change, a remaking of your minds.* When you said this, you did not add "according to your kind" as though you meant us to imitate others who had already led the way or to live by the example of someone better than ourselves. . . . when he has remade his mind and can see and understand your truth, he has no need of other men to teach him to imitate his kind. (13.22)

In this passage, Augustine condemns not just perverse imitation but imitation as perverse. Here, conversion is a solitary experience of reconstruction by which the self becomes other than what it was, becomes other than anybody, other than a self.

Although the two functions of conversion seem to contradict each other directly, Augustine is unwilling to surrender either one. Just one page before this passage he argues in praise of the work of the evangelists, who serve "as a pattern to the faithful by living among them and rousing them to imitation," adding that the soul "keeps itself intact by imitating those who follow the example of Christ your Son." He concludes with a suggestion that imitation does not even require effort: "Be as I am, says Paul, for I am no different from yourselves."

If imitation and remaking can be compared, respectively, to "defense" and "offense," it is apparent that conversion cannot quite free itself from the defensive strategy of imitation; and that conversion therefore remains earthbound and, in a sense, unconverted. Oddly enough, the act of conversion, requiring as it does an assent to imitation, contains a resistance to conversion: the term designates not only a principle of radical change in life, but also a principle of recalcitrance and unchangeability. But this discontinuity within the concept of conversion enables us to articulate the relation between conversion$_1$ and conversion$_2$. For if imitation is the special province of conversion$_1$, then perhaps remaking should be seen as the function of conversion$_2$, which translates the self out of selfhood and into discourse. The autobiographical act consequently provides a means both of confirming the subject's faithful imitation of models and of renouncing imitation altogether by transposing the self into the key of textuality.

What relation does conversion have to the unconverted life that precedes it? What happens in conversion? To what is conversion opposed? If we are to understand autobiography, we must understand conversion, but Augustine seems unable to provide a clear answer; he does not even seem to have recognized his own contradiction. Eugene Vance has tackled this question, however, arguing that Augustine converts in Book 8 at the precise moment when he decides to permit the "transgression" of his autobiographical text by the Word of God. Renouncing eloquence and the profession of rhetoric, Augustine, according to Vance, suffers a "death in language" that is also a "death to himself," and this double death is the essence and basis of conversion.

But Vance is undecided about language in the same way Augustine is undecided about imitation. Vance equates the violence at the moment of decision, when Augustine tears his hair, hammers his forehead, hugs his knees and so forth, with the beatings the young Augustine had received at school. These beatings prove to Vance that language learning is "an institution of fallen society . . . acquired through institutionalized rites of violence" (p. 19). They are allied with the later self-flogging as signs of "the transgression of his identity by the word of another. This," says Vance, "is the single violence of death in language, except that in the latter case Augustine's death to himself is the drama of salvation." A large exception, for it means that this "single violence" can embrace both the fall and salvation—and also the "ordeals of martyrdom," to which Augustine compares his school beatings in 1.4. The point here is that Vance's attempt to define conversion in terms of language acquisition has not defined the event as much as it has extended the idea of conversion to other events remote from it in structure and valence. Arguing for a tight definition of conversion, Vance has in fact been forced to open up the concept and make it permeable to a vast conceptual range.

Vance's loss of control testifies not so much to his confusion as to the conceptual strangeness of conversion; and so in a certain sense I am sympathetic to his argument. But I am in no way sympathetic to his claim that Augustine's conversion is marked by the transgression of his own identity, his own word, by the identity or word of another. Where does Augustine—where does anyone—ever use his "own" language? Of what would such a paradisal language consist?

We do not have to look far for a counterargument to this romantic notion of an individual language, for in Book 1 Augustine notes how, first through gestures, then facial expressions, and finally through language itself the infant learns by memory and imitation to repeat the signs made by others, to participate in the language and the community that always precedes its wishes or intentions. The very first instinct of the self—surely genetically imprinted as a form of biological "imitation"—is to seek precisely the transgression of the self by the "word of another." This is original desire, transgression by the alien word. Only through such transgression can the child acquire wishes and intentions at all; only through such transgression can anyone achieve a self. The imitation of models in conversion$_1$ does not constitute a radical break with previous behavior, but rather a particular adaptation of the first "behavior" we learn. Perhaps this is why conversion is so often described by Augustine and others as a "second birth."

The fact that we are never free from impingement by the "word of another" leads to another quarrel with Vance (and with almost every other reader of Augustine's), this time in his claim that conversion can be assigned to a definite temporal moment. The self emerges from, and constantly defines itself through, the conversion of instinct or impulse into language, which means that conversion cannot be localized in a single event. No moment of consciousness is "pre-conversion." Nor, we must remember, does the subject ever achieve a "post-conversional" condition, for conversion, as we discovered, always contains its own inhibition, its own antidote. Conversion is a constant, ceaseless process capable of absorbing any value, any thematization: It is the unchanging condition of our existence. Insofar as the *Confessions* pivots on conversion, it simply projects into a plotted, linear depiction of human action the manifold operations of language, whose double epitomes are figured as the "moment of conversion" in Book 8 and in the writing of the autobiographical text itself. Language does not provide a document of conversion, nor is it the scene of conversion. Language *is* conversion.

At this final frontier, we look over onto a view of autobiography as a particular organization of the "conversional" aspects of language acquisition and use. In learning language, human beings situate themselves in a system that both precedes and exceeds them. They imitate others and they become themselves. They discover human kinship and aspire to transcendence through a medium that is arbitrary and inert. They express themselves and submit themselves to the rules of the code. They come to consciousness, they transgress, they convert, they testify. Autobiography is an intensification of all these processes, all these paradoxes. Perhaps this is why autobiography so resolutely resists definition. Autobiography, we could say, is as easy to define as conversion, and as impossible.

If autobiography is not a mode like the lyric poem or the tragedy, its luminous indeterminacy makes it all the more intriguing as a subject of inquiry than these genres, whose formal limits mark a limit to their conceptual resonance. Autobiography is one of those instances in which the marginal example indicates a larger category than the typical, for it is a barely "literary" mode that contains within itself the category of "life" by thematizing and exemplifying the conversion from one condition to the other.

In the final pages of the *Confessions*, Augustine compares the individual to the cosmos and remarks that in forming the ur-material of the universe into heaven and earth, God had "converted" it: "For, by undergoing a change which bettered it, it was turned towards that which cannot change, either for better or worse, that is, towards you" (13.3). From the first instant of time, therefore, the Word creates and converts, so that not only the autobiographer but the world is already the product of conversion.

At this moment Augustine may sound to modern ears complacent in a way that typifies a certain limitation in the interest or attractiveness of autobiography itself. The confident assertion that the world is the infinitely receptive home of conversion accords all too well with what seems to many the nineteenth-century bias of the form. Indeed, many such self-representations seem to reflect the assurances of a coherent and metaphysically unproblematic existence within an elaborately secured culture, in a preconverted, stable world. The revelations of twentieth-century writers seem the expressions of selves altogether more improvisatory, ad hoc, and provisional than their predecessors; their writings may seem to indicate that autobiography as a mode of self-expression that confirms, depicts, and enacts conversion is through. Our writers are more likely to insist on the failures of conversion. One form of this insistence is the currently fashionable argument that autobiography is a fictive, that is, untrue form incapable of fully representing, much less transforming, existence. Such arguments may direct our attention to the life of the body in time, the act of writing itself, the fact of life after autobiography, and all the myriad acts that fall below or outside the decorums of representation. These are aspects of the self that don't make it into the text, that resist transformation, idealization, and narrative closure.

But we shouldn't sell conversion short as an expansive idea that comprehends the entire autobiographical self. Conversion has not only "always already" happened. As Augustine was literally the first to admit, it is also always imminent, always yet to occur. Insofar as the world exists, it is the product of conversion; yet insofar as it is changing, it is also unconverted. As it is with the world, so with the autobiographer: her text bespeaks conversion, but her life awaits it.

Works Cited

Arendt, Hannah. *The Human Condition* (Chicago and London: Univ. of Chicago Press, 1958).

Augustine, *Confessions*, trans. R. S. Pine-Coffin (Harmondsworth: Penguin, 1979).

Burke, Kenneth. *The Rhetoric of Religion: Studies in Logology* (Boston: Beacon Press, 1961).

de Man, Paul. "Autobiography as De-facement," *Modern Language Notes* 94 (1979): 919–30.

Freccero, John. "The Fig Tree and the Laurel: Petrarch's Poetics," *Diacritics* (1975): 34–40.

Gadamer, Hans-Georg. "On the Problem of Self-Understanding," in David E. Linge, trans. and ed., *Philosophical Hermeneutics* (Berkeley, Los Angeles, London: Univ. of California Press, 1977): 44–58.

Vance, Eugene. "Augustine's *Confessions* and the Grammar of Selfhood," *Genre* VI: 1 (1973): 1–28.

5

James Gronniosaw and the Trope of the Talking Book

Henry Louis Gates, Jr.

[a] disingenuous and unmanly *Position* had been formed; and privately (*and as it were in the dark*) handed to and again, which is this, that the *Negro's*, though in their Figure they carry some resemblances of Manhood, yet are indeed *no Men*.

the consideration of the shape and figure of our *Negro's* Bodies, their Limbs and Members; their Voice and Countenance, in all things according with other Mens; together with their *Risibility* and *Discourse* (Man's *peculiar* Faculties) should be sufficient Conviction. How should they otherwise be capable of Trades, and other no less Manly imployments; as also of *Reading and Writing*; . . . were they not truly Men?

MORGAN GODWIN, 1680

Let us to the Press Devoted Be,
Its *Light* will *Shine* and *Speak Us Free*.

DAVID RUGGLES, 1835

Language, for the individual consciousness, is on the borderline between oneself and the other. The word in language is someone else's.

MIKHAIL BAKHTIN

I

The literature of the slave, published in English between 1760 and 1865, is the most obvious site to explore for determining the usage of trope

This chapter appeared in *The Southern Review*, 22, no. 2 (1986): 252–72. Copyright © 1986 by Henry Louis Gates, Jr. Reprinted by permission of the author.

of race in Anglo-African texts as an ultimate sign of difference. Indeed, "race," writing, and difference constituted a nexus of issues that informed the shaping of all black texts published in this period. Between 1770 and 1815, black writers figured "race," writing, and difference in the trope of the Talking Book.[1] After 1815, "freedom and literacy" became the trope that revises that of the text that speaks in literature of the slave.

"The literature of the slave" is an ironic phrase, at the very least, and an oxymoron at its most literal level. "Literature," as Samuel Johnson used the term, denoted an "acquaintance with letters or books," according to *The Oxford English Dictionary*. It also connoted "polite or humane learning" and "literary culture." While it is self-evident that the ex-slave who managed, as Frederick Douglass put it, to "steal" some learning from his or her master and the master's texts, was bent on demonstrating to a skeptical public an acquaintance with letters or books, we cannot honestly conclude that slave literature was meant to exemplify either polite or humane learning or the presence in the author of literary culture. Indeed, it is more accurate to argue that the literature of the slave consisted of texts that represent *impolite* learning and that these texts collectively railed against the arbitrary and *inhumane* learning that masters foisted on the slave to reinforce a perverse fiction of the "natural" order of things. The "slave," by definition, possessed at most a liminal status within the human community.[2] To read and to write was to transgress this nebulous realm of liminality. The slave's texts, then, could not be taken as specimens of a black "literary culture." Rather, these texts could only be read as testimony of defilement: the slave's *representation* of the master's attempt to transform a human being into a commodity, and the "slave's simultaneous verbal witness of the possession of a "humanity" shared in common with Europeans. The slave wrote not primarily to demonstrate humane letters, but to demonstrate individual membership in the human community.

This intention cannot be disregarded as a force extraneous to the production of a text, a common text that I like to think of as the "text of blackness." If we recall Ralph Ellison's apt phrase by which he defines what I am calling "tradition," "a sharing of that 'concord of sensibilities'" which the group *expresses*," then what I wish to suggest by the "text of blackness" perhaps is clearer. Black writers to a remarkable extent have created texts that express the broad "concord of sensibilities" shared by persons of African descent in the Western hemisphere. Texts written over two centuries ago address what we might think of as common "subjects of condition" that continue to be strangely resonant, and "relevant," as we approach the twenty-first century. Just as there are remarkably few literary traditions whose first century's existence is determined by texts created by *slaves*, so too are there few traditions that claim such an apparent unity from a fundamental political *condition* represented for over two hundred years in such strikingly similar patterns and details.

Has a common experience or, more accurately, the shared *sense* of a common experience been largely responsible for the sharing of this text of blackness? It would be foolish to argue against an affirmative response to this rhetorical question. Nevertheless, shared experience of black people *vis-à-vis* white racism is not sufficient "evidence" on which to argue that black writers have shared patterns of *representation* of their common subject for two centuries—unless one wishes to argue for a "genetic" theory of literature, which the biological sciences do not support. Rather, shared modes of figuration result only when writers *read* each other's texts, and seize on topoi and tropes to revise in their own texts. This form of revision is a process of *grounding*, and has served to create curious formal lines of continuity between the texts that, together, constitute the shared text of blackness, the discrete "chapters" of which scholars are still establishing.

What seems clear on reading eighteenth-century texts created by black writers in English or the critical texts that responded to these black writings is that the production of "literature" was taken to be the central arena in which persons of African descent could, or could not, establish and redefine their status within the human community. Black people, the evidence suggests, had to represent themselves as "speaking subjects" before they could even begin to destroy their status as "objects," as commodities, within Western culture. In addition to all the myriad reasons for which human beings write books, this particular reason seems to have been paramount for the black slave. At least since 1600, Europeans had wondered aloud whether or not the African "species of men," as they most commonly put it, *could* ever create formal literature, could ever master "the arts and sciences." If they could, then, the argument ran, the African variety of humanity and the European variety were fundamentally related. If not, then it seemed clear that the African was destined by nature to be a slave.

Why was the *creative writing* of the African of such importance to the eighteenth-century's debate over slavery? I can briefly outline one thesis: After Descartes, *reason* was privileged, or valorized, among all other human characteristics. *Writing*, especially after the printing press became so widespread, was taken to be the *visible* sign of reason. Blacks were "reasonable," and hence "men," if—and only if—they demonstrated mastery of "the arts and sciences," the eighteenth-century's formula for writing. So, while the Enlightenment is famous for establishing its existence on man's ability to reason, it simultaneously used the absence and presence of "reason" to delimit and circumscribe the very humanity of the cultures and people of color that Europeans had been "discovering" since the Renaissance. The urge toward the systematization of all human knowledge, by which we characterize the Enlightenment, led directly to the relegation of black people to a lower rung on the Great Chain of Being, an eighteenth-century metaphor that arranged all of creation on a vertical scale from animals and plants and insects through man to the angels and God himself. By 1750, the Chain had become individualized; the human scale slid from "the lowliest Hottentot" (black South Africans) to "glorious Milton and Newton." If blacks could write and publish imaginative literature, then they could, in effect, take a few Giant Steps up the Chain of Being, in a pernicious game of "Mother, May I?" As the Rev. James W. C. Pennington, an ex-slave who wrote a slave narrative and was a prominent black abolitionist, summarized this curious idea in his prefatory note "To the Reader" that authorizes Ann Plato's 1841 book of essays, biographies, and poems: "The history of the arts and sciences is the history of individuals, of individual nations." Only by publishing books such as Plato's, he argues, can blacks demonstrate "the fallacy of that stupid theory, that *nature has done nothing but fit us for slaves, and that art cannot unfit us for slavery!*"[3]

Not a lot changed between Phillis Wheatley's 1773 publication date of her *Poems* (complete with a prefatory letter of authenticity signed by eighteen of "the most respectable characters in Boston") and Ann Plato's, except that by 1841 Plato's attestation was supplied by a black person. What we might think of as the black text's mode of being, however, remained pretty much the same during these sixty-eight years. What remained consistent was that black people could become "speaking" subjects only by inscribing their "voices" in the written word. If this matter of recording an authentic "black" voice in the text of Western letters was a matter of widespread concern in the eighteenth century, then how did it affect the production of black texts, if indeed it affected them at all? It is not enough simply to trace a line of shared argument as "context" to show that blacks regarded this matter as crucial to their texts; rather, evidence for such a direct relationship of text to context must be found in the black texts themselves.[4]

The most salient indication that this idea informed the writing of black texts is found in a topos that appears in five black texts published in English by 1815. This topos assumed such a central place in the black use of figurative language that we can call it a trope. It is the trope of the Talking Book, which first occurs in James Gronniosaw's 1770 slave narrative, and was then revised in other narratives published by John Marrant in 1785, Cugoano in 1787, Equiano in 1789, and John Jea in 1815. Not only does this shared but revised trope argue forcefully that blacks were intent on placing their individual and collective "voices," as it were, in the text of Western letters, but also that even the earliest writers of the Anglo-African tradition *read* each other's texts and "grounded" these texts in what soon became a "tradition."

The trope of the Talking Book is the "ur-trope" of the Anglo-African tradition. Bakhtin's metaphor of "double-voiced" discourse, figured within the black tradition most literally in representational sculptures of *Esu-Elegbara's* twin mouths and implied in the Signifying Monkey's function as the *rhetoric* of a vernacular literature, comes to bear in black texts through the trope of the Talking Book. In the slave narrative that I explicate in this essay, making the (white) written text "speak" with a (black) voice is the initial mode of inscription of the metaphor of the double voiced. This metaphor has proven to be of such fundamental import to the Afro-American literary tradition that it can usefully be thought of as the central informing metaphor of that tradition, its hidden "figure in the carpet," its speaking voice from within the woodpile. In Zora Neale Hurston, the concept of a doubled voice is complex, oscillating as representation among direct discourse, indirect discourse, and a unique form of free indirect discourse that serves to privilege the speaking voice. In Ishmael Reed's novel, *Mumbo Jumbo*, the double-voiced text emerges as the text of ultimate critique and revision of the rhetorical strategies at work in the canonical texts of the tradition. Finally, in Alice Walker's *The Color Purple*, the double-voiced text assumes the form of the epistolary novel in which revision manifests itself as a literal representation of a protagonist creating her self by finding her voice, but finding this voice in the act of *writing*. The written representation of this "voice" is a rewriting of the speaking voice that Hurston created for her protagonist of *Their Eyes Were Watching God*. Walker, in this brilliant act of "grounding" herself in the tradition by *Signifyin(g) upon* Hurston's rhetorical strategy, "tropes" Hurston's trope by "capping" (*metalepsis*), and *inverts* Hurston's effect of creating an "invisible" writing that "speaks," by creating an "invisible" speaking voice that, as it were, can only write!

The explication of the trope of the Talking Book enables us to witness the extent of intertextuality and presupposition at work in the first discrete "period" in Afro-American literary history. But it also reveals, rather surprisingly, that the curious tension between the black vernacular and the literate "white" text, the spoken and the written word, between the oral and the printed forms of literary discourse, has been represented and thematized in black letters at least since slaves and ex-slaves met the challenge of the Enlightenment to their humanity by writing themselves, literally, into being through carefully crafted representations in language of "the black self." Literacy, the very literacy of the printed book, stood as the ultimate parameter by which to "measure" the "humanity" of authors struggling to define the African self in Western letters. To establish a collective black "voice," through the sublime example of an individual text, and thereby to register a black presence in letters, most clearly motivated black writers, from the Augustan Age to the Harlem Renaissance. Voice and presence, silence and absence have been the resonating terms of a four-part homology in our literary tradition for well over two hundred years.

The trope of the Talking Book became the first repeated and revised trope of the tradition, the first trope to be Signified upon. The paradox of representing, of "containing" somehow, the oral within the written, *precisely* when oral black culture was transforming itself into a *written* culture, proved to be of sufficient concern for five of the earliest black autobiographers to repeat the same figure of the Talking Book that fails to speak, appropriating the figure accordingly with embellished rhetorical differences. Whereas Gronniosaw, Marrant, and Jea employ the figure as an element of plot, Cugoano and Equiano, with an impressive sense of their own relation to these earlier texts, bracket the tale in ways that direct attention to its status as a figure. The tension between the spoken and the written voice, for Cugoano and Equiano, is a matter they problematize as a rhetorical gesture, included in the text for its own sake, "voicing," as it were, for the black literary tradition a problematic of speaking and writing. John Jea's use of this curious figure has become decadent in the repetition, with the god in the machine here represented literally as the God who springs from the text to teach the illiterate slave to read in a primal, or supernatural, scene of instruction.

This general question of the voice in the text is compounded in any literature, such as the Afro-American literary tradition, in which the oral and written literary traditions constitute separate and distinct discursive universes, discursive universes that, on occasion, overlap, but often do not. Precisely because successive Western cultures have privileged written art over oral or musical forms, the writing of black people in Western languages has, at all points, remained "political," implicitly or explicitly, regardless of its intent or its subject. Then, too, since blacks began to publish books they have been engaged in one form of direct political dialogue or another, consistently to the present. The very proliferation of black written voices, and the concomitant political import of these, led fairly rapidly in our literary history both to demands for the coming of a "black Shakespeare or Dante," as one critic put it in 1925, and for an authentic black printed voice of deliverance, whose presence would, by definition, put an end to all claims of the black person's subhumanity. In the black tradition, writing became the visible sign, the commodity of exchange, the text and technology of Reason.

II

The first text in which the trope of the Talking Book appears is James Albert Ukawsaw Gronniosaw's first edition of *A Narrative of the Most Remarkable Particulars in the Life of James Albert Ukawsaw Gronniosaw, An African Prince, As Related by Himself.* Gronniosaw's narrative of enslavement and delivery had by 1811 been published in seven editions, including American editions in 1774 and 1810, and a Dublin edition in 1790. In 1840, another edition was published simultaneously in London, Manchester, and Glasgow. It is this edition to which I refer.[5]

Reading and writing were of signal import to the shaping of James Gronniosaw's text, as presences and absences refigured throughout his twenty-four page narrative. While the 1770 edition bears as its subtitle the fact that Gronniosaw "related" his tale "himself," the 1774 edition, "reprinted" at Newport, Rhode Island, claims that his narrative was "written by himself." When referred to in subsequent editions to 1840, "related" or "dictated" replace "written by himself." It is the narrator's concern with literacy that is of most interest to our argument here.

Gronniosaw's curious narrative has not enjoyed a wide reading among critics, or at least has not engendered many critical readings, unlike the works of his eighteenth-century colleagues John Marrant and Olaudah Equiano. What we know of him stems only from his slave narrative, generally thought to be the second example of the genre, after the 1760 *Narrative of the Uncommon Sufferings and Surprizing Deliverance of Briton Hammon, A Negro Man, ...* While the two texts are narratives of bondage and "deliverance," and although they both use the figure of the "return to my Native Land," Gronniosaw's most clearly inaugurates the genre of the slave narrative, from its "I was born" opening sentence to the use of literacy training as a repeated figure that functions to unify the structure of his tale.[6]

Who does Gronniosaw claim to be? Gronniosaw states that he was born "in the city of Bournou," which is the "chief city" of the Kingdom of Zaara. Gronniosaw's mother was the oldest daughter of the "reigning King of Zaara," and he was the youngest of six children. Gronniosaw stresses his intimate relationship with his mother, and to a lesser extent with his maternal grandfather, but rarely mentions his father, whom we presume was not born to royalty, but wed royalty. Gronniosaw's identification of himself in his narrative's title as "An African Prince" helps to explain the significance of this rhetorical gesture. By representing himself as a "Prince," Gronniosaw implicitly tied his narrative to the literary tradition of "The Noble Savage" and to its subgenre "The Noble Negro."[7]

Gronniosaw, in other words, represents himself as no mere common Negro slave, but as one nurtured, indulged, and trained in the manner of royalty everywhere. Faced with what must have seemed a deafening silence in black literary antecedents, Gronniosaw turned to the fictions of the Noble Savage to ground his text within a tradition. He also turned to the tradition of the Christian confession, referring to the import of works of Bunyan and Baxter on his quest to learn the identity of "some great Man of Power," as he proudly tells us. James Albert Ukawsaw Gronniosaw, in other words, represents himself as an ebony admixture of Oronooko and the Lord's questing Pilgrim.[8]

One of the ironies of representation of the Noble African Savage is that he or she is rendered noble through a series of contrasts with his or her black countrymen. Oronooko, we recall, bears acquiline features, has managed through some miraculous process to straighten his kinky hair, and speaks French fluently, among other languages. Oronooko, in other words, looks like a European, speaks like a European, and thinks and acts like a European—or, more properly, like a European king. Unlike the conventions of representing most other Noble Savage protagonists, Oronooko and his fellow black princes in bondage are made "noble" by a *dissimilarity* with their native countrymen. He is *the* exception, and not in any way the rule. Several Africans gained notoriety in eighteenth-century England and France by claiming royal lineage, and even attending performances of *Oronooko* on stage, weeping loudly as they were carried from the theatre.

Gronniosaw seized on this convention of Noble Savage literature, but with a critical difference. To ground himself in the tradition of Bunyan, Gronniosaw figures his sense of difference as the only person in his grandfather's kingdom who understood, "from my infancy," that "some great Man of Power . . . resided above the sun, moon, and stars, the objects of our [African] worship." Gronniosaw's salient sign of difference is his inherent knowledge that there existed one God, rather than the many worshipped by all and sundry in the Kingdom of Zaara.[9]

The youngest Prince's noble beliefs led, as we might suspect, to an estrangement from his brothers and sisters, and even, eventually, from his father, grandfather, and his devoted mother. Gronniosaw represents his discourse with his mother thusly:

> My dear mother, said I, pray tell me who is the great Man of Power that makes the thunder. She said that there was no power but the sun, moon, and stars; that they made all our country. I then inquired how all our people came. She answered me, from one another; and so carried me to many generations back. Then, says I, who made the *first man*, and who made the first cow, and the first lion, and where does the fly come from, as no one can make him? My mother seemed in great trouble; for she was apprehensive that my senses were impaired, or that I was foolish. My father came in, and seeing her in grief, asked the cause; but when she related our conversation to him, he was exceedingly angry with me, and told me that he would punish me severely if ever I was so troublesome again; so that I resolved never to say anything more to her. But I grew unhappy in myself.[10]

Gronniosaw tells us that "these wonderful impressions" were unique in all the Kingdom of Zaara, a situation "which affords me matter of admiration and thankfulness." But his alienation increased to such an uncomfortable extent that when "a merchant from the Gold Coast" offered to take young James to a land where he "should see houses with wings to them walk upon the water" and "see the white folks," he beseeched of his parents the freedom to leave. The only family tie that he regretted severing was that with his sister, Logwy, who was "quite white and fair, with fine light hair, though my father and mother were black."

Gronniosaw's "white" sister, from whom he resists separation, is one of three curious figures used in the text to represent his inherent difference from other black people. On one occasion, he describes "the devil" as "a black man" who "lives in hell," while he by contrast seeks to be washed clean of the blackness of sin. Moreover, the woman ordained by God for him to marry turns out to be white, echoing his bond with his "white" sister. Gronniosaw's color symbolism privileges whiteness, as we will see, at the expense of his blackness.[11]

The young prince, of course, is traded into slavery, and sails to "Barbadoes" where he was purchased by a Mr. Vanhorn of New York. His subsequent adventures, motivated by a desire to live among the "holy" inhabitants of England ("because the authors of the books that had been given me were Englishmen"), took him to "St. Domingo," "Martinco," "Havannah," and then to London and to Holland, only to return to marry and raise a family in England. The remainder of his *Narrative* depicts the economic hardships he suffers from racism and from evil people generally, and his fervent devotion to the principles of Christian dogma.[12]

What is of concern to us about James Gronniosaw's *Narrative* is his repeated references to reading and writing. His second master in New York, a Mr. Freelandhouse, and his wife "put me to school," he writes, where he "learnt to read pretty well." His master and mistress, wishing to help him to overcome his spiritual dilemma about the nature of this One God ("the Author of all my comforts") whom he discovered at New York, gave him copies of "John Bunyan on the Holy War" and "Baxter's 'Call to the Unconverted.' " As an example of the "much persecution" that he received from "the sailors," Gronniosaw writes that "I cannot help mentioning one circumstance that hurt me more than all the rest."[13] Even this scene of cruelty turns on the deprivation of a book:

> I was reading a book that I was very fond of, and which I frequently amused myself with, when this person snatched it out of my hand, and threw it into the sea. But, which was very remarkable, he was the first that was killed in our engagement. I do not pretend to say that this happened because he was not my friend; but I thought it was a very awful providence, to see how the enemies of the Lord were cut off.[14]

It is his ability to read and write and speak the Word of the Lord that motivates Gronniosaw's pilgrimage to England, as it did Phillis Wheatley, to "find out Mr. [George] Whitefield." Since Gronniosaw informs his readers late in his text that "I could not read English," and since he describes his eloquent discourse on religion with "thirty-eight ministers, every Tuesday, for seven weeks together" in Holland, and since his two masters at New York bore Dutch names, it is probable that he was literate in Dutch.[15] By the age of "sixty," which W. Shirley in his "Preface" estimates to be his age at the time of publication, he spoke fluent English, in which, like Caliban, he learned first "to curse and swear surprisingly."[16]

If Gronniosaw first learned the master's tongue to curse and swear, he quickly mended his ways. Indeed, almost from the beginning of his capture, Gronniosaw seems to have been determined to allow nothing to come between his desire to know the name of the Christian God and its fulfillment. Gronniosaw represents this desire within an extended passage in which he uses the trope of the Talking Book. He first describes his pleasure at disregarding the principal *material* sign of his African heritage, an extensive gold chain that must have been remarkably valuable, judging by its description:

> When I left my dear mother, I had a large quantity of gold about me, as is the custom of our country. It was made into rings, and they were linked one into another, and formed into a *kind of chain*, and so put round my neck, and arms, and legs, and a large piece hanging at one ear, almost in the shape of a pear. I found all this troublesome, and was glad when my new master [a Dutch captain of a ship] took it from me. I was now washed, and clothed in the Dutch or English manner.[17]

Gronniosaw admits to being "glad" when his royal chain, a chain of gold that signified his cultural heritage, was removed from him, to be replaced, after a proverbial if secular "baptism" by water, with the "Dutch or English" clothing of a ship's crew. That which signified his African past, a veritable signifying chain, Gronniosaw eagerly abandons, just as he longs to abandon the language that his European captors "did not understand."

Gronniosaw's signifying gold chain is an ironic prefigurement of Brother Tarp's link to *his* cultural heritage, a prison gang, in *Invisible Man*. When Tarp tells Ellison's narrator that his chain "had a whole lot of signifying wrapped up in it," and that "it might help you remember what we're really fighting against," we not only recall Gronniosaw's willingness to relinquish this chain, but we also begin to understand why. James Albert Ukawsaw Gronniosaw has absolutely no desire "to remember what we're really fighting against." As Tarp continues, such a signifying chain "signifies a heap more" than the opposition between "*yes* and *no*" that it connotes, on a first level of meaning, for the escaped prisoner. It is these significations that Gronniosaw seeks to forget.[18]

If Gronniosaw willingly abandons his signifying chain of gold, then he also is willing to discard that chain of signifiers that composed whatever African discourse he greeted his Dutch enslavers with. This desire he represents in the black tradition's first use of the trope of the Talking Book, which follows the unchaining ceremony in the same paragraph:

> [My master] used to read prayers in public to the ship's crew every Sabbath day; and when I first saw him read, I was never so surprised in my life, as when I saw the book talk to my master, for I thought it did, as I

observed him to look upon it, and move his lips. I wished it would do so with me. As soon as my master had done reading, I followed him to the place where he put the book, being mightily delighted with it, and when nobody saw me, I opened it, and put my ear down close upon it, in great hopes that it would say something to me; but I was very sorry, and greatly disappointed, when I found that it would not speak. This thought immediately presented itself to me, that every body and every thing despised me because I was black.[19]

What can we say of this compelling anecdote? The book had no voice for Gronniosaw, the book—or perhaps the very concept of "book"— constituted a silent *primary* text, a text, however, in which the black man found no echo of his own voice. The silent book did not reflect or acknowledge the black presence before it. The book's rather deafening silence *renames* the received tradition in European letters that the mask of blackness worn by James Albert Ukawsaw Gronniosaw and his countrymen was a trope of *absence*.

Gronniosaw can speak to the text only if the text first speaks to him. The text does not, not even in the faintest whisper, a decibel level accounted for by the black man's charming gesture of placing his "ear down close upon it." Gronniosaw cannot address the text because the text *will* not address Gronniosaw. The text does not "recognize" his presence, and so refuses to share its secrets, or decipher its coded message. Gronniosaw *and* the text are silent; the "dialogue" that he records that he had observed between book and master eludes him. To explain the *difference* between his master's relations to this text and the slave's relation to the same text, Gronniosaw seizes on one explanation and only one: the salient difference was his blackness, the very blackness of silence.

Gronniosaw explains the text's silence by resorting to an oxymoronic figure, a figure in which voice and presence, (black) face and absence are conflated. Perhaps a more accurate description of the figure is that Gronniosaw conflates an oral figure ("voice") with a visual figure (his black face). In other words, Gronniosaw's explanation of the silence of the text allows for no other possibility but one; and it, he tells us, suggested itself on the spot: "This thought immediately presented itself to me, that every body and every thing despised me because I was black."

Gronniosaw's conflation of the senses, of the oral and the visual— the book refused to speak to me because my face was black—was a curiously arbitrary choice for figural substitution. After all, a more "natural" explanation might have been that the book refused to speak to him because he could not speak Dutch, especially if we remember that this scene occurs on the ship that transports the newly captured slave from the Gold Coast to Barbados, the ship's destination. This more logical or natural explanation, however, did not apparently occur to the African. Instead, the curse of silence that the text yielded could only be accounted for by the curse of blackness that God had ostensibly visited on the dusky sons of Ham. The text's *voice*, for Gronniosaw, presupposed a *face*, and a black face, in turn, presupposed the text's silence since blackness was a sign of absence, the remarkably ultimate absence of face *and* voice. Gronniosaw could achieve no recognition from this canonical text of Western letters—either the Bible or else a prayer book—because the text could not *see* him or hear him. Texts can only address those whom they can see. *Cognition*, or the act of "knowing" as awareness and judgment, presupposes the most fundamental form of *recognition* in Gronniosaw's text. It was his black face that interrupted this most basic, if apparently essential, mode of recognition, thereby precluding communication.

This desire for recognition of his "self" in the text of Western letters motivates Gronniosaw's creation of a text, in both a most literal and a most figurative manner. Literally, this trope of the (non)Talking Book becomes the central scene of instruction against which this black African's entire autobiography must be read. The text refuses to speak to Gronniosaw, so some forty-five years later, Gronniosaw "writes" a text that "speaks" his face into existence among the authors and texts of the Western tradition. As I have shown above, no less than five subsequent scenes of instruction (in a 24-page text) are represented in the *Narrative* through tropes of reading and writing, including the curious scene in which Gronniosaw (with admirable control, if obvious pleasure) explains to us that the white man who "snatched" his favorite book from his hands and "threw it into the sea" proved to be "the first that was killed in our [first military] engagement." Gronniosaw represents a sixty-year life in a brief text that depends for the shape of its rhetorical strategy upon six tropes of reading and writing. The rhetorical patterning of his autobiography forces us to conclude that Gronniosaw narrates a text to satisfy the desire created when his first master's seminal text, the prayer book, refuses to address him. Gronniosaw, in other words, narrates a text that simultaneously *voices, contains*, and *reflects* the peculiar contours of his (black) face. Given the fact that by 1770, only four black people are thought to have published "books" in Western languages (Juan Latino, Jacobus Capitein, Wilhelm Amo, and Briton Hammon), Gronniosaw's gesture was a major one, if its motivation as inscribed in his central trope is ironic.[20]

But is his a "black" face as voiced in his text? When I wrote above that the ship captain's text and its refusal to speak to the slave motivated the slave to seek recognition in other Western texts (as figured in his several scenes of literacy instruction), I argued that this motivation was both literal and metaphorical. By metaphorical, I mean that the "face" of the author at sixty is fundamentally altered from that (black) African face that the adolescent Gronniosaw first presented in his initial encounter with his first Western text. Gronniosaw is a precise narrator, and is especially careful to state what he means. We recall that the trope of the Talking Book occurs in the same paragraph as does his description of his eager abandonment of the gold chain that signifies his African heritage. Indeed, he presents his face before the ship captain's speaking text only after he has been "washed, and clothed in the Dutch or English manner." The text represents this procedure as if it were a rite of baptism, but a secular or cultural cleansing or inundation that obliterates (or is *meant* to obliterate) the traces of an African past that Gronniosaw is eager to relinquish, as emblematized in his gold chain: "I found all this troublesome, and was glad when my new master took it from me."

In the sentence immediately following, Gronniosaw tells us that "My master grew fond of me, and I loved him exceedingly," unlike the mutual disdain and mistrust that had obtained between him and his "first" master. We recall that the first master, along with his partner, had persuaded the unhappy adolescent to leave the Kingdom of Bournou to seek the land of "the white folks," where "houses with wings to them walk upon the water." His second master "grew fond" of the "new" Gronniosaw, the Gronniosaw who had willingly submitted to being "washed, and clothed in the Dutch or English manner." His old master had related to an "old" Gronniosaw, an unregenerated (black) African Gronniosaw whose alienation from his traditional belief system and from most of the members of his family had, in retrospect, persuaded him to seek "the white folks" in the first place. Gronniosaw, in other words, was now capable of being regarded "fondly" by his second master because he was no longer the "pure" cultural African that he was when enticed to leave his village.[21]

If he was, at this point in his *Narrative*, no longer the African that he once was, he was not yet the Anglo-African that he would become, and that he so wished to be. "Clothes," and we might add, a good washing, "do not make the man," the ship captain's text in its silent eloquence informs the "new" Gronniosaw. He was merely an African, sans signifying chain, cloaked in European garb. His dress may have been appropriately European, but his face retained the blackness of his willingly abandoned African brothers. Gronniosaw, as he placed his ear close on the text, was a *third-term*, neither fish nor fowl: No longer the unadulterated African, he was not yet the "European" that he would be. The text of Western letters could not accommodate his liminal status, and therefore refused to speak to him, because Gronniosaw was not yet *this*, while clearly he was no longer *that*. It was not enough, the text in its massive silence informs him, to abandon his signifying gold chain to be able to experience the sublime encounter with the European text's chain of signifiers. Much, much more "washing" and "reclothing" would be demanded of him to make the text speak.

Forty-five years later, Gronniosaw registered his presence and figured the contours of his face, in the text of his autobiography. At sixty, he was fluent in *two* European languages, Dutch and English, he was a freed man, he was sufficiently masterful of the "Calvinist" interpretation of Christianity to discourse "before thirty-eight [Dutch] ministers every Tuesday, for seven weeks together, and they were all very satisfied," and he was the husband of an English wife and the father of both her child (by an English first marriage) and their "mulatto" children. The Christian text that had once refused to acknowledge him, he had by sixty mastered sufficiently not only to "satisfy" and "persuade" others by his eloquence "that I was what I pretended to be," but also to interweave within the fabric of his autobiographical text the warp and the woof of Protestant Christianity and the strange passage from black man to white. The presence found in Gronniosaw's own text is generated by the voice, and face, of assimilation. What is absent, of course, is the African's black mask of humanity, a priceless heritage discarded as readily as a priceless gold chain. Indeed, Gronniosaw's text is free of what soon became in the slave narratives the expected polemic against the ungodly enslavement of blacks. It is also free of descriptions of any other black characters, except for the "old black servant that lived in the [Vanhorn] family," Gronniosaw's first masters in New York, and except for his reference to "a black man called the devil." It was the "old black servant" who taught Gronniosaw about the devil's identity, and who, we presume (along with other servants), taught him to curse. No longer could Gronniosaw claim that "every body and every thing despised me because I was black."

Gronniosaw's important text in the history of black letters Signifies upon, in its trope of the Talking Book, two texts of the Western tradition. The first text is that of William Bosman, entitled *A New and Accurate Description of the Coast of Guinea*. Bosman's account of his travels in Africa was published in Dutch in 1704, and was published in English at

London in 1705. By 1737, four Dutch editions had been published, as well as translations in French and German. In 1752, an Italian translation appeared. At least two more English editions have been published in this century.[22]

Bosman was the Dutch "Chief Factor" at the Fort of Elmira, on the coast of West Africa (popularly called Guinea at the time) in what is now Ghana. Bosman is thought to have been the "second most important Dutch official on the coast of Guinea from about 1688 to 1702." Bosman's tenth "Letter" is devoted to "the Religion of the *Negroes*" at "Guinea," another name for the "Gold Coast" that appears in James Albert Gronniosaw's *Narrative*. Indeed, it is probable that Gronniosaw's Dutch ship captain set sail from the Fort of Elmira. It is just as probable that Gronniosaw and Bosman were at Elmira within twenty-three years of each other, if W. Shirley's estimate of Gronniosaw's age in 1770 is correct. If he has *underestimated* Gronniosaw's age, then it is conceivable that the two men could have been at Elmira at the same time. What is more probable is that Gronniosaw knew Bosman's Dutch text, especially "Letter X."[23]

Bosman's "Letter X," according to Robert D. Richardson, has had an extraordinary influence on the development of the concept of "fetishism" in modern anthropology, by way of Pierre Bayle's *Historical and Critical Dictionary* (1697, 1734–38) and Charles de Brosses's *Du culte des dieux fetiches* (1760), with the latter asserting that fetishism, as practiced by blacks in West Africa, was the most fundamental form of religious worship. Auguste Comte's declaration that a "primary, fetishistic, or theological stage" was central to the development of a society depended on de Brosses's 1760 theory of fetishism. Bosman's observations have proven to be central to the discourse on religion so fundamental to the development of anthropology in this century.[24]

Bosman's "Letter" begins with an assertion that "all the Coast *Negroes* believe in one true God, to whom they attribute the Creation of the World." This claim, of course, at first appears to be at odds with Gronniosaw's claim that he alone of all of the people in the Kingdom of Zaara held this belief. But Bosman quickly adds that for this belief in the *one* God the coastal blacks "are not obliged to themselves nor the Tradition of their Ancestors." Rather, the source of this notion is "their daily conversation with the *Europeans*, who from time to time have continually endeavoured to emplant this notion in them." The initial sense of *difference* that Gronniosaw strives so diligently to effect between himself and his African kinsman (his monotheism as opposed to their polytheism) is prefigured in Bosman's second paragraph.[25]

What is even more relevant here is that Bosman's account of the Ashanti people's myth of creation turns on an opposition between gold, on one hand, and "Reading and Writing," on the other. As Bosman recounts this fascinating myth:

> a great part of the *Negroes* believe that man was made by *Anansie*, that is, a great Spider: the rest attribute the Creation of Man to God, which they assert to have happened in the following manner: They tell us, that in the beginning God created Black as well as White Men; thereby not only hinting but endeavouring to prove that their race was as soon in the World as ours; and to bestow a yet greater Honour on themselves, they tell us that God having created these two sorts of Men, offered two sorts of Gifts, *viz*, Gold, and the Knowledge of Arts of Reading and Writing, giving the Blacks, the first Election, who chose Gold, and left the Knowledge of Letters to the White. God granted their Request, but being incensed at their Avarice, resolved that the Whites should for ever be their Masters, and they obliged to wait on them as their Slaves.[26]

Gold, spake God to the African, or the Arts of Western Letters: *choose*! The African, much to his regret, elected Gold and was doomed by his avarice to be a slave. As a footnote to Bosman's first edition tells us, the African's avarice was an eternal curse and his punishment was the doom of never mastering the Western arts and letters.

If the African at the Creation was foolish enough to select Gold over "Reading and Writing," James Albert Ukawsaw Gronniosaw, African man but European in the making, would not repeat that primal mistake. Rather, Gronniosaw eschewed the temptation of his gold chain and all that it signified and sought a fluency in Western languages through which he could remake the features, and color, of his face.

If Gronniosaw echoes Bosman, probably self-consciously, then he also echoed Kant, probably not aware of Kant's 1764 German text. Writing in *Observations on the Feelings of the Beautiful and Sublime*, Kant prefigures Gronniosaw's equation of his black skin with the text's refusal to speak to him. Kant, drawing on Hume's note on blacks in "Of National Characters," argues that "So fundamental is the difference between these two races of man, [that] it appears to be as great in regard to mental capacities as in color." Two pages later, responding to a black man's comment to Jean Baptiste Labat about male-female relations in Europe, Kant delivers this supposedly *natural* relation between blackness and intelligence: "And it might be that there was something in this which perhaps deserved to be considered; but in short, this fellow was quite black from head to foot, a clear proof that what he said was stupid." Gronniosaw, after Kant, presupposes a *natural* relation between black-

ness and being "despised" by "every body and every thing," including
the Dutch ship captain's silent primary text. To undo this relation,
Gronniosaw devoted his next forty-five years, until he was fully able to
structure the events of his life into a pattern that "speaks" quite eloquently, if ironically, to readers today.[27]

III

After 1815, the trope of the Talking Book disappeared from the black
literary tradition.[28] John Jea's extended revision, in which God answers
the slave's desperate prayers by emerging from the Bible and teaching
him to read, is the final usage of the trope.[29] After Jea's revision, or
"erasure" as I am thinking of it, the trope of the Talking Book disappears
from the other slave narratives published in the nineteenth century. No
longer is this sign of the *presence* of literacy, and all that this sign
adumbrates in the life of the black slave, available for revision after Jea
has "erased" its figurative properties by his turn to the supernatural.
Rather, the trope of the Talking Book now must be displaced in a
second-order revision in which the absence and presence of the *speaking*
voice is refigured as the absence and presence of the *written* voice. Jea's
scene of instruction, or midnight *dream* of instruction (did it actually
happen, he wonders aloud as we his readers wonder, or was it "only a
dream?" he asks), represents the "dream" of freedom as the "dream"
of literacy, a dream realized as if by a *miracle* of literacy. Jea's "dream"
is composed of elements common to the usages of his black antecedents,
but the central content of the trope has been expanded *disproportion-
ately* from its figurative associations to its most literal level, wherein an
"angel" teaches the slave how to read and thus escape the clutches of
the "devil" that keeps the slave in chains. Equiano's "angel" was the
white woman married to his master; Frederick Douglass's guardian "angel" was the white woman married to his master. Many of the post–
1830 slave narrator's "guardian angels" are also white women or children, related directly or indirectly by a marriage bond to the master.

These representations of the mastery of letters (literally, the
"ABC's") are clearly transferences and displacements of the "dream"
of freedom figured for the tradition by Jea's text, again in the most
literal way. Whereas Jea's Signifyin(g) relation to Gronniosaw, Marrant,
Cugoano, and Equiano is defined by a disproportionate expansion and
elaboration on the contents of their tropes, to such an extent that we
are led to conclude that these narrators could have saved themselves

loads of trouble had they only prayed to God intensely for six weeks to make the text speak, Jea's revision "erased" the trope (or Signified upon it by reducing it to the absurd) for the slave narrators who follow him in the tradition. They no longer *can* revise the trope merely by displacing or condensing its contents. Rather, Jea's supernatural *naming* demands that a completely new trope be figured to represent what Jea's revision has made "unrepresentable" without some sort of "censorship," *if* the narrator is to be "believed" and "believable" as one who is capable of, and entitled to, the enjoyment of the *secular* idea of liberty that obtains in a text of a life such as Frederick Douglass's. Because Douglass and his black contemporaries wish to "write" their way to a freedom epitomized by the abolition movement, they cannot afford Jea's luxury of appealing, in his representation of his signal scene of instruction, primarily to the Christian converted. Douglass and his associates long for a secular freedom *now*. They can ill afford to represent even their "previous" selves—the "earlier" self that is transformed, as we read their texts, into the speaking subjects who *obviously* warrant full equality with white people—as so naive as to believe that books "speak" when their masters "speak" to them. Instead, the post-Jea narrators *refigure* the trope of the Talking Book by the secular equation of the mastery of slavery through the "simple" mastery of letters. Their "dream" of freedom, figured primarily in tropes of *writing* rather than *speaking*, constitutes a displacement of the eighteenth-century trope of the Talking Book, wherein the "presence" of the human voice "in" the text is only implied by its absence as we read these narratives and especially their tropes of writing "against" the trope that we have been examining here.[30]

These narrators, linked by revision of a trope into the very first black chain of signifiers, implicitly Signify upon another "chain," the metaphorical Great Chain of Being. Blacks were most commonly represented on the Chain either as the "lowest" of the human races, or as first cousin to the ape. Since writing, according to Hume, was the ultimate sign of difference between animal and human, these writers implicitly were Signifyin(g) upon the figure of the Chain itself, simply by publishing autobiographies that were indictments of the received order of Western culture of which slavery, to them, by definition stood as the most salient sign. The writings of Gronniosaw, Marrant, Equiano, Cugoano, and Jea served as a critique of the sign of the Chain of Being and the black person's figurative "place" on the Chain. This chain of black signifiers, regardless of their intent or desire, made the first political gesture in the Anglo-African literary tradition "simply" by the act of writing, a collective act that gave birth to the black literary tradition and defined it as the "other's chain," the chain of black being as black people themselves would have it. Making the book speak constituted a motivated, and political, engagement with and condemnation of Europe's fundamental figure of domination, the Great Chain of Being.

The trope of the Talking Book is not a trope of the presence of voice at all, but of its absence. To speak of a "silent voice" is to speak in an oxymoron. There is no such thing as a silent voice. Furthermore, as Juliet Mitchell has put the matter, there is something untenable about the attempt to represent what is not there, to represent what is *missing* or absent. Given that this is what these five black authors sought to do, we are justified in wondering aloud if the sort of subjectivity they seek can be realized through a process that is so very ironic from the outset. Indeed, how can the black subject posit a full and sufficient self in a language in which blackness is a sign of absence? Can writing, the very "difference" it makes and marks, mask the blackness of the black face that addresses the text of Western letters, in a voice that "speaks English" in an idiom that contains the irreducible element of cultural difference that will always separate the white voice from the black?[31] Black people, we know, have not been "liberated" from racism by their writings, and accepted a false premise by assuming that racism would be destroyed once white racists became convinced that blacks were human too. Writing stood as a complex "certificate of humanity," as Paulin J. Hountondji put it.[32] Black writing, and especially the literature of the slave, served not to obliterate the difference of "race," as a would-be white man such as Gronniosaw so ardently desired; rather, the inscription of the black voice in Western literatures has saved those very cultural differences to be preserved, imitated, and revised in a separate Western literary tradition, a tradition of black difference.

Notes

1. The trope appeared in Garcilasso de la Vega's 1617 edition of *Historia General del Peru*, in an account of the confrontation between Pizzaro and the great Inca king, Atuahualpa. This is probably the black tradition's source of the figure. See Garcilasso de la Vega, *The Royal Commentaries of Peru*, Part II: *General History of Peru,* trans. Sir Paul Rycaut (London: Miles Flesler, for Samuel Hendrick, 1688), pp. 456–57. Jose Piedra located this reference for me.

2. My understanding of "liminality" arises from Robert Pelton's usages in *The Trickster in West Africa*. Houston A. Baker's usage is also relevant here, as taken from Victor Turner's work. See Baker's *Blues, Ideology, and Afro-American Literature: A Vernacular Theory* (Chicago, 1985).

3. James W. C. Pennington, "To the Reader," in Ann Plato, *Essays; Including Biographies and Miscellaneous Pieces, in Prose and Poetry* (Hartford: Printed for the Author, 1841), pp. xviii, xx. The italics are Pennington's.

4. See Sarah D. Jackson, "Letters of Phillis Wheatley and Susanna Wheatley," *Journal of Negro History*, LVII, No. 2 (April, 1972), 214–15, and William H. Robinson, *Phillis Wheatley in the Black American Beginnings* (Detroit: Broadside Press, 1975), pp. 15–18. See also "To the Publick," in *Poems on Subjects, Religious and Moral, by Phillis Wheatley, Negro Servant to Mr. John Wheatley, of Boston, in New England* (London: A. Bell, 1773), n.p.

5. For a full list of his book's editions, see Jahheinz Jahn and Claus Peter Dressler, *Bibliography of Creative African Writing* (Millwood, N.Y.: Kraus-Thomson Organization, 1975), p. 135. The 1770 edition was published by S. Hazard, with an Introduction by W. Shirley. The 1770 edition consists of 49 pages, but the 1840 edition I am using has 29 pages.

6. Briton Hammon, *Narrative* (Boston: Green & Russell, 1760), p. 14; James Albert Ukawsaw Gronniosaw, *Narrative*, p. 17.

7. See Wylie Sypher, *Guinea's Captive Kings: British Anti-Slavery Literature of the XVIIIth Century* (Chapel Hill: Univ. of North Carolina Press, 1942), pp. 103–55.

8. Gronniosaw, *Narrative*, p. 11.

9. Ibid., p. 3.

10. Ibid., pp. 4–5.

11. Ibid., pp. 3, 5, and 9.

12. Ibid., p. 14.

13. Ibid., pp. 10, 11, 13.

14. Ibid., p. 15.

15. Ibid., pp. 17, 21. George Whitefield, a central figure of the Protestant Great Awakening of the eighteenth century, appears frequently in black texts published before 1800. Gronniosaw, Phillis Wheatley, and Equiano, among others, refer to him or depict him as a character in their narratives.

16. Ibid., pp. 8, 9, and 19.

17. Ibid., p. 8. Emphasis added.

18. Ralph Ellison, *Invisible Man* (New York: Random House, 1982), p. 293. See the epigraph to Chapter Three.

19. Gronniosaw, *Narrative*, p. 8.

20. I say forty-five years later because W. Shirley, the author of the Preface to Gronniosaw's *Narrative*, deduces that he was "about fifteen years old" when "James Albert left his native country," and that at the time of publication, "He now appears to be turned of sixty."

21. See pp. 8, 10, 11, 14, 15, 19, and 21.

22. William Bosman, *A New and Accurate Description of the Coast of Guinea* (1705; New York: Barnes and Noble, 1967). These facts, as well as the biographical description that follows, are taken from Robert D. Richardson's headnote to his reprinting of "Letter X" in *The Rise of Modern Mythology, 1680–1860*, edited by Burton Feldman and Robert D. Richardson (Bloomington:

Indiana Univ. Press, 1972), pp. 41–42. All subsequent citations refer to this edition.

23. Elmira Fort, or "Castle," was the site of Jacobus Capitein's departure from Africa and his subsequent return. Capitein was one of the African children chosen to be educated in Europe as an experiment to ascertain the black's "capacity" for "progress" and "elevation." Feldman and Richardson, eds., *The Rise of Modern Mythology*, p. 42.

24. Margaret T. Hodgen, *Early Anthropology in the Sixteenth and Seventeenth Centuries* (Philadelphia: Univ. of Pennsylvania Press, 1964), p. 491. Feldman and Richardson, p. 42.

25. Feldman and Richardson, p. 44.

26. Ibid., pp. 44–45.

27. Immanuel Kant, *Observations on the Feeling of the Beautiful and the Sublime*, trans. by John T. Goldthwait (Berkeley: Univ. of California Press, 1960), pp. 111, 113.

28. Rebecca Cox Jackson, in an autobiographical manuscript (1830–32) not published until 1981, revises Jea's figure of the primal scene of literacy instruction. See *Gifts of Power: The Writings of Rebecca Jackson, Black Visionary, Shaker Eldress*, Jean McMahon Humez, ed. (Amherst: Univ. of Massachusetts Press, 1981), pp. 107–8.

29. John Jea, *The Life, History, and Unparalleled Sufferings of John Jea, the African Preacher* (Portsea, England: Printed for the Author, 1815), pp. 33–38.

30. On the relation between freedom and literacy, see Robert B. Stepto, *From Behind the Veil: A Study of Afro-American Narrative* (Urbana: Univ. of Illinois Press, 1979), pp. 3–32.

31. Recently published work by the linguist William Labov argues that "black English vernacular" is "becoming more different from standard English rather than more like it." See William K. Stevens, "Black and Standard English Held Diverging More," *New York Times*, March 15, 1985, p. A14.

32. Paulin J. Hountondji, *African Philosophy: Myth and Reality* (Bloomington: Indiana Univ. Press), p. 204, note 3.

6

Black Elk Speaks with Forked Tongue

G. Thomas Couser

Autobiography . . . expresses a concern peculiar to Western man, a concern that has been of good use in his systematic conquest of the universe and that he has communicated to other cultures; but those men will thereby have been annexed by a sort of intellectual colonizing to a mentality that was not their own.

Georges Gusdorf (p. 29)

Critical opinion has been almost unanimous in praising *Black Elk Speaks* as an authentic and authoritative Indian autobiography, thus reinforcing the popularity that has made it since the 1960s something of a cult classic. Its power and appeal are undeniable: Witness the frequent references to it in William Least Heat Moon's recent best-seller, *Blue Highways*, and its current invocation by Sioux attempting to regain control of sacred lands from the government. Indeed, it has been virtually canonized, both as autobiography and as Indian Bible. Critics have singled it out as a trustworthy narrative, an exception to the heavily edited—and thus corrupted—narratives gathered by anthropologists.

There are many interesting reasons for its exceptional reliability. Black Elk was distinguished from most "native informants" (as they are somewhat ominously called) not only by his status as a medicine man and visionary but also by the degree of his initiative in proposing the narrative, in choosing his collaborator, and in arranging the timing and circumstances of the narration. Equal weight has been given to the exceptional suitability and preparation for the task of his collaborator, John Neihardt, who was a mystic and an epic poet of the West. As a mystic, Neihardt had a spiritual affinity with Black Elk; as an amateur historian of the West, he was knowledgeable about Indian history and Indian religion; and as a poet, he had the skills to translate the transcribed narrative into compelling prose. Finally, there is the ritual adoption of Neihardt that in effect authorized the text.

One after another, the critics have praised Black Elk, John Neihardt, and the text they collaboratively produced (with the help of Black Elk's son and Neihardt's daughter). But the notion of the text as a valid one that offers an invaluable insight into Lakota culture has, until recently, rested on Neihardt's own account of the collaboration—presented first in his Preface and later added to in interviews with scholars—and on a reading of the text of *Black Elk Speaks* in isolation from the transcripts. Given the estimation of the book as a paragon of Indian autobiography, its inability to withstand close scrutiny made possible by recent developments in theory and recent publication of the transcripts is particularly distressing. But notwithstanding Neihardt's abundant talent, his exceptional empathy, and his noble intentions, *Black Elk Speaks* is not nearly as reliable as it appears or has been made out to be. Indeed, I want to argue that it unwittingly reenacts the process it so eloquently condemns: the appropriation and erasure of Lakota culture by whites.

Before detailing the shortcomings of *Black Elk Speaks* (the ways in which it is not—because it cannot be—an authentic Indian autobiography), I would like to acknowledge the considerable efforts Neihardt made to honor Black Elk's narrative. To read the recently published transcripts is to be impressed by the sheer scope and complexity of the job and the ingenuity and dedication involved. Neihardt apparently sensed that the narrative's meaning resided in the transaction as a whole rather than in its discrete message and attempted to convey the process by which it was produced. In his Preface, he explains the circumstances of his meeting Black Elk and arranging to record the story. And the first chapter is given over not to the story but to the ceremony by which Neihardt was adopted and renamed Flaming Rainbow and through which the narrative was released. Similarly, the book acknowledges its doubly collaborative nature throughout. Whole sections are spoken by several older tribe members who are present to supplement the narrative, with stories of events Black Elk did not witness, and to verify it. They give the narrative a communal dimension not only through their contributions but also by their recorded presence. Moreover, the use of shifters frequently reminds us of Neihardt's presence and of the surroundings, grounding the book in a particular spatial as well as temporal framework. Thus, Black Elk's "asides" (such as "when you look about you can see what it was they wanted") locate the narrative in a particular (sacred) landscape and remind the reader of the transaction that produced it. The language of the narrative—simple but dignified, vivid and detailed but concise—obviously accounts in part for the book's force and credibility. In particular, details of the translation effectively convey an Indian point of view. Whether or not the phrase yellow metal literally translates a Lakota term for gold, the term demystifies the substance and allows a reader momentarily to view it from outside a cultural perspective.

But the problems that remain are severe enough to vitiate the book's virtues. The point here is not that Neihardt was unequal to the task, but that the task was impossible; the failure was not one that could have been avoided by a more careful editor but one determined by culture. Nor does it make sense to bemoan the book's existence. As H. David Brumble has observed, bicultural documents like this one can teach us much about "the effects of cultures in collision, the effects of literacy, the history of autobiography, literature, and literary theory" (p. 2). *Black Elk Speaks* is best seen as a text that raises, and illuminates, a series of interesting problems pertinent to the authority of autobiography in America.

First there is the complicated issue of the translation of oral materials into written ones, for writing entails authorship and history, both alien to preliterate cultures. The idea of authorship reaches full development when the printed book makes possible, on the one hand, the close identification of an individual with a fixed text, and, on the other, the dramatic spatial and temporal extension of that individual/text (McLuhan, pp. 131–32). This bears directly, and ironically, on *Black Elk Speaks*: As we will see, in participating in the production of a book, Black Elk attained something like authorship but at the same time relinquished authority over his vision. History begins with writing because contradictions are easier to detect in texts, which are linear and static; thus, written documents, unlike myths, encourage—because they permit—correction, verification, and rationalization (Goody, pp. 11–14). Writing begs for—actually compels—editing, which is, after all, the superimposition of another authority over that of the text's primary producer.

Thus, when Black Elk's oral narrative is written down, it does not merely pass from one language to another; it passes from one mode of understanding the universe to another, from myth to history. This occurs despite Neihardt's conscious attempts to thwart the process; he tries, for example, to give the narrative a mythic quality by using Indian names (translated into English: Moon When the Cherries are Ripe) for months, years, and places. The inevitability and irreversibility of the process are suggested by the fact that Raymond J. DeMallie's publication of the transcripts of the interviews—avowedly an attempt to recover the historical Black Elk from Neihardt's interpretation—is far more heavily edited. DeMallie cannot retroactively revoke Neihardt's poetic license and cancel its effects; he must, by virtue of his profession as a scholar, *correct* Black Elk when he gets events out of order or confuses one with another. Thus, his attempt to restore the original "text" finally surrounds it with extensive scholarly apparatus; the narrative is further textualized, even intertextualized, as DeMallie identifies events with the help of published sources.

We must be grateful for the editing, for we compulsively seek to understand the narrative by inscribing it within our own history—indeed, it may be the only way we can grant its reality—but we must acknowledge that between the mythic world that Black Elk inhabited and recreated and the world we inhabit there remains a gulf created not just by language but by written texts. The problem is not merely academic; the relationship between oral and written agreements (promises, treaties) is perhaps the most vexed issue in the history of Indian/white relations.

The translation of oral into written narratives presents other less global problems—problems of accuracy and reliability, for example. Dennis Tedlock has argued that the performative qualities of oral literature—gesture, tone, timing, and sound effects—can be suggested, in freshly recorded narratives, by means of typographical effects (pp. 513–17), and Dell Hymes has shown how oral literature can be retranslated—recuperated—from original transcripts. Neither of these ingenious attempts to use typography to recreate oral forms helps much with *Black Elk Speaks*, for the transcripts are several removes from Black Elk's Lakota, which was rendered into idiomatic "Indian English" by his son, Ben Black Elk, then into Neihardt's standard English, which was recorded stenographically by his daughter.

Black Elk's language and gestures remain irrecoverable, yet it is good to bear in mind Hymes' warning that translations of Indian narratives and songs by their collectors are often inaccurate and his belief that literal translations are more valuable than literary ones. Since, according to Hymes, "literary" patterns are more often imposed on than discovered in native materials (pp. 38–39), Neihardt's talent and experience as a poet may have been liabilities rather than assets. Indeed, Blair

Whitney, the author of the Twayne volume on Neihardt, who necessarily sees *Black Elk Speaks* as part of his oeuvre, stresses the features it shares with his other work. Even DeMallie, who argues that Neihardt's free translation is likely to be "more faithful to the intended meaning than a strictly verbatim recording," concedes, "in a sense, Neihardt was already 'writing' Black Elk's story by rephrasing his words into English" (p. 32).

A scholar interested in assessing the accuracy or faithfulness of Neihardt's translation soon reaches an impasse beyond which one can proceed only by the strenuous exercise of intuition. A look at the transcripts impresses one with the superior "readability" and the greater dignity and consistency of tone of *Black Elk Speaks*; but one cannot know how close the effect is to the original Lakota or to Black Elk's "intended meaning," neither of which is available for inspection. And there is extratextual evidence, as we'll see later, that Black Elk was not entirely pleased with the book. Moreover, comparison of the text and the transcripts suggests that Neihardt was editing in terms of preconceptions about what Indian "longhairs" ought to be like.

A related issue is that of the genre and its genesis. In an MLA volume on Indian literature, the author of an essay on autobiography has claimed that, at its best, autobiography offers a "penetrating insight into the private world of the subject. . . . Nowhere else is such direct and intense contact possible as in the works that issue from recorded autobiography" (Sands, p. 56). But the assumption of a division between public and private selves, the assumption that Indian autobiography will be confessional, and that the genre can afford the best insight into tribal culture— all these are disturbing preconceptions. For, as Robert Sayre has noted, "Autobiography, as any editor thinks of it himself, depends on European and American concepts of *life, self,* and *writing.* The Indians obviously had no such thing" (p. 512).

Indeed, the very idea of autobiography involves an equation between a life and a book that is altogether alien to preliterate cultures; the implications of Indian participation in the form have not been sufficiently explored. In a sense, Indian autobiography is *always* collaborative, or at least bicultural, because the suggestion that life can take literary form is itself a kind of editing. Indeed, the suggestion that autobiography is possible and the questions that elicit its materials create the very kind of self-consciousness that is conventionally thought to generate the genre (Brumble, pp. 1, 3–4). In this sense, at least, the structuralists appear to be right; autobiography produces self-conscious selves, rather than vice versa.

The sources of the conventions of Indian autobiography are murky, but H. David Brumble has suggested that Neihardt's version of the genesis of this book may owe more to Paul Radin's introduction to the autobiography of Crashing Thunder than to the facts, and has pointed out that, whatever *its* source, *Black Elk Speaks* has helped to make the claim that "the *Indian* is eager to have the god-sent white man preserve the Indian's sacred knowledge" a convention of white-assisted autobiographies (p. 29). DeMallie has suggested that Neihardt and Black Elk may have had different expectations and purposes in the interviews—as much, I think, because this explains certain tendencies of the editing as it explains certain subsequent events: "Neihardt conceived of the project as writing Black Elk's life story, whereas Black Elk conceived of it as making a record of the Lakota religion" (p. 62). That is, the white writer imagined the end result as autobiography; the Lakota visionary, as communal or sacred history. In any case, the more closely one examines the text in its context, the more elusive its authority—and its author—becomes. To put it differently, the more one knows about *Black Elk Speaks*, the more one senses that it differs in degree rather than in kind from the white-produced Indian shows in which Black Elk participated, and that its proper epigraph might be his remark about Buffalo Bill's Wild West Show: "I liked the part of the show we made, but not the part the Wasichus [whites] made" (p. 221).

In addition to the problems inherent in any collaborative oral autobiography, *Black Elk Speaks* involves the issue of its visionary dimension. It has been prized above other Indian autobiographies partly because of its prophetic impulse. But, as I see it, the essential problem of reading the book lies in the fact that it is ghostwritten in two profoundly different and competing senses. First, as a visionary narrative, it is *ghost*written; it originates not with a living individual but with the ghosts of his ancestors and the spirits of the earth, and in an important sense its authority derives from them. But it is also ghost*written*, for it is committed to the page not by the narrator but by a surrogate, amanuensis, collaborator—call him what you will. Thus, the vision, if not the entire narrative, is twice mediated—first through Black Elk from his ancestors, then through Neihardt from Black Elk. (The medicine man, unlike the poet, admits that the vision is ineffable and that he is an imperfect vehicle.) Moreover, Neihardt became a medium in a second sense, after Black Elk's death, as the living person who answered questions on behalf of the deceased. Thus, while Black Elk sought to locate the narrative's authority in a communal and transcendent source, its basis slowly but inexorably shifted—from the supernatural to the secular, the tribal to the western, the communal to the individual, the Lakota to the English, the visionary to the written. Even though Neihardt's creative role has increasingly been recognized—because he insisted on it—most critics have not seen this as compromising the book's special status. We need to be reminded that, in the end, we see Black Elk not face to face but through a gloss, whitely; that is, we see him not only through a translation whose accuracy cannot be assessed but through a surface that obscures him by reflecting us.

Carol Holly's view best represents the canonical reading of *Black Elk Speaks*: "The shape that Neihardt lent to Black Elk's narrative, particularly through his arrangement and partial writing of the first and final chapters, both unifies the narrative and lends it an authenticity unequalled by the life stories recorded for the purpose of scientific study" (p. 120). And later: "Neihardt's structure for *Black Elk Speaks* reflect[s] and define[s] Black Elk's identity.... For these reasons, *Black Elk Speaks* represents a genuine marriage between native American consciousness and Western literary form, thus becoming what I take the liberty to call the first American Indian autobiography" (p. 121). It seems to me that this claim not only is not true but *cannot* be true. (For one thing, authenticity cannot be *lent*; or if it can, it can be recalled.) Still, for reasons I will explore later, the idea has been very attractive, especially to white readers.

It is not surprising that Hilda Neihardt Petri, who witnessed the recording of the narrative, should reiterate this self-contradictory claim in her Foreword to *The Sixth Grandfather*: "*Black Elk Speaks* is authentic; it does convey with faithful sincerity Black Elk's message. But in presenting this message to the reader, Neihardt created a work of art, and true art in all its forms is an intensification and greatly clarified form of communication" (p. xviii). But it is surprising that DeMallie expresses a similar attitude toward the text. While he warns that many have underestimated the extent of Neihardt's creative role, he adds that others have failed "to appreciate the sincerity of Neihardt's commitment to make the book speak for Black Elk faithfully, to represent what [he] would have said if he had understood the concept of literature and if he had been able to express himself in English" (p. xxii).

Indeed, DeMallie in a way compounds the problem, for after paying his respects to Neihardt, he claims in effect that *his* book does what Neihardt's failed to do: "The intention of this book is to allow readers direct access to Black Elk, the historical personage" (p. xxiii). This claim cannot be true either, for as DeMallie admits, the transcripts represent language at several removes from Black Elk's. DeMallie's presumption is not equal to Neihardt's, of course, and its source lies in scholarship rather than mysticism. Furthermore, his full account of the collaborative transaction reveals distortions in *Black Elk Speaks* and thus arms its readers against presumption. Neihardt was no doubt sincere in his belief in his spiritual affinity with the holy man. But the danger implicit in such a belief is apparent in a letter he wrote to his publisher, William Morrow: "There was a very peculiar merging of consciousness between me and Black Elk, and his son, who interpreted for me, commented on the fact. Very often it seemed as though [he] were only repeating my thoughts or my own poetry although he knows no English and is utterly unaware of the existence of literature. . . . Once he said, 'This man could make an ant talk' " (DeMallie, p. 41). We can never recover Black Elk's motives or intentions, but DeMallie's research permits us to see that he took somewhat less initiative than Neihardt claimed; that as early as the fall before the interviewing was done, Neihardt had conceived of the book as covering the story of Black Elk and his tribe up to the Battle of Wounded Knee; and that he intended to pay Black Elk for his time (p. 29). (There is no evidence that profit was an important motive for either party, but in view of the distaste expressed by many critics for the work of paid informants, it is wise to acknowledge that this privileged collaboration was not without an economic dimension.)

DeMallie's publication of the transcripts also makes very clear one of Neihardt's editorial practices, the consistent suppression of Black Elk's awareness of white western culture and technology (p. 52). When this extends to the substitution of descriptive phrases for the names of cities and towns, the results sometimes seem ironic: Omaha becomes "a very big town" and Chicago "a much bigger town" (Neihardt, p. 220). Without knowing what Black Elk's locations were, we should not make too much of this. But Neihardt's editing out of the narrative of biblical phrases such as "many were called but few were chosen" is part of his strategy of concealing crucial facts about Black Elk, facts still known to very few readers of the book: that he became a Roman Catholic early in this century and, more startling perhaps, served as a catechist and successful missionary to other Indians for decades thereafter. Black Elk's conversion to Christianity was probably less a matter of profound and total inner change than of accommodation to the repression of traditional religious practices. Although Black Elk gave up conjuring and healing completely, his conversion and career as a catechist evidently allowed him to continue to function in a traditional role and to participate in an ongoing communal life (DeMallie, pp. 23, 26, 92). At least, this helps explain his sudden willingness, even eagerness, to share his vision with

Neihardt some twenty-five years after his apparent renunciation of the old beliefs.

His conversion was, of course, viewed differently by the local priests, and the publication of *Black Elk Speaks* aroused considerable consternation among them. Indeed, the consternation was so great that in 1934 Black Elk "spoke" again; in a document signed by him and witnessed by his daughter and his priest, he reaffirmed his faith in Christianity. And in a letter to missionaries, he complained that he had realized not a cent of the promised profits and that Neihardt had denied his request to append an account of his conversion to the end of the narrative (DeMallie, pp. 59–63). In spite of this, he later participated in annual pageants in which he reenacted his practice as a healer, and he gave two more major interviews in which he passed on his teachings to white collaborators. (The first, given in 1944 to Neihardt, resulted in *When the Tree Flowered*; the second, in 1947 to Joseph Epes Brown, resulted in *The Sacred Pipe*.) Black Elk's behavior seems self-contradictory. But, taken as a whole, the evidence suggests that, rather than desiring to renounce *Black Elk Speaks*, Black Elk sought to appease the local authorities. It also implies that he saw little conflict between his roles as catechist and as repository of the suppressed and thus endangered religion of his ancestors.

Having granted his first set of interviews, Black Elk discovered that the authorities found his published "pagan" self inconsistent with their image of him (he had in fact been pictured on Church literature instructing his daughter in religion) and that they had a large stake in the ideas of consistency, orthodoxy, and conversion. Thus, he was caught between two irreconcilable "selves" (both produced in collaboration with white men), each of which claimed historical authority for itself. Unable to regain authority over his narrative, he could only generate other texts that would qualify his relationship to it and make his life livable again. That is, haunted by his own textually produced double, he found that his only escape lay in the creation of other texts and other selves. At this historical distance, it is not easy to know his motives or beliefs. What seems clear is that while generating a book served certain needs, it also entangled him among texts and created verbal reservations about him.

Neihardt's role as editor was especially decisive at the borders of the narrative, beginning with the title page. His daughter Hilda has cited the title as evidence of his desire to make the book Black Elk's from the start (p. xviii). But *Black Elk Speaks* is not Black Elk's speech. Thus, Neihardt's first gesture, intended to identify Black Elk as the

source of what follows, backfires because it displaces him from the first
to the third person. Nor is Black Elk what he should be called, necessarily; it is an unhappy medium between his Lakota name, Hehaka Sapa,
and his Christian name, Nicholas Black Elk. If Neihardt is to have
Flaming Rainbow after his name—thus doubling him—Black Elk ought
perhaps to have his Lakota name after his English one. The use of
names in Indian narratives is often complicated by the custom of using
various names over a lifetime (Brumble, p. 7), so Neihardt faced a
genuine dilemma, but his choice perfectly exemplifies his contradictory
desires to characterize Black Elk as an unreconstructed "longhair" and
to make him accessible to a white audience. The title page creates
uncertainty from the start as to who's entitled to what follows.

The book's style and content are problematical, too. Lacking the
original Lakota, we cannot decisively analyze the "translation." But the
consistency and dignity of tone of *Black Elk Speaks* are not only missing
from the transcripts, they may be found in earlier Neihardt works
(DeMallie, p. 52). One would expect the book's content to be more
straightforward: Surely the book's stated beliefs can be safely attributed
to Black Elk. But the case here is not simple either. According to Blair
Whitney, "Though Neihardt says Black Elk spoke through him, it is
equally correct to say that Neihardt speaks through Black Elk, since the
Sioux holy man asserts many of Neihardt's personal beliefs and dram-
atizes in his narrative some of Neihardt's own themes" (p. 93). Whitney
seems to view this as a happy coincidence, but in fact it is evidence of
a serious problem: Neihardt's background, which would seem to make
him the ideal (i.e., transparent) medium for the conveyance of Black
Elk's message, seems to have emboldened him to take liberties another
collaborator would not have taken. It might seem that concern with the
exact boundaries of Neihardt's and Black Elk's contributions to what
was already a collaborative account of tribal history is beside the point.
But the issue of boundaries is a loaded one in the text and one that
must be dealt with tactfully by its producers and its consumers. Moreover, there are disturbing implications in Whitney's casual but revealing
reversal of the usual account of the collaboration: There is an important
sense, as we will see, in which Black Elk became Neihardt's medium.

Two other aspects of the narrative are especially problematic. One is
its focus on Black Elk; as Sally McCluskey points out, the transcripts
include more description of ritual than the finished book and, as she
reports, Neihardt referred to the use of the first person as "a literary
device" (p. 232). Thus, while the book retains some element of communal tribal culture, it omits a good deal, too. As a result of the editing,

McCluskey asserts, "Black Elk appears here as a priest second, a man first" (p. 233). Needless to say, this may not be the way he perceived or presented himself. Here is more evidence that Neihardt's editing, which he may have thought would make the narrative *more* autobiographical, was what made it "autobiographical" in the first place.

The narrative's chronology also subtly imposes alien conventions and world views on the narrative. In an interview with McCluskey shortly before he died, Neihardt stated that "he had to fashion Black Elk's story from many days of talk, many reminiscences recalled not necessarily in order" (p. 232). Chronology is so conventional in Western autobiography that it seems a natural, even inevitable, ordering principle. But to commit *this* narrative to a time-line is to privilege historical time over mythic time; it violates the Lakota sense of time as cyclical rather than sequential. The premise of both Black Elk's vision and the Ghost Dance religion is of communication with a world that transcends simple chronology. The cumulative effect of these decisions is to shape the book according to expectations irrelevant to Lakota culture; the medium (Western autobiography) becomes the message.

The narrative's opening lines take on a peculiar irony in the light of McCluskey's discoveries: "My friend, I am going to tell you the story of my life, as you wish; and if it were only the story of my life, I think I would not tell it" (p. 1). Here Black Elk concedes more than he knows to his collaborator, since he is telling his story not only in *response* to Neihardt's wish but also in the *way* that Neihardt wishes (or, more properly, *wills*). This passage is further complicated by McCluskey's revelation that it is entirely Neihardt's invention (p. 237). What appears to be Black Elk's defense, to his collaborator, of the distinctively Lakota qualities of his narration is actually that collaborator's indirect explanation to his white readers of qualities he has partially bleached out of the text. This is not Black Elk, historical personage, speaking through John Neihardt, his passive instrument; it is Neihardt, self-proclaimed author of the book, speaking through the mask of Black Elk, which is to say, creating a literary character by means of invented speech. (An additional irony accrues because passages like this are conventional opening gambits for Western autobiographies: Franklin, Thoreau, and Adams—to name a few classic American autobiographers—all begin their narratives with strategies designed to deflect the charge of egotism.)

Now, in collaborative autobiography, it may never be possible to tell just where the work of one party leaves off and the other begins. But here we have a remarkable thing: a text that seems to establish a clear boundary—by means of the shift from "frame" to "narrative" and by the use here of the first- and second-person pronouns—only to have it erased by a later collaboration between the author and a third party. Neihardt's admission, intended to correct the impression that he had merely recorded the narrative, makes it evident that Black Elk's speech was not quoted but reconstructed (and at times invented), that there was no clear distinction between the words of one and those of the other, after all. (Ironically, DeMallie points out that the most frequently quoted passages are those known to be contributed by Neihardt [p. 55].) If, as Bakhtin believed, dialogue is a form of struggle between the participants on the territory of the utterance, and if, as his interpreters say, "This territorial concept of the word requires a politics of representation" [p. 15], then the evidence suggests that *Black Elk Speaks* is governed by a form of (at best) benevolent dictatorship. What is true in one sense of the opening paragraphs is true in another of the entire text: It is an act of ventriloquism, told not by Black Elk through Neihardt but vice versa.

The ending also reveals Neihardt's designs and preconceptions. In claiming credit for the narrative's organization, in his interview with McCluskey, he asserted that he concluded with the Battle of Wounded Knee because he considered that to be the most dramatic event. He also acknowledged that he shaped the whole for a white audience: "The translation—or rather the *transformation*—of what was given to me was expressed so that it could be understood by the white world" (pp. 238–39). It should be remembered here that when Neihardt first approached Black Elk, it was in quest of material about the Ghost Dance religion for his poem cycle, which was to end with that battle as the climax of white conquest of the West. Though a different book resulted from his visit, the ending was the same—and, in this sense, at least, it was a foregone conclusion.

Indeed, the end is forecast in the third paragraph, where the story is described as that of a "mighty vision, given to a man too weak to use it . . . and of a people's dream that ended in bloody snow" (p. 2). But although much did end there—one does not want to minimize the significance of the battle—Black Elk's life did not, nor did his vision. Indeed, he maintained the dream long afterward, and it was the burden of his vision to deny the finality of such events. The orientation of his vision is toward a redemptive future; the progress of the narrative, by contrast, is toward a disaster that seems the fulfillment of all that precedes it. While the narrative structure merely implies that tribal culture ended with the battle, the final paragraphs say so explicitly: "I did not know how much died there. . . . And I, to whom so great a vision was given in my youth—you see me now a pitiful old man who has done nothing, for the nation's hoop is broken and scattered. There is no center any longer, and the sacred tree is dead" (p. 276).

But these paragraphs, like the first three, are Neihardt's creation, and so are the attitude of failure and the tone of despair they impart. (DeMallie suggests that Neihardt may have misread the tone of humility conventional in Lakota prayer as expressing an attitude of hopelessness toward history [p. 56].) The effect of the premature ending is to dismiss Black Elk's reservation life as nonexistent; this parallels and reinforces the effect of Neihardt's suppression of his Christianity. It is evident, in reading the transcripts, that the remembering consciousness is one informed, if not dominated, by a Christian perspective. But because of its erasure of phrases and attitudes characteristic of the semiassimilated reservation Indian, *Black Elk Speaks* gives the impression of a consciousness remote in time from, but close in spirit to, the life of the Plains. There is a certain truth in this, of course, but the effect of such editing is to characterize Black Elk as a man who has aged but not changed—certainly not grown—in the intervening years.

The editing does not stop the clock exactly—if anything, it emphasizes the march of time—but it arrests Lakota history in both its personal and communal dimensions. To end the narrative so *conclusively* with the Battle of Wounded Knee is the literary equivalent of killing off the survivors; it is a subtle but insidious form of cultural genocide. The effect is to encourage white readers to indulge in an uncomplicated pathos at the demise of a noble way of life rather than to compel them to contemplate its survival in assimilated forms. While Neihardt's translation records the vision in a compelling, because preternaturally clear, prose, he fails to devise a narrative form that can present it in any but a pathetic and nostalgic way. Thus, the narrative does not entirely transcend that romantic cliché, the song of the dying Indian.

If, as Henry Adams declared, autobiography is the literary equivalent of suicide—the taking of one's life in prose—and biography is the literary equivalent of murder—character assassination in print (pp. 512–13), then collaborative autobiography is a kind of literary mercy-killing, in which one party agrees to have his or her life taken by a sympathetic other. But with literary as with literal euthanasia, it is not always clear who is being merciful to whom. And when the already complicated act involves members of different, and historically hostile, races, then the transaction becomes especially perilous.

If anthropologists are accused, by literary critics, of murdering tribal culture to dissect it, then anthropologists might accuse Neihardt of murdering Black Elk to resurrect him—to give him immortality in literary form, as a martyr. One irony of this would be that, even as he suppressed his Christianity, Neihardt may have helplessly encoded his life in terms of Christian mythology. Indeed, one troubling feature of the collaboration is that it casts a white man as the only true disciple of the Lakota prophet or Messiah, for Neihardt sees himself as the perpetuator and disseminator of the faith. However, in the terms of the narrative, he is equivalent to Wovoka, who proves to be a false savior. For Black Elk finally recognized Wovoka's vision as a corrupt one that unwittingly conflated Sioux and Christian mythology. (The historical ironies here are terrible, for although the Ghost Dance religion was essentially a syncretic, pacifist crisis cult, its enthusiasm so threatened reservation administrators that it was brutally suppressed.)

It is especially ironic that Neihardt's own revelations began to expose the flaws in a seemingly seamless collaboration. His admission that he wrote the first and last paragraphs is devastating, for it literally changes the formal boundaries of the narrative, the point at which the Lakota wor(1)d meets the white wor(1)d. As Neihardt encroaches on Black Elk's verbal territory, the book unintentionally inscribes in itself the process it explicitly and eloquently condemns: the historical expropriation of Indian lands by whites, if not by violence, by means of manipulative verbal contract.

But when we have grasped the implications of Neihardt's editing, we may see that we should not have required his testimony or the revelations of McCluskey and DeMallie to expose the book's self-contradictions. For its own tropes—they are, ironically, almost all Neihardt's, for the use of metaphor was one of his strategies for giving the book the power of poetry—deconstruct it. Its lament for the displacement of the tribe from round tipis based on sacred archetypes to frame houses based on Western models comments on the use of a framed narrative and the confinement of an oral narrative to blocks of print. Black Elk's childhood fear of being "rubbed out" by Wasichus is ironically realized by Neihardt's editing, which erases some of his distinctive Lakota features, even as it exaggerates others. Finally, the condemnation of the white hunters who slaughtered buffalo for their tongues indicts the process by which the white reader acquires and consumes Black Elk's preserved speech.

Apparently, Black Elk surrendered his most precious possession, his vision, to Neihardt in the hope that he could smuggle it intact out of the reservation, on which tribal religion had been literally outlawed.

But the narrative remains confined within the invisible reservations of its own unconscious ethnocentrism. What is surprising is not that the narrative is tainted with ethnocentrism, but that it passed for genuine for so long. The reason for this is perhaps not far to seek: the truth of Indian/white relations is so intolerable that we try desperately to escape it. Lacking historical instances of harmonious relations between the races, we invent literary ones. Witness the well-documented tradition of idealized relations between white and colored males in the novels of Cooper, Melville, Mark Twain, and others. Most critics of *Black Elk Speaks* have treated it as a historical example of communication and cooperation between majority and minority races when it may be just another fictional one.

Neihardt's narrative speaks with a forked tongue in many senses. (Ironically, judging from the transcripts, Black Elk never used the phrase forked tongue, though he complained about the Wasichus' lies.) It speaks with a divided tongue in the way that all collaborative auto-biography must, because it conflates two consciousnesses (and in this case cultures and languages) in one undifferentiated voice. And it deceives by not fully acknowledging the extent and the tendencies of its editing. The book also falsifies because of the contradictory senses in which it contains the historical tensions between Wasichus and Lakotas. Superficially, it contains (includes) them as its subject, and clearly indicts them. But surreptitiously it contains (confines) them by attributing them to a distant past and erasing them from the present. In this way it *conceals* them, rendering them invisible under its gloss. Thus, the book's greatest deception is its most subtle one—its pretense that the means of its production escaped the cultural imperialism the text condemns. The Preface claims that the collaboration was mutual and egalitarian—in effect, that it took place outside the historical conditions it describes. But the editing is clearly implicated in—it encodes—cultural imperialism.

It is, finally, the book's metaphors, whatever their source, that expose the text's contradictions. For the text undoes what it says, by reenacting the process it condemns. While Black Elk repeatedly refers to the present predicament and his vision points to a distant future, the narrative produced is largely retrospective; Black Elk's attempts to free the narrative from chronology are defeated by Neihardt's editing, especially by its truncated ending, which severs the tragic past from the present. Black Elk remains marooned, confined to the black road of print that marches inexorably across the page. His speech is preserved here as Lakota culture is preserved on the reservation: in conditions neither wholly of its making nor freely of its choosing. Neihardt, too, is caught in a trap of his own creation. In making *Black Elk Speaks* autobiography (rather than sacred history), he made it less Indian; in trying to make it more Indian (editing out evidence of assimilation), he made it less autobiographical (a less accurate record, apparently, of Black Elk's life)—until Indian autobiography is revealed to be a misnomer, if not an oxymoron, like collaborative autobiography. For all these reasons, the voice of *Black Elk Speaks* always and inevitably speaks with a forked tongue.

Works Cited

Adams, Henry. Letter to Henry James, 6 May 1908. In *The Education of Henry Adams*. Ed. Ernest Samuels. Boston: Houghton Mifflin, 1973.

Brumble, H. David, III. *An Annotated Bibliography of American Indian and Eskimo Autobiography*. Lincoln: Univ. of Nebraska Press, 1981.

Clark, Katerina, and Michael Holquist. *Michael Bakhtin*. Cambridge: Harvard Univ. Press, 1984.

DeMallie, Raymond J., ed. *The Sixth Grandfather: Black Elk's Teachings Given to John G. Neihardt*. Lincoln: Univ. of Nebraska Press, 1984.

Goody, Jack. *The Domestication of the Savage Mind*. Cambridge: Cambridge Univ. Press, 1977.

Gusdorf, George. "Conditions and Limits of Autobiography." Trans. James Olney. In *Autobiography: Essays Theoretical and Critical*. Ed. James Olney. Princeton: Princeton Univ. Press, 1980. 28–48.

Holly, Carol. "*Black Elk Speaks* and the Making of Indian Autobiography." *Genre* 12 (Spring 1979): 117–36.

Hymes, Dell. *"In Vain I Tried to Tell You"*: *Essays in Native American Ethnopoetics*. Philadelphia: Univ. of Pennsylvania Press, 1981.

McCluskey, Sally. "*Black Elk Speaks*—And So Does John Neihardt." *Western American Literature* 6 (Winter 1972): 231–42.

McLuhan, Marshall. *The Gutenberg Galaxy*. London: Routledge and Kegan Paul, 1962.

Neihardt, John. *Black Elk Speaks, Being the Life Story of a Holy Man of the Oglala Sioux*. New York: Morrow, 1932.

Sands, Kathleen Mullen. "American Indian Autobiography." In *Studies in American Indian Literature*. Ed. Paula Gunn Allen. New York: MLA, 1983.

Sayre, Robert F. "Vision and Experience in *Black Elk Speaks*." *College English* 32 (1971): 509–35.

Tedlock, Dennis. "Toward an Oral Poetics." *NLH* 8, No.3 (Spring 1977): 507–19.

Whitney, Blair. *John G. Neihardt*. Boston: Twayne, 1976.

7

Dialogue in Antebellum Afro-American Autobiography

William L. Andrews

Of what use is dialogue to an autobiographer? What risks does an autobiographer take when he or she novelizes a narrative by introducing dialogue into its predominantly monologic mode of address? This is one of the more problematic issues we can raise in the criticism of auto-biography, whether we study it in terms of its historical credibility, rhetorical purpose, or literary value. We know that the increasing in-cidence and varying uses of dialogue in American literature of the nine-teenth century signaled great changes in the evolving form and function of American prose style.[1] What I want to talk about here is the signif-icance of dialogue to the evolution of Afro-American narrative in the nineteenth century, focusing on the genre of autobiography in its crucial formative years between 1845 and 1865.

In the two decades before Emancipation, black autobiography served as a kind of sociocultural crucible in which some of the era's most interesting literary experiments were conducted in how to tell the truth about experience, in this case, Afro-American experience. By the mid-nineteenth century, black autobiographers had recognized that their great challenge was much more than just telling the truth; they had to *sound* truthful doing it, or else risk the failure of their rhetorical enter-prise. Thoreau might demand of every writer "a simple and sincere account of his own life,"[2] but he didn't explain how one could invest such an account with sincerity and credibility, especially if one were of a race generally assumed by white Americans to be inherently untrust-worthy. One thing is clear to the reader of early black autobiography, however. The genre treated Thoreau's desiderata for autobiography—

sincerity and simplicity—as mutually reinforcing and needful and thus cultivated its own version of the Protestant plain style.

The aim of this plain style was, ostensibly at least, a strictly mimetic rendering of the facts of Afro-American life. Nothing that might prompt the reader to suspect that he or she was reading fiction could be allowed in a text. Slave narrators were particularly sensitive to the charge of having fictionalized their stories for ulterior purposes. They knew that much of their audience would concur with a noted leader of the American Anti-Slavery Society who wrote in 1839: "simple-hearted and truthful" as fugitive bondmen from the South might appear to be, one "must recollect that they are slaves—and that the slave, as a general thing, is a liar."[3] Critics of the slave narrative usually accused their authors of lying when they discovered facts that sounded "exaggerated." In response, black autobiographers promised to understate the facts of their experience in the hope that this gesture of insincerity, this tacit admission of self-censorship, would inspire white confidence in their sincerity. A second way in which black autobiography tried to confirm its sincerity was by admitting nothing that smacked of "the imagination" into its discursive agenda. One reason why the *Narrative of the Life and Adventures of Charles Ball* (1836) was so popular was that its editor promised to be "no more than the recorder of the facts detailed to him by another," rendering them in a style "as simple" and "as plain as the laws of language would permit." The goal was to "exhibit, not to [the reader's] imagination, but to his very eyes, the mode of life" that slaves had to live.[4] Indeed, one of the best guarantees that William Lloyd Garrison could give Frederick Douglass's *Narrative* (1845) was that nothing in it had been "drawn from the imagination." Rather than "exaggerate," Douglass had deliberately "come short of the reality" of slavery as he knew it.[5]

Twentieth-century historians and literary critics have shown a similar preference for and confidence in the plain style over most forms of imaginative expression in antebellum black autobiography. Probably the most eminent historian in the field has suggested that "literary flourishes" in a text are one of the more prominent earmarks of white editorial meddling with a black person's story. The most recent literary history of slave narratives posits "the sentimental novel" as the origin of many of the "literary embellishments" that ex-slaves introduced into their accounts. "Many narratives were full of long passages of dialogue," in which a "black Joseph Andrews or Pamela" might be found discussing "the moral and spiritual dangers which assailed every slave of sensibility." We need not worry about being deceived by such imaginative corruptions of the slave narrative, however, for, as another major critic of black autobiography reminds us, the more fictitious a slave narrative, the more it "reads like a novel, replete with reconstructed dialog and false sentiment."[6]

In the literary history of Afro-American autobiography, books that display, almost to the point of flaunting, literary self-consciousness have often been distrusted as fictional pretenders to the real thing—dangerous supplements, we might call them today, that threaten by amplification and artfulness the essential truth that presumably inheres in the plain style.[7] As the quotations that I have just cited attest, dialogue is often treated as one of the most suspect of these supplements to monologic simplicity and straightforwardness. I would like to argue in response to this suspicion that dialogue in autobiography, black or white authored, is a feature of what Bakhtin has called the "novelization" of narrative, a phenomenon that helps to keep any genre, in this case mid-nineteenth-century slave autobiography, in "a living contact with unfinished, still evolving contemporary reality."[8] The "reality" that slave narratives evoke for us through dialogue is not so much what people actually said as what they were doing (or trying to do) in and through certain conventions of discourse. An autobiographer who "dialogizes" his or her narrative is often more important to us as a dramatizer of basic sociolinguistic realities that structured the relationships of blacks and whites in slavery than as a recorder of spoken discourse. Dialogue in slave narratives tells us something about the negotiation of power that goes on in discourse, whether between a master and a slave or a black autobiographer and a reader.

The crucial fact attending all concrete discourse in Bakhtin's view is this: "language, for the individual consciousness, lies on the borderline between oneself and the other. The word in language is half someone else's." Before someone appropriates a word for his or her own purposes "it exists in other people's mouths, in other people's contexts, serving other people's intentions: it is from there that one must take the word, and make it one's own." To speak or to write is to enter "a dialogically agitated and tension-filled environment of alien words, value judgments and accents." To use language, therefore, is to engage in a power struggle, for "language is not a neutral medium that passes freely and easily into the private property of the speaker's intentions." It belongs to the other, and "expropriating it, forcing it to submit to one's own intentions and accents, is a difficult and complicated process."[9]

Consider, for example, the dialogue between William Wells Brown and his St. Louis master, Dr. John Young, after Young informed his slave that he intended to sell him. Appealing to the doctor's sense of fair play and familial responsibility, Brown's expostulation with his master concludes with "will you sell me to be carried to New Orleans or some other place?"

> "No," said he, "I do not intend to sell you to a negro trader. If I had wished to have done that, I might have sold you to Mr. Walker [a slave-trader to whom Brown had been hired out the previous year] for a large sum, but I would not sell you to a negro trader. You may go to the city, and find you a good master.
> "But," said I, "I cannot find a good master in the whole city of St. Louis."
> "Why?" said he.
> "Because there are no good masters in the state."
> "Do you not call me a good master?"
> "If you were you would not sell me."
> "Now I will give you one week to find a master in, and surely you can do it in that time."

Having extracted this concession from his master, Brown went to St. Louis, spent a couple of days visiting his mother and his incarcerated sister, and then ran away to Illinois. After his apprehension and return to slavery, Brown's master summoned him and "asked me where I had been? I told him I had acted according to his orders. He had told me to look for a master, and I had been to look for one. He answered that he did not tell me to go to Canada to look for a master."[10]

This is a prototypical instance of the "dialogizing" of black autobiography. What we witness here is something more than the expected verbal dictation of power from a master to a slave. We discover instead an exchange between two interlocutors that immediately belies the idea of the unquestioned authority of the one over the other. In fact, this is a verbal sparring match in which the white and black man are contending for mastery of the word "master." Young unwittingly introduces this loaded word into the discourse, assuming that he has control over the word, assuming, implicitly, that this word is exempt from Bakhtin's "dialogic imperative," which keeps all signification in flux and subject to "competing definitions for the same things." As soon as Young lets the word out of his mouth, Brown snatches it and starts to signify on it. That is, he "dialogizes" it in a manner peculiar to the oral culture of black America. Signifying on the term "good master," Brown reiterates Young's language to reverse and confuse the relationship between himself and *his* master. Like all signifying, Brown's constrains Young (and the implied reader of the *Narrative*) "to attend to all potential meaning carrying symbolic systems in speech events—the total universe of discourse," or, what Bakhtin would call the "heteroglossia" surrounding the word "master."[11] Expropriating the white man's language, tricking it out in his own sly idiom, and then returning it "dialogically," the signifying slave lays claim to the right to redefine terms like "master" and "slave." This is the prelude to redefining himself as a freeman.

For ex-slaves like Brown, it was essential to show that the master-slave relationship was not monologic, but rather dialogic. Though standard abolitionist propaganda stressed the absolute power of master over slave, "novelized" slave narratives insist, through repeated instances of dialogue between whites and blacks, that the terms of the master-slave relationship were not *dictated* from the one to the other in an "I talk—you listen" fashion. In fact, those terms were often the subject of negotiation in and through dialogic verbal jousts, some taking the form of jokes, other escalating into speech acts of defiance.[12] During such dialogic negotiation, what speech-act theorists would call the appropriateness conditions of master-slave discourse were suspended along with the rules that limited the language of that discourse to the master's meanings. Dialogue, therefore, often became a liminal phase in the master-slave relationship, when neither master nor slave was in full control of the situation, when they implicitly agreed to an "indeterminacy" of outcome to their verbal combat. Within such indeterminacy, we must remember, lies a margin of freedom, even for slaves that would seem to be the most powerless. This is especially important to recognize in that most "dialogized" of antebellum black autobiographies, Harriet Jacobs's *Incidents in the Life of a Slave Girl* (1861).

It is not a coincidence that the first autobiography written by a female slave in the United States contains more reconstructed dialogue than any male-authored slave narrative. Jacobs knew that many apologists for slavery were fond of depicting the slave owner as the benevolent patriarch of his extended plantation family, who presided over all his dependents with biblically sanctioned authority. Jacobs also knew that when abolitionists attacked the "patriarchal institution," they singled out black women as its special, nearly hopeless victims, totally "unprotected" from their master's lust for power and forced, therefore, to be "entirely subservient to the will of their owner."[13] Jacobs "dialogized" her narrative because she was unsatisfied with both characterizations of plantation patriarchalism. The dialogues she creates between herself and white men, especially her master, Dr. Flint, tell us more about male-female power relationships under slavery than we are likely to find in any other antebellum source.

Most of the discourse between Jacobs and Flint occurs when the white man hopes to cajole or coerce his slave into submitting to his various demands. It should be noted that most of these dialogues pivot on arguments over the slave woman's right to speak certain words in certain contexts, to define herself through language that her master denies is applicable to her. It should also be noted that in none of these debates is the verbal struggle resolved absolutely in favor of the master. Between Jacobs and Flint the word "love" is constantly at issue. "Do you love this nigger?" the doctor impatiently inquires when young Harriet asks permission to marry a free Negro carpenter. When she replies, "Yes, sir," Flint thunders, "How dare you tell me so!"[14] By putting these words in Flint's mouth, Jacobs underlines the fact that it is the *telling* as much or more than the *feeling* of love that angers the master. He can tolerate the idea of her pairing up with a black man (so long as it is one of his slaves), but he cannot abide hearing her talk about love, for this is a word that signifies a feeling to which he would deny her access. To name the feeling is to know the difference between what Flint and the young carpenter desire of the slave woman. Flint tries immediately to reclaim the empowering word: "I supposed you thought more of yourself; that you felt above the insults of such puppies." Jacobs neatly parries the attempt to redefine love as "insult": "The man you call a puppy never insulted me, sir; and he would not love me if he did not believe me to be a virtuous woman." The doctor's response is to give his slave "a stunning blow," an obvious sign that, having lost the verbal combat, his only recourse is physical violence. The slave woman makes a verbal rejoinder, "How I despise you!" which caps the argument over whom she loves by identifying unmistakably whom she hates.

Shrieking "Silence!" and demanding never to hear Harriet speak of the freeman again, Flint tries once more to repress the "dialogic imperative" that underlies the competition between the master and slave for the right to define and apply the word love. However, he cannot simply take the word out of commission; it is the only route through which he can learn anything about the slave woman's secret affections. Thus, after the birth of Jacobs's first child, with the doctor desperate to know who his rival is, he tries first to shame, then threaten, then wheedle the information out of her, but with no success. Finally, after extracting her admission that the child's father is white, he returns to the crucial word. "He sprang upon me like a wolf, and grabbed my arm as if he would have broken it. 'Do you love him?' said he, in a hissing tone." Jacobs's reply is the perfect squelch. "I am thankful that I do not despise him" (p. 92). This evades the question of how she feels about the unnamed white man while echoing the conclusion of her previous interview with Flint. It is an act of verbal obfuscation that leaves Flint tormentingly ambivalent about the manner and degree of his response to Jacobs. Nothing that Jacobs can say in these interviews can free her of her master, but her repeated "dialogic" struggles with Flint testify to the power she could and did exercise against his attempts to manipulate and dominate her.

In dialogues like this one, Harriet Jacobs illustrated graphically the discursive nature of male-female power relationships under racist patriarchalism. What is striking is the structure, as much as the content, of this dialogue. The white man does not simply issue commands that the black woman silently obeys. The pretenses of patriarchalism require that in some cases he talk her into submission to him. If the slave woman seizes the right opportunities with presence of mind, she may talk her way out of the most abject forms of humiliation. The relationship of master and concubine is interstitial, somewhere between that of master and slave and husband and wife. The source of the power of the master over his concubine is not sanctioned in law or instituted in recognized praxis; it is relative only to the individual instance and the informal ties that bind the two parties together. Under such circumstances, power is much more likely to be negotiable than to be absolutely fixed in either party. And power, as Jacobs shows us, is negotiated through speech acts, through dialogue in which the woman constantly matches wits with the man in order to define a margin of option for herself. Jacobs does not imply that the average slave woman could have done what she was able to do in her verbal bouts with Flint. Few slave women could risk talking back to their masters as she did; one who forgot "that it was a crime for a slave to tell who was the father of her child" is sold away from Dr. Flint's plantation early in *Incidents*. This victim of Flint upbraids him with his promise "to treat me well," but the white man is immovable. "You have let your tongue run too far; damn you!" he replies (p. 24). Jacobs, by contrast, knows just how far her tongue can get her, and when to use it to purpose.

Instances of dialogue provide moments of comic release from the oppressive pattern of white-to-black dictation that threatens to enclose many slave narratives in tragedy. Though Jacobs's discourse with Flint is almost never humorous, it plays a comic role in her story nonetheless by reinforcing her inner resources and preparing her for her eventual triumph over patriarchal slavery at the end of her book. Moreover, through dialogue we sometimes receive a distinctly comic perspective on patriarchal authority that reduces it through ridicule to a level that makes it easy for the black protagonist to "talk down" to it condescendingly. This occurs in Jacobs's account of her repartee with a gang of white marauders who use Nat Turner's insurrection as an excuse to rob, horsewhip, and kidnap unprotected blacks in the area. When these "low whites" arrive, spoiling for a chance to "exercise a little brief authority" over Jacobs and her grandmother, both women indulge themselves in sassy rejoinders to the "soldiers," knowing that they are "in the midst of white families who would protect us" (p. 99).

> My grandmother had a large trunk of bedding and table cloths. When that was opened, there was a great shout of surprise; and one exclaimed, "Where'd the damned niggers git all dis sheet an' table clarf?"

> My grandmother, emboldened by the presence of our white [male] protector, said, "You may be sure we didn't pilfer 'em from *your* houses."

On discovering the young slave woman can read and write, the captain of the patrol demands all her letters.

> I told him I had none. "Don't be afraid," he continued, in an insinuating way. "Bring them all to me. Nobody shall do you any harm." Seeing I did not move to obey him, his pleasant tone changed to oaths and threats. "Who writes to you? half free niggers?" inquired he. I replied, "O, no; most of my letters are from white people. Some request me to burn them after they are read, and some I destroy without reading." (p. 101)

This unwelcome, unexpected knowledge "put a stop to our conversation." The white men complete their search by sampling Grandmother Martha's preserves and then depart, pronouncing "a malediction on the house."

In this comic scene, the black women skillfully play off one class of male power against another and, for a time, they enjoy the freedom of their interstitial position between the "better" and the "low" class whites in their region. As narrator, Jacobs reconstructs the scene with a freedom approaching that of a caricaturist. First she recounts in general terms the ruthlessness of these troops of feral white trash "terrifying and tormenting the helpless." Then, through their dialogue with the black women, she transforms these rampaging "demons" into bumbling dimwits who are easily made the butts of ridicule. For once, Southern whites, not slaves, speak in a dialect removed from dignified English; the narrator must intervene editorially to help us make sense of cracker vernacular like: "Don't wonder de niggers want to kill all de white folks, when dey live on 'sarves' [meaning preserves]" (p. 101). For a moment, the power of the word backed by women's wit seems more than a match for the crude strength of these gabbling male ignoramuses.

But should we be wondering how true all this is, how much credibility we ought invest in this scene? Given the many doubts that have been raised about Jacobs's narrative as a highly fictionalized account,[15] should we question her judgment in employing the skills of a Southwestern humorist to skewer the patriarchy in this scene? Obviously not. When slave narrators like Jacobs or Brown opted for dialogue as a way of telling their stories, they were also opting for, indeed demonstrating in favor of, freedom, in this case, literary freedom. Jacobs and Brown are in a sense liberating their narratives from the fetters of monolithic facts and monologic voice. What else would we expect of two free people than that they tell their stories freely? Whether we call this sort of behavior in a text something positive, like free "novelizing," or something negative, like phony fictionalizing, will be a function of our own sense of how much an autobiography owes to the past or to the self when fidelity to each makes a conflicting demand on the writers. By the mid-nineteenth century black autobiographers had learned that they could not serve two masters—the past and the self—equally. Self-expressiveness through dialogue presides over retrospective mimesis in the autobiographies of a Harriet Jacobs or a William Wells Brown because of such writers' commitment to the ideal of freedom, not just as the theme of their life quests or as the moral aim of their narratives, but as the distinguishing characteristic of their style of storytelling.

Notes

1. Richard Bridgman, *The Colloquial Style in America* (New York: Oxford Univ. Press, 1966), pp. 62–77.

2. *Walden and Civil Disobedience*, ed. Owen Thomas (New York: Norton, 1966), p. 1.

3. Gerrit Smith, "Letter to Editor of the Union Herald," *Emancipator*, 3 January 1839, p. 146, col. 2.

4. See the Preface to *Slavery in the United States: A Narrative of the Life and Adventures of Charles Ball* (New York: John S. Taylor, 1837).

5. See Garrison's Preface to the *Narrative of the Life of Frederick Douglass*, ed. Houston A. Baker, Jr. (New York: Viking Penguin, 1982), p. 38.

6. John W. Blassingame, *The Slave Community* (New York: Oxford Univ. Press, 1972), p. 233; Frances Smith Foster, *Witnessing Slavery* (Westport, Conn.: Greenwood, 1979), pp. 58–59; Charles H. Nicholas, *Many Thousand Gone* (Leiden: E. J. Brill, 1963), p. xiii.

7. The idea of the "dangerous supplement" is Derrida's, of course. See *Of*

98   STUDIES IN AUTOBIOGRAPHY

Grammatology, trans. Gayatri Chakravorty Spivak (Baltimore: Johns Hopkins Univ. Press, 1976), pp. 144–45.

8. M. M. Bakhtin, *The Dialogic Imagination*, ed. Michel Holquist, trans. Caryl Emerson and Michael Holquist (Austin: Univ. of Texas Press, 1981), p. 7.

9. Ibid., pp. 293–94.

10. *Narrative of William W. Brown* (Boston: American Anti-Slavery Society, 1847), pp. 64–65.

11. See Claudia Mitchell-Kernan's discussion of signifying as a verbal duel that extends language "to cover a range of meanings and events" outside standard usage. "Signifying," *Mother Wit from the Laughing Barrel*, ed. Alan Dundes (Englewood Cliffs, N.J.: Prentice-Hall, 1973), pp. 311–14. For an illuminating discussion of the applicability of the act of signifying to the interpretation of Afro-American literature, see Henry Louis Gates, Jr., *The Signifying Monkey: A Theory of Afro-American Literary Criticism* (New York: Oxford Univ. Press, 1988), particularly Chapter II, "The Signifying Monkey and the Language of Signifyin(g): Rhetorical Difference and the Orders of Meaning."

12. An excellent example of joking in this form can be found in the verbal trick played by a slave named Pompey on his master in Peter Randolph's *Sketches of Slave Life*, 2nd ed. (Boston: the Author, 1855), pp. 64–65. A dialogue of defiance is recorded in Douglass's *My Bondage and My Freedom* (New York and Auburn: Miller, Orton & Mulligan, 1855), pp. 292–93, in the interchange between Henry Harris and the St. Michael's constables.

13. A representative example of the celebration of slavery as a patriarchal institution appears in C. G. Memminger, *Lecture Before the Young Men's Library Association of Augusta, April 10th, 1851* (Augusta, Ga.: W. S. Jones, 1851), p. 14. See Willie Lee Rose, "The Domestication of Domestic Slavery," in her *Slavery and Freedom*, ed. William W. Freehling (New York: Oxford Univ. Press, 1982), pp. 21–22, 29–30. Female abolitionists were among the most outspoken refuters of the myth of plantation patriarchalism. See Harriet Beecher Stowe, *The Key to Uncle Tom's Cabin* (Boston: J. P. Jewett, 1853), p. 333, and L. Maria Child, *An Appeal in Favor of That Class of Americans Called Africans* (New York: John S. Taylor, 1836), p. 23.

14. Harriet Jacobs, *Incidents in the Life of a Slave Girl*, ed. L. Maria Child (Boston: the Author, 1861), p. 61. Further quotations from *Incidents* are taken from this edition.

15. Until Jean Fagan Yellin's "*Written by Herself*: Harriet Jacobs' Slave Narrative," *American Literature*, 53 (November 1981), pp. 478–86, which establishes Jacobs's authorship of *Incidents*, the book had been treated as a work of doubtful authenticity by many who felt that Jacobs's editor, L. Maria Child, had done much of the writing.

8

Is the Slave Narrative a Species of Autobiography?

John Sekora

I

Since the Enlightenment every age has seemingly viewed itself as unique, special, distinctive. Voices of every generation have shouted that they stood at some pivotal point in the movement of human history. And as surely, later generations have declared that their ancestors were wrong. Are we not bound together to testify—if not shout—that something extraordinary, something distinctive is at work in our own time—if only in the modest, academic enterprise of biography and autobiography?

We can demonstrate with ease (at least to our contemporaries) that we are present at the creation of a new understanding of life-writing. Speaking of autobiographical studies generally, James Olney has remarked the sudden, unpredicted, unprecedented appearance of a large number of papers and monographs on the form. Speaking of life stories by and about women, Carolyn Heilbrun has noted "an explosion" of new books and new theories since 1970. Speaking of Afro-American writing, Arnold Rampersad marks the passing of a heroic age of autobiography into a different but present age of biography. Speaking of that distinctively American form of life-writing, the slave narrative, Darwin Turner and I have called attention to the plethora of critical studies published since 1969—more, that is, in the last fifteen years than in the previous 150.

Perhaps we are all encircled by generational chauvinism. Equally likely, however, we are onto something. One measure of the power of autobiographical study is the intensity of resistance it has spurred among our colleagues. While some traditional critics dismiss autobiography as a minor form, hardly deserving of the honorific of *genre*, some contemporary theorists dismiss all genre criticism as thoroughly discredited. Others say the very notion of autobiography contradicts the concept of a transmissible form or tradition. Similar arguments abound about Afro-American writing. Rampersad reports challenges to his use of European theories to explain Afro-American lives. Although some historians see only factual value in the slave narratives, some literary critics would segregate them as an ur-literary form. In one of the baldest of dismissals of the narratives, several critics have denied them any distinctive place because, they say, all American writing deals with bondage. What all this suggests is that life-writing is disturbing—and to an unusual degree. Disturbance breeds resistance, and resistance provides more glib answers than articulated (and difficult) questions.

Few forms of life-writing have been more disturbing than the slave narratives. And few have met more resistance. Indeed, one can say that after the Civil War they were subjected to cultural repression, a repression only recently and partially abated. Notwithstanding fifteen years of scholarly activity, something important remains—a profound categorical uncertainty. The issue is particularly pressing because virtually every student of Afro-American writing now seeks to *use* the narratives as starting or leaping-off point for one type of study or another. Rampersad argues eloquently that "no single genre holds sway over a culture as powerfully as does autobiography over Afro-American literary expression" and traces the autobiographical hold back to the power of the narratives. Describing the impulse for her own writing, Alice Walker states simply, "Our literary tradition is based on the slave narratives." It is no detraction from the herculean studies of recent years to note that almost all begin with what is essentially a conclusion. What is now needed is to discover and to explain how the genre of the slave narrative emerged from an earlier historical context in which the literary category of "slave narrative"—name and practice alike—did not exist. I have taken for my title the central question remaining to be answered. Yet the question of autobiography is compassed by others. Does the category slave narrative signify one thing or several? Is it a unified genre? If so, around what principle or practice? From what earlier Afro-American and/or Anglo-American forms did it emerge? And, if not autobiography, what else can it be?

Fully to answer such questions would require a powerful union of theory and history. The ideal account of the slave narrative would, I presume, mediate between the formal analysis of individual texts and a doubled, decade-by-decade history—of narrative forms and of the evolution of social life in America, particularly in the institution of slavery. Far more modestly, I propose here to look at two moments (or periods) in that history, in order to suggest that the type of question one asks largely determines the quality of answer, and that all such questions are more problematic than once believed. For in American writing the slave narrative is unique; it resembles other forms, but other forms do not resemble it. Slavery was indeed the great divider of human beings, one from another. And we must know what we do not know about the slave voice in the slave narrative.

II

Although slave writing has without doubt been repressed for more than a century, the name slave narrative has been expanded and extended from the earlier nineteenth century to the present day. A short list of the types of writing given the heading by the Library of Congress would include: about 100 narratives that received separate publication—as broadside, pamphlet, or book—between 1760 and 1863; more than 400 brief accounts of slave lives first printed in abolitionist periodicals from about 1830 to 1863; book-length collections of the periodical accounts; about 50 narratives gathered by the American Freedman's Inquiry Commission in 1863; about 80 book-length accounts published between the end of the war and the turn of the century by women and men, like Booker T. Washington, who were born into slavery; the 2194 interviews of former slaves gathered by the WPA in 1936–38 and published together for the first time in 1972; hundreds of letters to and from slaves that are preserved in manuscript collections; novels like *Black Thunder* and *The Autobiography of Miss Jane Pittman*; and recent works like *Roots* and *All God's Dangers*.

With such a spectrum of writings termed slave narratives, one can as easily speak of bibliographer's confusion as of a Protean literary form. Originally reserved for the separately published antebellum accounts, the term and its extension over time and circumstance speak of a generic power present even in times of institutional neglect. (It is in fact an issue that merits its own study.) Eighteenth-century examples, like many other American prose works, used "narrative" prominently in their titles, often as the first substantive word; the phrases "runaway slave," "fugitive slave," "escaped slave" were regularly added early in the nineteenth century. By the early 1830s at the latest, sponsors, printers, and reviewers were writing without dispute of a distinct literary genre. It is clear that readers, from whom there is more direct evidence, were by then calling accounts of slave life as related by present or former slaves "slave narratives."

What this sketch of usage indicates is a large act of historical displacement. Questions of name, origin, and autobiographical nature are shifted from the eighteenth century to the nineteenth. And because we cannot interrogate the other writings of the early slave narrators as we can Manly, Defoe, or Fielding for a definition of the early novel, we rest content with the much later lucubrations of white sponsors and readers. When and where may we hear the slave's voice unmuted?

That is the first of several vexed questions. Because no earlier instance has been uncovered, Briton Hammon's fourteen-page narrative of 1760 has borne great weight as progenitor. William L. Andrews, one of the most astute critics of Afro-American narrative, provides both category and criteria when he states, "In my view, the history of black American autobiography begins with the publication of the first discrete narrative text in which an Afro-American recounts a significant portion of his life: *A Narrative of the Uncommon Sufferings and Surprizing Deliverance of Briton Hammon, A Negro Man* (1760)." Like other commentators, Andrews calls especial attention to two portions of the text: its title page and its opening paragraph.

This opening page, no more elaborate than most eighteenth-century prose works, outlines story and appeal alike. It also identifies Hammon as a black American and presumably a slave of Winslow and places his story in the popular form of the captivity narrative. Dozens of tales of Indian captivity had been published between 1680 and 1760, all fashioned to represent the trials of a devout Christian in the savage and heathen hands of an Indian tribe. The title page likewise advertises two elements uncommon to the form: It will describe the Indians of Florida (not well known in the Northeast) and it will center on a black man whose spiritual error was to flee "his good old Master's" protection.

The opening paragraph, in italics and bearing a heading "To the Reader," is a finely wrought sentence usually taken as identifying Hammon as a slave (there is no other indication in the text), someone disabled from interpreting the higher meaning of his own story.

Hammon's *Narrative* raises many of the issues inherent in antebellum slave writing, especially (in a dictated story) that of who controls the tale. But before citing them, one must place another captivity narrative alongside Hammon's. His was printed in Boston by Green and Russell. Also published in Boston (presumably) earlier in 1760 was the tale of captivity of a young white man, Thomas Brown, whose title page sug-

A

NARRATIVE

Of the

UNCOMMON SUFFERINGS,

AND

Surprizing DELIVERANCE

OF

Briton Hammon,

A Negro Man,---- Servant to

GENERAL WINSLOW,

Of *Marshfield*, in NEW-ENGLAND;

Who returned to *Boston*, after having been absent almost Thirteen Years.

CONTAINING

An Account of the many Hardships he underwent from the Time he left his Master's House, in the Year 1747, to the Time of his Return to *Boston*.—How he was Cast away in the Capes of *Florida*;---the horrid Cruelty and inhuman Barbarity of the *Indians* in murdering the whole Ship's Crew;---the Manner of his being carry'd by them into Captivity. Also, An Account of his being Confined Four Years and Seven Months in a close Dungeon,---And the remarkable Manner in which he met with his *good old Master* in *London*; who returned to *New-England*, a Passenger, in the same Ship.

BOSTON, Printed and Sold by GREEN & RUSSELL, in Queen-Street. 1760.

Title page of *A Narrative of the Uncommon Sufferings and Surprizing Deliverance of Briton Hammon, A Negro Man.*

A

NARRATIVE, &c.

AS my Capacities and Condition of Life are very low, it cannot be expected that I should make those Remarks on the Sufferings I have met with, or the kind Providence of a good GOD for my Preservation, as one in a higher Station; but shall leave that to the Reader as he goes along, and so I shall only relate Matters of Fact as they occur to my Mind ---

ON Monday, 25th Day of *December,* 1747, with the leave of my Master, I went from *Marshfield,* with an Intention to go a Voyage to Sea, and the next Day, the 26th, got to *Plymouth,* where I immediately ship'd myself on board of a Sloop, Capt. *John Howland,* Master, bound to *Jamaica* and

Opening paragraph of Briton Hammon's *Narrative*.

A plain

NARRATIVE

Of the

UNCOMMON SUFFERINGS,

and

REMARKABLE DELIVERANCE

OF

THOMAS BROWN,

Of *Charleſtown*, in *New-England* ;

Who returned to his Father's Houſe the Beginning of Jan. 1760, *after having been abſent three Years and about eight Months :*

C O N T A I N I N G

An Account of the Engagement between a Party of *Engliſh*, commanded by Maj. *Rogers*, and a Party of *French* and *Indians*, in *Jan.* 1757 ; in which Capt. *Spikeman* was kill'd ; and the Author of this Narrative having receiving three Wounds (one of which thro' his Body) he was left for Dead on the Field of Battle :---

How he was taken Captive by the *Indians*, and carried to *Canada*, and from thence to the *Miſſiſippi* ; where he lived about a Year, and was again ſent to *Canada* :---During all which Time he was not only in conſtant Peril of his own Life ; but had the Mortification of being an Eye-Witneſs of divers Tortures, and ſhocking Cruelties, that were practiſed by the *Indians* on ſeveral *Engliſh* Priſoners ;--one of whom he ſaw burnt to Death, another tied to a Tree and his Entrails drawn out, &c. &c.

THE THIRD EDITION.

BOSTON : Printed and Sold by FOWLE and DRAPER at their Printing-Office in *Marlborough-Street*. 1760.

[Price 8 Coppers.]

Title page of *A Plain Narrative of the Uncommon Sufferings, and Remarkable Deliverance of Thomas Brown, Of Charlestown, in New-England.*

gests a relation to Hammon's. The January 1760 date and the appearance
of at least three printings within the year suggest that the Brown narrative may have been published before Hammon and may have been
its immediate model. The prefatory paragraph to Brown, again finely
wrought, is strikingly similar.

While the implications of the Hammon *Narrative* merit a full monograph, its immediate relevance can be stated briefly. Does it matter that
this earliest of slave narratives is not at all about the legal institution of
Anglo-American slavery? Does it matter that all we know positively of
Hammon's life as a black man is a single word on a title page? Does it
matter that the slave narrative as a form begins fully encased in the
trappings of another—some would say white and hostile—literary mode?
Does it matter that the immediate model for this significant black story
may be an insignificant white youth about whom nothing is known?
Does it matter if the agent for both Hammon and Brown is the same
anonymous white amanuensis? Does it matter for autobiography if personal, individual experiences and language are suppressed in favor of
the orthodox and the conventional? Finally, does it matter for the integrity of either autobiography or Afro-American narrative that black
narratives are printed apparently only when they bear the imprimatur
as well as the nihil obstat of some white institution?

One's judgment about such questions will rest on one's view of most
eighteenth- and early nineteenth-century narratives. For they do tend
to be shaped into familiar, popular patterns of criminal confession,
spiritual pilgrimage, gospel labors, and Franklinesque success story, as
well as captivity tale. Put another way, slave writing was simply con-
scripted into the movements and vagaries of American printing and
bookselling.

III

Hammon's *Narrative* represents a watershed in Afro-American writing;
yet it is but a moment in a long history. What is arresting is that the
contours of that moment coincide almost exactly with those of the great,
three-decade-long golden age of the slave narrative. In the years from
1831 to the Emancipation Proclamation, more slave narratives were
printed in America than any other literary form. It was the age of
Douglass, Wells Brown, Pennington, Josiah Henson, Ellen and William
Craft, Linda Brent, Harriet Tubman, and Sojourner Truth. It was a
time when, according to Charles H. Nichols, "almost any victim of

A

NARRATIVE, &c.

AS I am but a Youth, I fhall not make thofe Remarks on the Difficulties I have met with, or the kind Appearances of a good GOD for my Prefervation, as one of riper Years might do ; but fhall leave that to the Reader as he goes along, and fhall only beg his Prayers, that Mercies and Afflictions may be fanctified to me, and relate Matters of Fact as they occur to my Mind.--

I was born in *Charleftown*, near *Bofton* in *New-England*, in the Year 1740, and put an Apprentice by my Father to Mr. *Mark White* of *Acton*, and in the Year 1756, in the Month of *May*, I inlifted into Major *Rogers*'s Corps of Rangers, in the Company commanded by Capt. *Spikeman*.---

We march'd for *Albany*, where we arriv'd the firft of *Auguft*, and from thence to *Fort-Edward.* I was out on feveral Scouts, in one of which I kill'd an *Indian*.

On

Opening paragraph of Thomas Brown's *Narrative*.

slavery could get published." The term slave narrative possessed a full-ness of signification: an exposure of slavery recounted by a present or former slave.

Notwithstanding these differences, the institutional imprint is yet deeper than it had been in 1760. For the slave writer is enfolded in a loose but elaborate network of abolitionist clergymen, politicians, merchants, writers, editors, printers, and advocates that is transatlantic in scope and resources. For literary purposes, the forces of slavery and antislavery alike have been marshalled and institutionalized. By the late 1830s some eighty antislavery societies were formed across the Northeast and into the Midwest. About half were organized by white groups, and of these nearly thirty took part in the printing of narratives.

Defining the inner meaning of slavery to a tepid and confused Northern white audience was the initial public task of most of the abolitionist societies. If they were to issue an alternative text of the American story, they were obliged to make it not only national but also psychologically compelling and rhetorically persuasive. Materially, their instruments were the printing press, the lecture platform, and the pulpit. In addition to a regular flow of gifted speakers, their vehicles included sermons, petitions, and pamphlets; whole newspapers and parts thereof; weekly, monthly, and quarterly journals; ballads, broadsides, and poetry; gift annuals and other collections; essays, dramas, novels, and travel books. It is but small tribute to the power of the word to recall that Garrison had been apprenticed as a printer—"a trade which probably produced more abolitionist activists, in both Britain and America, than any other." Vitality in abolition meant that its text must *move*—through New England, New York City, Pennsylvania, the new farm lands from upstate New York across Ohio and Illinois, and into Canada. Garrison wrote in 1832 that it would be the purpose of antislavery societies "to scatter tracts, like rain-drops, over the land, on the subject of slavery." The Declaration of Sentiments adopted by the American Anti-Slavery Society at its founding convention vowed that the organization will "circulate unsparingly and extensively anti-slavery tracts and periodicals."

It is because the world of the abolition movement was so verbal, so dedicated to the printed record, that we can be certain of its strategies. For Garrison, Tappan, Weld, and others, former slaves were required in one role—as witnesses to the horrors of bondage. Less articulate fugitives would, when identified, be questioned, their stories transcribed and then verified and published. For articulate fugitives, the role was greater; like Douglass and about thirty others, they would be encouraged to serve as full-time antislavery agents and lecturers. Speaking about their lives under slavery was their primary duty; writing was secondary, valuable insofar as it reached areas that lecturers could not cross and brought in funds otherwise untapped. Thus, the abolitionist design for both lectures and narratives was a collective one: to explain slavery to an ignorant audience, not to chart an individual life. Reviews and announcements routinely stated that "former slaves have a simple, moving story to tell," using the singular noun to signify a collective account. Black expression was expected to be collective in yet another sense. A slave lecturer or narrator was normally preceded and followed by several white figures who supplied introductions, testimonials, affidavits, seals of approval.

As with Hammon nearly a century earlier, the demands of antislavery sponsors seem to raise several questions of literary authority. Does it matter who controls the shape of the story—author or sponsor? Does it matter that the facticity demanded by sponsors may preclude individual personality? Does it matter that the process begun with a series of collectively gathered questions could result in a volume collectively written? Does it matter that a slave's story is sandwiched between white abolitionist documents, suggesting that the slave has precious little control over his or her life—even to its writing? Does it matter that several people in Garrison's circle alleged that most black agents—including the great Douglass—had no stories until abolitionists gave them one? Does it matter that the very sponsors of slave narratives attempt to muffle the slave voice?

IV

I should like to indicate why the easy answer to such questions is the wrong one. If I have been fair in reporting some prima facie issues regarding the publishing of the slave narrative at its beginning and its flowering, then we may not be much closer to answering my initial question. But we can better understand why it has never been satisfactorily answered before: The usual methods of historical scholarship are inadequate to it. To search for the slave presence in the institutional clutter of sources, composition, sponsorship, or ideology is actually to look in specifically those places where, by definition, it cannot reside.

I noted earlier a curious historical displacement in the naming of the slave narrative. That displacement persists in all critical investigations that privilege sponsoring institution over author. Its logical conclusion is to deny, not only that the slave narrative is autobiographical, but also that it is an Afro-American form at all. Some version of this displacement has been at work since the end of Reconstruction. In no other way can one explain the expulsion of the narrative from the center of our literary history (even of the Civil War) to its furthest margins. There, at the margins, to deny the narrative a place as autobiography is to doubt its literary status altogether. All that is left is a historically bound, critically uncertain category, no more vital than that of petitions to Henry VIII. Edward Said has written: "Any philosophy or critical theory exists and is maintained in order not merely *to be there, passively around everyone and everything*, but in order to be taught and diffused, to be absorbed decisively into the institutions of society or to be instrumental in maintaining or changing or perhaps upsetting these institutions and that society." To deny the authority of the narrative is to poison the well of Afro-American writing.

The older method for discussing the antebellum narrative as autobiography—preferred, for instance, by Arna Bontemps—is simply to *stipulate* the position at the outset as a given. Bontemps could always point to the later writings of Douglass or Wells Brown or Pennington to establish that each believed his narrative to be his own authentic life story. But relatively few slave writers left later accounts; most are, like Hammon, nearly anonymous. (It is revealing that students of the captivity narrative have no difficulty in accepting the *Narrative* of Thomas Brown as autobiographical.) The important criticism of recent years assumes both autobiography and institutional constraint. It assumes that the early narrative is not a doubtful or contaminated genre, but merely a mixed one—one that separates itself from captivity stories as readily as does, say, *Robinson Crusoe* from spiritual autobiography. And it assumes that antebellum America did not possess a single, homogeneous, and linear literary tradition. Rather it possessed, before its official founding, at least two literatures.

What I take to be the primary lesson of recent criticism and theory is that the narratives must be studied carefully, not merely used as a springboard for another mode or period. For if the slave voice has grown less audible to us since Reconstruction, the reason is likely to lay as much in our capacity to hear as in the strength of the voice. And they must be studied as a group, as a black and collective species of autobiography, and as a unique genre with a distinctive history. Within that history, each new narrative both supports and subverts the series as a whole. Hence, Briton Hammon's presence as subject of a captivity tale for a time expands the scope of the captivity narrative, but also creates the terms of possibility for the slave narrative. As a slave writing a spiritual autobiography undermines that form but strengthens alternative life stories for slaves, so the meaning of one narrative (and the proper answer to its questions) is a later one. The eighteenth-century tale of Indian captivity is easily turned to the nineteenth-century story of Southern bondage. One escape teaches another.

Historically, the narrative as form was too large and too potent to be colonized. Each example moreover is itself a multilayered network of relations, containing varieties of diction, rhetoric, and syntax that it shares with other forms of discourse and that it orders for a particular effect. Future literary history will illuminate for example the nuances of difference between white- and black-sponsored stories (like those in the *North Star*), between religious and abolitionist groups and among the latter, and between stories of the 1830s and those of the 1850s. It will attend more closely to recurrent topoi that modify the symbolic order of the narratives. Folk elements, superstitions, plays on names and naming, metaphors of migration and rebirth, images of exile and confinement and defilement all have the effect of disturbing, then inverting the narrative form. Many writers were quite aware that they were reshaping for their own lives the Christian story of the crucifixion within the national crisis of human slavery; they were not humbled.

Finally a new literary history will engage in radical strategies to hear the imposed silences of the narratives. It will attend to the gaps, the elisions, the contradictions, and especially the violations. It will decode suppressed texts and recover concealed lives. The narrative is the only moral history of American slavery we have. Outside its pages, slavery for black Americans was a wordless, nameless, timeless time. It was, according to Peter Walker, time without history and time without imminence, the only duration slaveholders would permit. The narrative changed that forever. It gave means and measure of fixity in a life of flux, and in this sense to recall one's history is to renew it. The written narrative encouraged a recollection that could be tested, corrected, replenished. Such recollection could then be united with other life stories to inscribe a history, a time beyond personal memory, a time beyond slaveholders' power. The narrative is both instrument and inscription of a powerful collective memory. New literary history will attempt to recapture that power. It will turn institutional purposes on an angle, transform objects into subjects, and abolish the abolitionists.

9

Scripture of the Self: "Prologue in Heaven"

Georges Gusdorf
Translation by Betsy Wing

We may date the earliest scripture of self at the beginning of the beginning, that is to say, back in the first instant of the Creation. From
this perspective, the esteemed Jean Jacques Rousseau, chosen by some
as the point of origin, seems to stand out slightly, a minor, late figure,
the heir to a very long past, though not an unworthy heir; for he was
initiated through the double tradition of both Holy Scripture and literature, which make one more a man (*humaniores litterae*). Christian
space-time on which, like it or not, we depend coincides with the sphere
of influence of a discourse that was first spoken, then written down.
The first chapter of Genesis, relating the creation of the world, is punc-
tuated by the much repeated formula: "God said" ("God said: let there
be light!...."). The Word of God is accessible to us in the form of
Scripture; Western culture throughout most of its history was developed
as a sacred philology. From the very beginning a flood of problems arise:
who spoke? for whom? in what tongue? and who wrote? in what period?
in what idiom? The book of Genesis cannot be considered as God's
account of God's work, God's autobiography. There has been a lot of
argument to ascertain whether or not the Creator expressed himself in
Hebrew—an easy way out that does not hold on examination. The same
question arises about Adam and the words the Creator and his creature
exchanged. Same question again for the one, traditionally identified as
Moses, who wrote the Scriptures. We wonder in what form and under

This chapter appeared in *The Southern Review*, 22, no. 2 (1986): 280–95. Copyright ©
1986 by Georges Gusdorf. Reprinted by permission of the author.

what conditions the sacred writer was entrusted with what he passed on to posterity.

The creation of Language precedes the creation of man. The first word, creating, gives rise to beings; then a second word intercedes to name the beings once they are created: "God called the light day and He called the darkness night" (Genesis 1:5); "God called the vastness heaven" (1:8), "God called what was dry Earth and He called the great mass of waters Sea" (1:10). The naming of realities works to set these realities in place once they are called into being; man, created in his turn, will inherit a realm already organized into linguistic reasoning. The imposition of the name seems the last moment, the completion of creation, a sort of second creation, capable of clearing the way for intelligibility in the midst of first reality's reign of confusion. Next in the procession of beings comes the advent of man, created by God "in His image" (1:27). One of the signs of this likeness is the power to impose names. "From the earth, Eternal God formed all the animals of the fields and all the birds of the sky, and he had them approach man to see what He would call them, so that every living thing should bear the name man gave it. And the man gave names to all the beasts, to the birds of the sky, and to all the animals of the fields" (2:19–20).

Given the extreme conciseness of the narrative of Genesis, the place occupied in it by language seems particularly meaningful. God creates a speaking man, and man speaks even before he has been endowed with a companion like himself; in the first stage of biblical history, Adam can only converse with God. Once humanity has been split in two, Adam is still the one to impose a name on his wife: "Adam gave his wife the name of Eve" (3:20). From then on the characters of the sacred drama, God, Adam, Eve, and the serpent, will communicate among themselves through the circuitous route of speech, from which the other residents of the first Garden are excluded. Speech, at the beginning of the world, is not a later, seemingly adventitious component, it is what constitutes the real and what founds identity. Only the God of the Bible has no name, or rather it is He whose name cannot be spoken by the creatures; the divine name concentrates within itself so much sacred power that human reality could not bear hearing the secret designation whose mere approach remains forbidden to mankind.

God's breath on the clay earth engendered human form. Man's word is another breath creating a reality in spirit and in truth; it is able to initiate being. An uttered word exposes the innermost human recesses to inspection and judgment by others. Language, an outpouring of thought, is thought's externalized form, which, once expressed, is able to return to its point of departure. Thus, it becomes consciousness, an inner speech, man's discourse to himself, self debating with self, by virtue of which the individual's destiny is formed. Deprived of speech, the mind would fall back into confusion analogous to an animal's, with an unclear consciousness, clinging to the life of the present moment, joy or pain drifting with time, like the torpor of sunbathers on the beach who have made their minds a blank. In an anecdote recounted by Diderot, the Cardinal says to the big chimpanzee in the King's Garden: "Speak and I will baptize you!" The monkey has all man's attributes and could be mistaken for one; the final sign of belonging to the human race is the ability to speak. If the chimpanzee begins to speak, he crosses the line separating animality and humanity; he is capable of receiving a baptismal name, the sign consecrating his insertion in Adam's lineage.

Speech, when uttered, both taps meaning and makes it ostensible, but a word is fleeting; speech is a precarious thing, subject to memory's erosion. A verbal sentiment or consent is not likely to hold up for long with use. Writing offers breath a second incarnation, first formulated in terms of language, then materialized through substantial, extrinsic sorts of reality. It is the memory and the commemoration of spoken utterances, which thus will be able to confront the very one who, having spoken them, might very well have forgotten them. Writing, the word's imprint on an outside space, does not merely clothe it, coating discourse. It snares the word and confers a different form of existence on it. Consciousness never stops shifting, escaping itself, either in denial or loss of memory. The inscription of thought confers on it the value of finality. Once written, the word moves from continuity to simultaneity. The written text sets out a consolidated, meaningful, whole contemporaneous; it is able to be skimmed over in any direction, on panoramic display for the reader's intelligence.

To the spoken word, in all its transience, writing adds the virtue of permanence. This stability is already to be found in the naming of man, which enunciates the principle of his identity. The essence of a human being is announced by the name he bears, which has been imposed on him by the sacrament of baptism. The patronymic has a transcendent meaning. When God says to Moses: "I know you by name" (Exodus 33:12), it does not mean: "I know what your name is"; God gives Moses to understand that nothing of his innermost being or of his fate is hidden from Him. The name of a being carries within itself a magic power; the one who knows the name has a power over the being thus named. This is attested to by certain procedures of the occult sciences which must not be considered as empty superstitions; rather, beneath their obvious absurdities and insanities, they conceal anthropological significance. Moreover, something of this natural magic of the name subsists in the fact that writing the name, the material imprint of identity, is making public a person's visible mark, inimitable in itself (or, at least, very difficult to imitate); since a mere signature authenticates a legal action or a financial document. The signature is generally recognized as making ostensible the essence of a man in all of life's common practices.

The mythical narrative of Genesis is situated in the universe before writing, an archaic universe in which the spoken word reigns in actuality. Writing comes later, when Adam's descendants invent the techniques of civilization. The Hebrew people, during the vicissitudes of their history, came in contact with historical empires, Mesopotamia and Egypt, in which writing played a major role. At the moment that God's covenant with the Jewish people was sealed, "The Lord said to Moses: Come up to me on the mountain, and stay there; I will give you stone tables, the law and commandments that I have written so you can teach them" (Exodus 24:12). God engraved in stone the tables of the law, the code of laws for a good and moral life, imposed on his chosen people. This entails an entire ritual and a constitution for the use of the Israelites. These holy writings, within the book of the Bible, are the heart of the Holy Scriptures, the word of God embodied forever as an inscription in the memory of all those who take their inspiration from the Judeo-Christian tradition. This memorandum, which includes the Ten Commandments, among other prescriptions, after thousands of years remains one of the fundamental texts of the West. And when lawmakers of the Revolution drew up the list of the rights of man and of the citizen, they could not help referring to the tables of Moses in the formulation and presentation of their document. The Tables of Sinai have created a mental space, have defined the postulates of an axiomatics within which, despite the denials and rebellions of one group or another, Western humanity has never ceased to place itself. Even someone declaring himself liberated and emancipated, in the context of the general moral laxity, betrays latent guilt often by insisting too much. From Moses to Freud and his ridiculous, Ubu-esque epigones a tradition of continuity reveals that the biblical law has not ceased making its influence felt, in accordance with the nature of a clear conscience or of the unconscious.

For his part, Adam is not subject to Mosaic law. His law is an unwritten law, in accordance with the nature of the word, spoken and heard then perpetuated by tacit agreement. Something new develops with Eve's appearance, the result of creation by means of schizogenesis. For Adam, this splitting in two of the first personality starts a dialogue of one equal with another, which differs specifically from the relation of dependence binding him to God. Doubtless, the existential question posed by self-knowledge is opened, starting with this event. During his solitude Adam was a complete being, androgynous by nature, that is to say, exempt from the problematic instituted by the division of the sexes. With Eve's appearance, Adam discovers he is endowed with a companion like himself, but at the price of the loss of a portion of his integrity. From then on he must seek outside himself this complementary being who will restore his lost unity to him. Duality can be seen as a fall before the Fall, and certain gnostics have interpreted it in this way.

Sexual differentiation has consequences: each, from then on, is the other's complement, but at the same time, the other's opposite, antagonist and mirror as well. Each reflects to the other a different image from the spontaneous consciousness that one may have of oneself. Woman reveals man to himself as man, and man reveals woman to herself as woman. Thus, a disorder on the level of identity makes its appearance, the beginnings of a guilty conscience. Each one, led to ask himself what he is for the other, must question himself about what he is in himself. The existence of others is perceived in a mode of lack and dissatisfaction, of dependency in relation to this other whose tributary I am and who will never give me anything other than precarious and revocable satisfactions. It is language between men that institutes the rule of misunderstanding in accordance with the nature of imperfect communication.

Traditionally, the problem of evil is viewed through the perspective of the forbidden fruit and the Fall. But the psychodrama is foreshadowed, in a latent mode, from the moment dialogue is instituted within the original couple. Evil would not have come into the world if Adam had stayed alone in paradise; but is paradise possible for a lone man? The other's appearance creates a risk, but risk is not solely negative; it can take on the positive value of enrichment. The interplay of same and other forces one to go beyond appearances, in a deepening of the relationship binding me to myself; I am not what I am, what I believe I am. But who am I? Soul-searching requires the pursuit of self. Adam before Eve, in his first state of beatitude, had no reason to keep a diary; at the very most he might have been able, as steward of the Garden, to keep some track of the days in an account book. The diary becomes possible, and perhaps necessary, with the appearance of the Other, who disrupted the established mental order. Because of the Other and the questions he never stops asking me, I become my own interlocutor, in order to react to those disturbing influences that come from this absolutely separate partner apart, whose attitudes and behavior are unpredictable. Such an encounter creates a need to settle accounts, not merely with the Other, but with oneself. Tolstoy's journal is like this, frequently settling the scores inevitably generated by married life.

Finally, if the couple is the cause of soul-searching and reflection, it also establishes a new situation in relation to the Third Person in this sacred drama of the beginning. Adam and Eve are two before God; equal dialogue between the two spouses is a specifically different relationship from the unequal one established between the couple and God. This new situation will provoke the tragedy following on the entrance of the serpent, who is to disrupt the order of relations through the seductive power of the word—henceforth in the service of bad faith. Woman, seduced by the serpent, seduces her spouse in turn, with well-known results. The covenant is broken; the founding contract making Adam happy steward of the Garden is retracted. Adam and his descendants are to experience history's vicissitudes, the torments of wandering, crime, and death.

Before the Fall, hence before any discrimination between good and evil, soul-searching and self-knowledge are to experience an abrupt acceleration caused by Adam's compelling need to understand what is happening to him. Consuming the tree's fruit gives rise to a transmutation of appearances; in the light of irrevocable guilt, the relationship to the world instituted by that first innocence gives way to a new consciousness. "The eyes of both were opened, they knew that they were naked, and sewing fig leaves together they covered themselves with them" (Genesis 3:7). From the moment of this radical origin, guilt takes up residence in the sphere of sexuality. The consciousness of sin engenders a procedure for concealment; concealment first of the sexual organs, then of the guilty ones themselves. "Man and woman hid themselves far from the face of the Eternal God, amongst the trees of the garden" (3:8).

Guilty conscience flees God's presence; it attempts to hide its sin by concealing. To keep the meaning of one's life and the suspicion of one's own shamefulness for oneself will be one of the ultimate aims of private scriptures, written to hide a secret, to avow something too shameful without really avowing it. The secret doesn't work with God. So we have the curious event related in the Bible: "The Lord God called the man and said to him: Where are you? He answered: I heard your voice in the garden, and I was afraid because I was naked and I hid myself" (3:9–10). How can one dream of hiding from God? And besides, why does God need to ask the question, He who plumbs the depths of heart and loins, and from whom nothing could be hidden? Certainly, in the biblical text that is not God speaking; God cannot not know where Adam is; He doesn't have to wait for him to acknowledge what he has done; the idea of hiding behind trees to escape His glance is absurd. The question "Adam, where are you?" is not God asking Adam, it is Adam asking himself; he no longer knows where he is. In a state of disobedience, which changes his position in the economy of the world, he feels the need to position himself again. His own voice, risen from the depth of his consciousness, suggests the critical questioning. "Conscience, instinct divine, immortal and heavenly voice..." is uttered here, in this instant, for the first time in the Judeo-Christian myth-history of humanity.

The official commentators have made no mistake about it. Milton, in *Paradise Lost*, recounted the scene at length. God asks:

> What art thou Adam, wont with joy to meet
> My coming seen far off? I miss thee here,
> Not pleas'd, thus entertain'd with solitude,
> Where obvious duty erewhile appear'd unsought.
>   ... or what change
> Absents thee, or what chance detains? Come forth.
>   (*Paradise Lost*, X, 103–8)

The couple responds to his invitation,

> ... discount'nanct both, and discompos'd;
> Love was not in thir looks, either to God
> Or to each other, but apparent guilt,
> And shame, and perturbation, and despair,
> Anger, and obstinacy, and hate, and guile...
>   (X, 111–14)

Adam knows full well that it is futile to hide anything:

> ... though should I hold my peace, yet thou
> Wouldst easily detect what I conceal.
>   (X, 135–36)

And the poet's grandiose evocation gives us to understand how the first judgment of the Fall, the judgment that man brings against himself by acknowledging his guilt, marks the threshold of the history of humanity, which, from this moment on, at the beginning of time, awaits the Last Judgment whose judgment is the abolition of history. At the end of the poem, Milton evokes the first couple making their way outside the Garden:

They hand in hand with wand'ring steps and slow,
Through Eden took their solitary way.

(XII, 648–49)

The poet's sumptuous orchestration of the dry biblical tale sets up a correlation between the new geographical world, the earthly realm entered by the couple turned out of Paradise, and the new psychological and moral world, the new inner space that henceforth dwells in them. Shame and confusion, despair, hatred, guile, as well as misunderstanding in the very heart of the couple now are on the agenda for their days and their nights. Adam is under sentence for having let himself be drawn in as accomplice to his companion's guilty weakness. The poor woman does not understand what is happening to her; beclouding passions expose her to dangerous mental confusion. Breaking the pact with God has incurred God's wrath against His creature, and this new experience brings with it the creature's anger against other and against self. In the peaceful light of that first innocence, man caused man no problems; after the Fall he causes problems. The self-knowledge that was self-evident be⸍ nes something at stake in existence, the goal of a search both indis| .isable and impossible to complete.

Another commentator of the Scriptures, Jacob Boehme, emphasizes the paradoxical question that God asks Adam:

Why then does God say to him: "Where are you?"; of course, He saw Adam, but Adam didn't see God, because his eyes were turned away from the Lord, turned from the divine world to focus on time, the external world, the ophidian world of Good and Evil, death and destruction. . . . The property that he had lost, the principle of light, said to him: Where are you Adam? that is to say: seek me, therefore see me again, I have come to restore myself to you!

(*Mysterium Magnum*)

In this eschatological game of hide-and-seek between man and God the new relationship of a lost transparency is instituted. The hidden man and the hidden God are mutually in search of each other *per speculum in aenigmate*, in the mystery of the absence of being, which, according to Boehme's and Milton's Christian expectations, will only be solved in the compensatory mystery of the Redemption. When Michel Foucault announces in *Les Mots et les choses* that "these days one can only think in the void of man's disappearance," he is referring to an interpretation of Nietzsche which is, moreover, suspect. Perhaps an archaeological investigation of the etymologies of this thought would have to go all the way back to the account in Genesis. Adam, the first man, institutes his

thought in the emptiness of his own disappearance, of the sudden oc-
cultation of his life's meaning, of self-awareness that dims in the dimming
relationship with God. And out of this will be born the huge, compensatory labor of self-examination in order to return to God.

One of the most important characteristics of our time is the loss of
eschatological meaning, the incapacity to go beyond the limits of the
present situation to the source of meaning. The consequence of the
effacement of first origins and final ends is the abolition of the immanent
intelligibility of the meaning of life. The question "Adam, where are
you?" issues an order for self-knowledge. Somewhat later the same
question will be asked again of the next biblical generation—asked by
God of Cain, the murderer of his brother Abel: "The Lord said to Cain:
Where is your brother Abel?" (Genesis 4:9). A false question here
again, occasioned by the recurrence of human guilt; God is not unaware
of Abel's whereabouts. The question put to Cain invites him to ask
himself where he is in his heart of hearts; the examination of his conscience is quickly accomplished, and Cain answers: "I shall be hidden
from your face; and I shall be a fugitive and a vagabond on earth"
(4:14). First Adam's wandering, then Cain's wandering define the common law for errant man in quest of his place in a vast world and in the
spaces of self-knowledge where each man, hidden from God, discovers
that he eludes himself.

In an illustration of Hebrew wisdom, Martin Buber tells of Rabbi
Schneour Zalman, imprisoned at Saint Petersburg, receiving a visit in
his cell from the police chief who discovers him deep in thought. "At
the sight of the prisoner's tranquil visage, bathed in serenity and a radiant
power, the officer guessed the quality of this prisoner." Conversation
begins and the officer, "a great reader of the Holy Scripture," asks to
have some light shed on certain obscurities. "And how," he ends up
asking, "should we understand it when God, the omniscient, calls Adam
and says to him: 'Where are you?' " "Do you, yourself," Rabbi Zalman
replies, "faithfully believe that the Scripture is eternal and that it em-
braces every time, every generation and even every individual?" "Yes,
I believe that." "Then," the Tsaddik replies, "think that God at every
moment calls every man and asks in this way: 'Where are you in your
world? Having spent so many days and years there, where are you now?
. . . It is forty-six years now that you have been alive, where are you?'
Hearing the mention of his exact age, the other pretended to keep calm,
exclaiming: 'Bravo!', and thumping the Rabbi on the shoulder, but fear
made his heart tremble" (*Les récits hassidiques*).

Judeo-Christian revelation inscribes the development of the human race between eschatological coordinates, in relation to which it is possible for each individual to pinpoint his own position between a beginning and an end predestined by the Creator of the world. No matter what one person or another has to do in life, or what course he follows, the question of questions: "Where are you?" refers to eschatological horizons. In the last analysis it is in relation to these that the adopted positions take on meaning.

Another of Buber's hassidic tales relates the story of Rabbi Eisik, a pious man tortured by hideous poverty, who is ordered in repeated dreams to go seek a treasure hidden on the bridge at Prague. Finally he arrives there with great difficulty; his searches yield no result, but the captain of the guard at a nearby palace notices that he is up to something. When questioned, Rabbi Eisik tells the officer his dream and the officer makes fun of him: "Oh you poor wretch, what if we had to rely on dreams! Me for one, after a dream I had, I would have had to take to my heels too, running all the way to Krakow to the house of a Jew, a certain Eisik, Yekel's son, just to look under his oven! Can you imagine! Since half the Jews there are named Eisik and the other half Yekel, I can just see myself one after the other going into these houses and turning them upside down. . . . " The holy man understands the divine lesson, returns home, and consecrates the treasure to the construction of a new synagogue. The moral of the story, according to the narrator, "is that there is something that you can find nowhere in the world, not even at the home of the Tsaddik; nonetheless, there does exist a place where you can find it, this treasure" (*Les récits hassidiques*).

Birth and death do not define the true beginning and end of the human journey; there does indeed exist a biological logic of growth and decline, a historical logic of events, but these are sequences that do not carry their own internal and final justification. The material linking of vital phenomena, the fateful coincidences of minor social events, inscribed within the oceanic tangle of minutely detailed, universal totality, prevent ascribing any meaning whatsoever to an individual existence. The ant in the ant hill, the termite in its swarm make no sense by themselves or in themselves. Nature makes itself known on a grand scale. Who would dream of taking into account a separate molecule, a particle in the infinity of the universe?

It seems that the existence of a meaning particular to the human being as individual is a supernatural phenomenon. Because he is endowed with consciousness, man emerges from the common law of the animal ranks; this consciousness makes him a responsible being; he is given to himself as a problem to resolve, a situation to clarify. It is not enough to adapt himself to the demands of the present, to face the requirements and needs that make their claim from moment to moment. Even if elementary needs are satisfied, the question of meaning is compelling as a second, or a first question. Man is a metaphysical being, a being of distances and surpluses, whose journeys and wanderings are inscribed in a space that is neither physical nor geographical, a space defined by expanding the values of Being. It is illuminated by a consciousness of either plentitude or deficiency, depending on whether the creature feels his state to be one of proximity or of estrangement in relation to the radical origin of this truth.

Rabbi Eisik set out from Krakow to Prague to find the treasure that was at home. Time was lost in wandering, lost time and wasted life, but in the end the reward was found in the sure knowledge gained and in the construction of the synagogue where the covenant with God would be commemorated. T. S. Eliot sums up this adventure of paradise regained:

> We shall not cease from exploration
> And the end of all our exploring
> Will be to arrive where we started
> And know the place for the first time.
> (*Four Quartets*)

The whole problem of self-knowledge is laid out here, in the evocation of this course. The pilgrim willingly believes that the center of the world is found at his pilgrimage place. Wrong. The center is found in the place he left, to which the end of his course returns him, the same place yet another, for the vision of it is transfigured by the experience of the pilgrimage. Proving oneself to oneself—crossing inner borders—is richly replenishing to a wandering consciousness that pays this price to discover the true center.

Self-knowledge, existential questioning, cannot be reduced to the dimensions of a psychological problematic, in which the states of the soul would each refer to each other according to circuits of some natural intelligibility with, when all is said and done, a typology, a characterology and a psychotherapy, backed up by prescription of a few tranquilizers if necessary. Still less is it possible to transfer the anxiety of existing to a sociological plane, devoted to demonstrating various conditionings linked to the system of production or to nothing at all, or even devoted like others to enclosing itself within the universe of some rhetoric's discourse, with ready-made formulas meant to entrap anyone believing he can speak the meaning of his life in words that are his own, whereas he speaks like everybody, that is to say like nobody (since man, just as easily, does not exist). In this case, moreover, the one who boxes up other people's discourses exists no more than they, and speaks in order to say nothing.

If, for lack of another interpretation, one takes the biblical text seriously, it seems that scriptures of the self are not just graphic documents, written or typed. Nor are they stylistic exercises, texts on texts, reflections referring to other reflections, dilatory linguistic phenomena with no reference to a first word. Scriptures of a self are both investigations of the self and works of the self, investigations of a meaning and meaning of an investigation. Subject and object overlap each other, intending a communion of meaning, a communication that is always refused under cover of symbolisms and myths that both say and do not say, that offer themselves at the same time they conceal themselves and vanish though scarcely offered; but that nonetheless indicate a viewpoint, an invitation to pursue the endless quest whose goal would be there, at the very end of this procession to which mirrors invite, infinitely reflecting each other.

Man is free to live his life in the immediate, from moment to moment, according to the range of various demands and constraints, without considering the whole, being content with the routes imposed by social custom and the vital stages of life. One can be content with taking life as it comes, with no thought of before or after. Up to the catastrophe this was Adam's existence, entirely taken up with the present. The breaking of the covenant, rousing God's anger, introduces a discontinuity; from that point on nothing is the same. Expulsion from the Garden, introduction to a new space, corresponds also to a transfer in time, situating the creature between a weighty past of memory and a dreadful future. For the woman, who from now on is to give birth in pain, for the man subjected to the curse of working with the sweat of his brow, existence has become a hazardous adventure, between the former mystery and the mystery afterwards.

Adam's descendants find they are subjected to the same conditions restricting their fate, without having been personally party to the initial Fall. If they want to understand the fate imposed on them, they must find, outside the limits of their experience, a knowing of knowing, a principle of intelligibility escaping the common law of knowledge, going all the way back to preconditions and preliminaries, the foundations of presence to the world, at the level of the mystical, constitutive authority of the eschatology of personal life.

One of the books of the Bible is devoted entirely to a parable of the existential anxiety of man, who is prey to a radical disorientation and who desperately struggles to find his place again. Job is a righteous and pious man, whom God showered with blessings; unlike Adam he did not betray the sacred commandments. Then, without having deserved it, he finds himself victim of a challenge flung by Satan at God; stricken in his wealth, his family, his body, he sees himself reduced to the worst misery and despair. Adam, at least, knew the reason for the curses that struck him; Job's misfortune is all the more irreparable since he finds no reasonable justification.

The complaint of this righteous sufferer tells of the loss of familiar markers and usual facts. Job no longer knows where he is, he no longer knows where he is in relation to this God who seems to hide from him: "Oh if I knew where I might find him! . . . But when I go East He is not there; when I go West I do not find Him" (Job, 23:3, 8). To the question God asked, "Adam, where are you?" Job asks: "Eternal Lord, where are you?" which comes down to saying: "Job, where are you?" And God's response makes known that there is something impious about this question; the creature has no right to question his Creator: "Where were you when I laid the foundations of the earth?" (38:4). God alone, who carried out the work of those six days, is master of meaning; He alone is able to answer the fundamental problems: "Where is the path that leads to where light stays? And darkness, where does it dwell?" (38:19).

Like his ancestor Adam, Job finds himself confronted with trouble that is inescapable yet insoluble. "Where then does wisdom come from, where does intelligence reside? . . . It is hidden from the eyes of all living. . . . It is God who knows its path" (28:20, 23). To know himself would be to find his place in the economy of creation, to make his peace with God and man. But God's designs obey no human logic; God's justice is not the same as man's. It is not for us to elucidate this mystery, and yet we never stop colliding with it in fresh confrontation. To know ourselves would be to understand the order of the universe and God's design. This knowledge is forbidden us; nevertheless, obstinate, agonized, we cannot resist seeking it, as if the quest contained its own justification in knowing that we do not know.

Numerous myths of evil and the Fall exist outside the Judeo-Christian tradition, in widely differing cultures. This investigation of foundations is, for one who self-questions, a voyage to the center of oneself: for those who do not want to lead an unthinking life, this is one of the principal means of access to self-knowledge.

Henri Charles Puech mentioned this problematic in his studies on the gnostic movement in the first centuries of Western culture. The questions that adepts of this spirituality ask themselves are: "What was I? What am I? What will I be?" questions that they generalize as "What were we? What are we? What will we be?" Consequently, "subjective experience and individual reflections, transposed onto an impersonal level, are formulated as if they were theoretical truths, in the form and within the framework of a doctrine or myth which systematizes, clarifies, or justifies them" (*En quête de la Gnose: La Gnose et le temps*, I, p. xxiii). The way taken by gnostics, at least at the beginning, is the way of self-knowledge. "The uneasiness felt on contact with sensible truths will lead to regarding present existence as bad, classing it as degenerate and consequently regarding it as following upon a fall. Not merely the fall into which we plunged because of our birth as flesh, but one going much further back, long before, to the dawn of human history, or even for manicheans to the principle of the formation of the world: fall of the first man, of Adam or 'Primordial Man,' of 'Archetypical Anthropos.' Whence the considerable interest that gnostic writing attaches to the narrative of the first chapters of Genesis" (p. xxiv).

Gnostic ways of thinking basically agree with the biblical narrative of the creation. The Greek word *gnosis* evokes only the notion of knowledge, but knowledge par excellence, which is "an attitude, not just psychological or purely intellectual, but total, 'existential', engaging life, behavior, destiny, the very being of the whole man; ... it corresponds to the successive steps taken by an individual who has set out in pursuit of his own identity" (xiv). To reach this end, the person concerned comes to regard himself as more and more foreign to the world. "The desire to 'be himself,' to 'belong to himself' is joined in him with nostalgia for 'another world,' a transcendent world superior to space and time, a place of 'true Life,' of 'Tranquility,' of 'Plentitude,' from which he is temporarily 'in exile,' but to which he will return and where he has truly never ceased to be. In short, throughout his long journey, the gnostic does no more than hope to discover (to rediscover) and to recover— beyond the weak and false 'image' reflected to him by the appearances of a world that 'alienates' him from himself—his personal, authentic, innate being. From one end to the other he bends himself to 'knowing' ('reknowing' and 'recognizing') who he is, and consequently, to becoming (to re-becoming) fully what he is. Since self-questioning results in a return to self, throughout the process 'gnosis' for him is merged with the seeking, encountering and resumption of himself. Abstractly, it is the act of an *I* in search of its *self*" (p. xv).

Gnostic spirituality, a broad movement both within Christianity and outside it, thus seems to set out a metaphysical and religious representation of the hunt for personal being that underlies the existential questioning of self-knowledge. A gnostic text, *Actes de Thomas*, quoted by Puech as the epigraph to his work, perfectly sums up this quest: "To seek myself and know who I was and who I am, in order to become once more what I was." Incarnation in space and time imposes constraints on a human being, stifling and depriving him of the plentitude of self-consciousness. The recovery of being implies implementing procedures that cloak meaning in a true asceticism. There is a necessary analogy with the situation of an individual who begins by making the first decision to seek self by way of autobiography or diary. The gnostic's initial experience is one of lack, of deficient being. "His present condition here below can only seem to him a paradox, an anomaly, an accident resulting from some catastrophe, an episode in a drama where he is temporarily victim" (Puech, p. xvi). This original situation of the individual who discovers he is lost in the labyrinth of contradictions is lived by gnostics in the mode of mythical interpretation; justifications of the present refer to precedents and to consequences in the form of sacred drama, of the same order as the biblical schemata of paradise regained.

The gnostic, victim of the world's misfortune, asks himself: "Who then am I? I, so astonished and suffering so to find myself in it, feeling myself 'cast' here, downcast, disappointed, destitute?" ... "Who am I?" in conformity with the well-known formula employed by the gnostics to define "knowledge," is expanded into: "What was I? Who am I now? What will I be? What will I become?" or, in the first person plural: "Who were we? What have we become? In what direction, towards what are we hastening?"; "Where do we come from? Where are we? Where are we going?" The answers that *gnosis* is supposed to provide converge on the same certainty: there the gnostic draws the assurance of his own eternity. In the end the quest for being will have its reward; the initiate will learn that "he cannot cease to be what he is in himself, as he was and where he was at the beginning. He is thus guaranteed that what he will be can only be identical to what he has been, the first principle and the end merging into an identical timeless essence, the future rejoining the past and uniting with it in actuality of the eternal present" (p. xvi).

Throughout the history of the West, not all those who set out to undertake scripture of self have been disciples of the gnostic masters, whose existence must even have been unknown to most of them. But in the orchestration of this metaphysico-religious movement, one can sense certain overtones of the never-ending philosophy, echoing in Plato as much as in Heidegger. The related intentions make one think that questions and motivations of self-knowledge cannot be reduced to writing games or parlor games. Montaigne, Amiel, Karl Philipp Moritz, Jung Stilling, Goethe, Chateaubriand, and their emulators right up to Michel Leiris, all those pilgrims in the labyrinth of self-knowledge cannot be considered as amateur rhetoricians who, thanks to the leisure granted them by a bourgeois career, enjoy skipping scriptural pebbles on the surface of their existence. Their own existence and, more broadly, human life in general are not self-explanatory. Gnosticism presupposes that there is no direct access to the meaning of life; a second revelation must be sought, a revelation of revelation. Human life in its historical development is a coded message, whose sense can only be grasped at the price of a deciphering that puts in question the decipherer's reasons to exist. Whence the attempt to take in hand and concentrate the natural expansion of life, in order to dig out its roots and clarify its meaning, the conquest, at the price of a silent asceticism, of interior space. Through this initiatory procedure the subject attains higher degrees of self-knowledge. An existential advancement that is the price for obtaining greater transparency of self to self, though never that translucency of clarification that the seeker dreamed of at the beginning of his search.

Scriptures of the self are glosses on the *I*, a gnosticism of the *I*, beginning with the ontological experience of lack of being, the call of being. But, right from the outset, the metaphysical demand is repressed and restrained within the limits of personal identity; the subject remains an *I*, who refuses to transfer his problematic to the level of *we*. Mythological interpretations, held in check, are unable to expand into sacred representations, although sometimes certain themes of a personal myth come through, invocations of the individual *daimon* who is seeking his life in the spaces within. At the heart of the original confusion, the mess must be untangled in order to show plainly the figure of a progress that justifies life by giving it a meaning. Only the *I*'s word is the *I*'s work; it reacts with the mysterious substance of the *I*, regrouping it within, always introducing something like a new defiance to analysis. The hunt for being could never know fulfillment, but it preserves its end in itself in the maintenance of this vigilance that sums up, in its essentials, the asceticism of hailing, *salve*, salvation, what is at stake in the knowledge of self by self. Gnosticism, the knowing of knowing, where subject and object overlap each other, knowing with no distance, irreducible to discursive intelligibility.

10

Toward Conceptualizing Diary

Felicity A. Nussbaum

Diary and journal, works written to the moment rather than from a retrospective time and stance, have seldom been the subject of theoretical discussion. Some reasons for the neglect of these serial narrative forms are practical, while others relate to critical assumptions: Diaries often remain unpublished documents; their length may make reading tedious and difficult; they lack the formal cohesiveness that lends itself to New Critical readings; and, despite their articulation of human chronology, diaries are not classic realist texts. Donald Stauffer is typical of formalist critics in his argument that we should ignore diary when he writes, "The diary makes no attempt to see life steadily and see it whole. It is focussed on the immediate present, and finds that the happenings of twenty-four hours are sufficient unto the day. It becomes, therefore, not the record of a life but the journal of an existence, made up of a monotonous series of short and similar entries. Furthermore . . . the diary has scant claim to consideration, for it makes no pretense to artistic structure."[1] In many ways the status of diary in the 1980s parallels the status of autobiography in the 1950s that James Olney has described so acutely.[2] Now, in a postmodern theoretical context, as we begin to relinquish demands for theme, pattern, structure, and certain meaning, it is, I think, an auspicious moment to consider the formerly unread and unreadable—the voluminous autobiographical constructs that defy nineteenth- and twentieth-century generic paradigms.

This historical discussion of diaries and journals takes its theoretical impetus from the work of such writers as Althusser, Lacan, Derrida, and Foucault.[3] What postmodern theory can provide us here is that ideas about the "self" are constructs rather than eternal truths; that the canon can be revised to consider any text as a representation of reality and identity; and that writing the history of any set of conventions that we identify as a genre is a dialogue between the present and the past. It assumes that these texts may be read as modes of signification, as linguistic representations derived from the many discourses available at a particular historical moment. In that context, we can begin to conceptualize diary and journal as we expose the manifold meanings, silences, and discontinuities in the texts, and question the assumptions about experience and identity that the texts ratify and challenge. Here I will begin to consider the historical origin, development, and appropriation of the diary, particularly in its early seventeenth- and eighteenth-century history in England. In diary and journal, linguistic constructs of the self (or, more accurately, the significations of the subject) are produced through social, historical, and cultural factors; and the "self" both positions itself in the discourses available to it, and is produced by them. I will suggest that autobiographical texts in this early period hold within them competing systems of representation that construct the "self," and that the discourse of diary is particularly open to a series of coterminous and contradictory subject positions.

Though a theory of diary has not yet evolved, the genesis of thinking about autobiography as a genre has often been assigned to 1809 when Robert Southey apparently coined the word in the *Quarterly Review*.[4] The search through the eighteenth century for examples of autobiography is usually an attempt to seek antecedents of the post-Romantic version of self-fashioning, and historians of autobiography have been unable to read the eighteenth century except as failed versions of the later fruition. The twentieth-century constructions of eighteenth-century autobiographical writings either reduce the history of the self from 1660–1760 to a predictable group that may have influenced Rousseau's and Wordsworth's precursors, or they leap over the period with scant attention to diffuse forms. For Roy Pascal, for example, the development of "autobiography" is inextricably tied to Romanticism and its belief in man's centrality and uniqueness. Pascal identifies "the classical age of autobiography" as extending from Rousseau's *Confessions* (1782) until Goethe's *Poetry and Truth* (1831).[5] Such works, Pascal argues, hold in common an attitude toward the self that celebrates its uniqueness, and an attempt to relate external reality to that unified and autonomous self. These autobiographers structure their narrative and make meaning from the universal in their experience. John Morris argues that good autobiography is simultaneously "a chronicle of experience" and "a judgment of it."[6] It presents a powerful and virtuous example for modern man to imitate, a model of the heroic life. When these definitions are applied to the autobiographical texts produced in the eighteenth century, however, they seem to me to be irrelevant and inadequate, for even the canonical eighteenth-century texts are more discontinuous than critical urges toward formalist coherence have suggested. Constructs of the self, such as Boswell's *London Journal* or Franklin's and Gibbon's autobiographies, are multilayered revisions by themselves and others, their public coherence only arrived at through assiduous editing by later generations.

The twentieth-century conceptualizations of classical autobiography would suggest that there are no landmark canonical works between Bunyan's *Grace Abounding* (1666) and the burgeoning of the 1760s with Rousseau in France, Franklin in America, and Boswell, Burney, Cowper, and Gibbon in England. Discussions of autobiography seldom include within their purview such works as the diaries, journals, and annals of Pepys, Evelyn, Swift, Wesley, Piozzi, Johnson, the later journals of Boswell, or any of the large numbers of women's autobiographical fragments or serial autobiographies that were written before the nineteenth century gave form and definition to the genre.[7] In the main, critical readers of autobiography still assume that the most typical autobiography is one that presents a coherent core of a self with a beginning, middle, and end, and that embodies a later self that derives from a former self; thus, nonfictional serial narrative forms, which allow contradictions to coexist without assimilating the dissonance, do not fit autobiographical conventions and have not been considered. I am using diary here to mean the daily recording of the thoughts, feelings, and activities of the writer, entered frequently and regularly; and I am using journal interchangeably, though often diaries are considered to be the less elaborate form. A diarist such as John Wesley, for example, kept diaries that were little more than lists of activities he assigned to a precise hour, but he later expanded them into a more discursive narrative journal.

In the sixteenth century the modern usages of the words diary and journal began to appear. When diary is used in the title of seventeenth- and eighteenth-century texts, it often refers to medical, astronomical, or metereological accounts—or, as in the case of the popular *Ladies Diary* (1752), it means a kind of almanac or even a housekeeper's pocket book. Such diaries, seldom designed for publication, were instead kept as private record books. Most of the diaries included in William Matthews's *British Diaries: An Annotated Bibliography of British Diaries Written Between 1442 and 1942* (Berkeley, 1960) were not *published* in the eighteenth century and so did not reach the public domain until the nineteenth or twentieth centuries. The diaries that *were* published in the eighteenth century are not introspective or personal but are most often travel or military—sea diaries or daily accounts of battles. Matthews's list is not exhaustive, but among those he cites, I can find only one that is both written and published in the sixteenth century, and approximately 25 in the seventeenth century. Fewer than 20 were both written and published between 1700 and 1750, and 23 between 1750 and 1800. By the nineteenth century diaries were frequently published relatively soon after they had been written and without waiting for the death of the author. The diary, in other words, was largely a private document in the seventeenth and early eighteenth century, but by the nineteenth century it was both a private and a public document, no longer confined to secrecy.

Though diaries and journals certainly existed earlier than the seventeenth century, that historical period marks the moment of *proliferation* of the serial autobiographical text.[8] Just what social, cultural, and historical shifts occurred that may have contributed to the diary's proliferation at that historical moment can be mentioned only briefly here, but among the relevant factors may be increasing secularization; a shift from oral communication to widespread literacy and print technology that signals a change in the articulation of consciousness; new conceptualizations about time and the way it should be employed; an assumption that "man" is a unitary, consistent, and rational "self," a philosophy taking its roots in empiricism and idealism; and an expanded concern for the creation of the private realm of the individual. I will deal only with the last two—identity and privacy.

Postmodern theory recognizes that the self is less a reified thing than an ideological construct articulated in the language available to the individual at a particular historical moment. The coherent and stable human self who originates and perpetuates the meaning of experience and history is the construct of modern philosophical thought. This view, one that we have long associated with common sense, takes its origin in the assumption of empiricism—that knowledge is the product of experience—and of idealism—that a universal human nature exists outside the confines of history. Recent thinkers such as Lacan, Foucault, and Althusser, have reconsidered the universality and essence of human nature and substituted a human subject constituted by history, language, and culture.[9] This reformulated self is a product of specific discourse and of social process. Individuals construct themselves as subjects through language, but the individual—rather than being the source of his or her own meaning—can only adopt positions within the language available at a given moment. The poststructuralist concept of the self redefines a self as a position, a *locus* where discourses intersect. We *believe* that the different positions make an autonomous whole, but that *feeling* that we are constant and consistent occurs because of memory. If human subjects attend to inconsistencies and contradictions, the self may seem less self-evident. As Mieke Bal has written on subjectivity, "The discourses [language] produces are (located in) common places, be it institutions, groups or, sometimes, and by accident, individuals. Those common places are the places where meanings meet." Thus, we both recognize and misrecognize ourselves in language, but it is part of the function of ideology to restrain the importance of language to compel us to construct a self.[10]

The self presented in diary lacks an obvious center and a smooth continuity in its intermittent form and content, and thus may call into question the dominant humanist assumption that man is the center of meaning. At its inception in the seventeenth century, the diary, tolerant of multiple subjectivities and discourses, is especially resistant to representing the self as a unified, rational, and intentional subject. Critics writing about diary have certainly sensed these contradictions. William Matthews, for example, described the way in which diary works against a fixed identity when he wrote that "the diarist can see only the pattern of a day, not the pattern of a lifetime; if he is a true diarist, one day is likely to be at odds with another for any reader who thinks of people as having fixed characters."[11] The journals of Pepys or Wesley or Boswell describe discrete moments of experience, contest a coherent and stable self, and violate the assumptions of dominant ideologies at the same time that they also set forth the humanist discourse of the self. I would like to suggest that in the late seventeenth century, the diary may be an important and often unpublished site of contest between the ideologies of the unitary self and the more discontinuous subject. Diary serves the social/historical function of articulating a multiplicity of contestatory selves, of unstable and incoherent selves at an historical moment when that concept is itself the object of contest.

The period between John Locke's *Essay on Human Understanding* (2nd ed. 1694) and David Hume's *Treatise of Human Nature* (1739–40) spawned fifty years of philosophical debate on the issue of personal identity. Hume's *Treatise of Human Nature* indicates that he has trouble making his ideas on identity consistent. He writes, "It is certain there is no question in philosophy more abstruse than that concerning identity and the nature of the uniting principle, which constitutes a person."[12] Hume assumes that a uniting principle exists, but here, as in the appendix, he finds himself unable to name it. This question has recently taken on new significance in the uncovering of an important debate on identity. Christopher Fox has pointed out that philosophers have inaccurately suggested that the philosophical debate began with Hume while he argues that Locke first posed the problematics of identity. The debate on identity parallels the historical moment of the proliferation of diary. Fox considers Stillingfleet, Shaftesbury, Berkeley, Butler, Clarke, and Collins; and he assigns the modern neglect of the issue to our assumption that Locke's writings were not controversial, and that steeped in our own self-reflexivity, we are not sufficiently observant of the same in the early eighteenth century. Locke defines personal identity as "a thinking intelligent Being, that has reason and reflection, and can consider it self as it self, the same thinking thing in different times and places."[13] It is consciousness that constitutes the self, and the same self, in past, present, and future. It is Locke's radical idea, that others intuit and debate, I think, that it is not a self that takes shape but many selves—and perhaps there is no self at all but only a collection of moments of consciousness, many of which may be contradictory to each other. Joseph Butler, for example, in an essay on personal identity, fears that Locke finds personality to be impermanent, "that it lives and dies, begins and ends continually: that no one can remain the same person two moments together, than two successive moments can be one and the same moment . . . *since it is not substance, but consciousness alone, which constitutes personality*: which consciousness, being successive, cannot be the same in any two moments, nor consequently the personality constituted by it."[14]

One of the ways the diarist may worry over identity is in setting the past and present self in contest in this diurnal record. While diary creates a record of the past, its discourse produces a crisis of attention to the present, a shift to a series of current events rather than narrative perspective on the personal past, that puts autobiographical writing in combat with itself. Among the most prominent of those who fear the implications of a self without memory is Hume, who writes, "For how few of our past actions are there, of which we have any memory? Who can tell me, for instance, what were his thoughts and actions on the first of January 1715, the eleventh of March 1719, and the third of August 1733?" Hume assumes no one has such a memory, but, paradoxically, the diarist who insists on attention to the present creates memoranda that formulate that memory. Hume presses on with his inquiry: "Or will he affirm, because he has entirely forgot the incidents of these days that the present self is not the same person with the self of that time and by that means overturn all the most established notions of personal identity."[15] Hume seems to recognize that the loss of memory, the lack of evidence of the past, threatens cherished ideas of identity, while at the same time a diary record of remembered days may also offer proof of the discontinuous self. The diarist or journalist may record himself in order to produce an enabling fiction of a coherent and continuous identity; or he may record himself and recognize, to the contrary, that the self is not the same yesterday, today, and tomorrow.

In addition, diary creates and tolerates crisis in perpetuity. While more formal autobiography urges a crisis moment, an epiphany of transformation from a former self to a new fixed self, particularly prevalent in spiritual autobiography, such change occurs perpetually in the intermediate time and space of the diary. Ambiguity and ambivalence replace certainty; change may be the only constant in the daily depiction of self. And the diary may also subversively suggest that these moments of tedium and monotony, of repetition and the mundane, signify only themselves. In other words, nineteenth-century assumptions about the transcendental or providential purposes for recording despair or self-reflexivity may not have been anticipated by the seventeenth- or eighteenth-century diarist or journalist, and should not be assumed.[16]

The diary is also secret. Much of eighteenth-century writing—journal, diary, letter, epistolary novel—rests uneasily on the perplexing boundary edge between the private and public worlds. And it is in that privatization of self, that division between public and private self, that journal is born. More permanent than spoken speech, it is a private working out of what cannot and is not ready to be published; it may explore positions in discourses not suitable for public scrutiny.[17] Among those who were the most prolific diarists were individuals with secrets to tell, especially women and dissenters. The impulse to keep the diary as a self-reflexive narrative rather than an account of public or historical activity centers in religious discourse and women's autobiographical writing. Very prominent among the first published *introspective* diaries, in which the self is the subject, are works by such women as Elizabeth Bury (Bristol, 1720), Deborah Bell (London, 1702), and Mrs. H. Housman (London, 1744). It is, in fact, possible that women invented such a form, that they began the idea of private, and later, public articulation of quotidian organization of internal experience. Historically, it seems likely that journal, poised as it is between spiritual autobiography and the *bildungsroman* secular autobiography of the nineteenth century, represents a liminal form when past constructions of human nature no longer suffice to express private seventeenth-century experience, and the self cannot be shrunk or constricted into the crisis and transformation paradigm that many nineteenth-century autobiographers found more compatible to the public representation of their experience. It is poised between past and future, self and other, public and private, universal and particular.

Historians have argued that the later seventeenth century is distinct from the sixteenth century in its demands for privacy and autonomy. According to Lawrence Stone's history of the family during that period, the desire for privacy parallels the increased development of affective individualism that is well established by 1750.[18] It seems that as demands for emotional bonds increased, the desire and demand for autonomy and privacy also grew. In addition to greater privacy demands surrounding sexual activities and excretion, architectural structures signal that psychological movement toward privacy—Stone gives examples such as the corridor, the ha-ha, and the dumbwaiter—which are physical manifestations of the need for privacy. A new individualism coincides with an increased inferiority, an increased demand for the personal expression of the individual will. In general, the history of England in the period I am discussing evidences greater demand for privacy in relation to bodily and psychic space. Similarly, Elizabeth Eisenstein has remarked on the growing atomization of the reading public: Communal solidarity was displaced by the assumption of society as "a bundle of discrete units."[19] Printing, she suggests, increased the bifurcation between public and private, society and self.

The diary signifies a consciousness that requires psychic privacy in a particular way. Though the diary is not always strictly secret, it usually *affects* secrecy, and it is often sold today with lock and key. It is a private and personal revelation that cannot be spoken to anyone except the self. It is a confession to the self with only the self as auditor and without the public authority; but, on the other hand, it becomes necessary at the point when the subject begins to believe that it cannot be intelligible to itself without written articulation and representation. It is a way to expose the subject's hidden discourse, perhaps in the hope of "knowing" the self when the subject is still the sole censor and critic of his or her own discourse. Before diaries were published, they provided a way to keep the truth about oneself out of the tangled skein of power before the subject is constructed by the human sciences. It would seem that the diary might arise when the experienced inner life holds the greatest threat.

It was this secret and forbidden aspect of diary, of its boundary edge between private and public, that Boswell spoke to when he wrote, "I have therefore determined to keep a daily journal in which I shall set down my various sentiments and my various conduct, which will be not only useful but very agreeable. . . . I was observing to my friend Erskine that a plan of this kind was dangerous, as a man might in the openness of his heart say many things and discover many facts that might do him great harm if the journal should fall into the hands of my enemies. Against which there is no perfect security. . . . I shall be upon my guard to mention nothing that can do harm."[20] Writing of modern confession, but equally applicable, I think, to eighteenth-century diary, Stephen Spender has written, "I think it is because the inner life is regarded by most people as so dangerous that it cannot be revealed openly and directly. An antidote that can be applied at the very moment of revelation needs to be applied to this material. The antidote was once the Church. Today it is the vast machinery of psychological analysis and explanation."[21]

We can have no reviews of diaries, no forcing them through the dominant ideologies; perhaps they are the site of tensions between historical truth which must, for public consumption, be fitted into poetic truths. Precisely because diary and journal often are not subjected to the public scrutiny of publication, of moving the articulation of experience through the process of the public consciousness, they potentially subvert it. The marginalized and unauthorized discourse in diary holds the power to disrupt authorized versions of experience, even, perhaps to reveal what might be called randomness and arbitrariness of the authoritative and public constructs of reality.[22]

The journal and diary in seventeenth- and eighteenth-century England, like chronicle and annal, frequently defy current definitions of narrative form, for they often do not overtly assign meaning, nor come to conclusions. What are diary's secrets at a given historical moment? What events are worth reporting, and which kinds of representations are omitted? What, in its absence, makes diary different from more narrative autobiographical forms? How does she or he locate events in human time, given that, particularly in the eighteenth century, the notion of events located in divine time was profoundly questioned? We translate our reality into its narrative representation as a way of assigning meaning and substituting the reality for its representation. Narrative requires a reiteration of events that have occurred, but it also requires the assignment of meaning to the events. Diary, simultaneously preserving and evaluating, makes meaning inherent in the choice of words, the sequence of phrases, and the assignment of dialogue to self or other. The articulation of the event is itself an evaluative act—word itself a representation of reality complicated by self, culture, and history. Diary and journal are representations of reality rather than failed versions of something more coherent and unified.

Finally, it seems to me that the diarist, like the annals writer, may well attempt to imitate human chronology without overt rearrangement, evaluation, or closure. Who or what adopts the authority for the self may remain unresolved, for diary need submit itself only to the authority of the problematic self—there are no tropological, biblical, or classical models—no public to which the diary must conform; no Other dares to contest the private unpublished recording of experience. The annalist and, by the analogy I am drawing, the diarist, eschew the authority for the events and for their recounting. Diary, unlike more finished forms of narrative, need not display "the coherence, integrity, fullness, and closure of an image of life that is and can only be imaginary," as Hayden White has written of narrative.[23] That plenitude of a life may have been Pepys's and Swift's and Wesley's and Boswell's desire—but it may also have been their fear that only in the imagination can such order occur, and the representation of reality that was available to them was, then, something different from history, something that recounted events in their incoherence, lack of integrity, scantiness, and inconclusiveness—diary and journal.

Diary is the thing itself, not a failed version of autobiography, *itself* a mode of perceiving reality and a signifying system within the discursive practices available in the social-cultural domain. The diary delivers narrative and frustrates it; it simultaneously displays and withholds. The diary articulates modes of discourse that may subvert and endanger authorized representations of reality in its form as well as its discourse of self or subject.[24] It seems likely that from the seventeenth century until the late eighteenth century, diary and journal represented one important site of the dangerous and secretive, a site that was only later conceptualized as the divided mind of conscious and unconscious psyche. That both the hidden or secretive *and* the public and available were aspects of reality was a dangerous presentiment of the eighteenth century as manifested in diary and journal, and it has been the traditional reading of the history of early nineteenth-century autobiography that has buried that irrational and dangerous notion underground by taming the radical, making it "useful" in the achievement of self, and turning the un-shaped ungainly self of the journal and diary into an autobiographi-cal form that most resembled the nineteenth-century realistic novel.

Notes

1. Donald Stauffer, *The Art of English Biography Before 1700*, (Cambridge: Harvard Univ. Press, 1930), p. 55. Arthur Ponsonby, *English Diaries: A Review of English Diaries from the Sixteenth to the Twentieth Century with an Intro-duction on Diary Writing* (London: Methuen, n.d.) offers a descriptive history. Other scholarly, though not theoretical, discussions include the introduction to *The Diary of Samuel Pepys*, I, 1660, ed. Robert Latham and William Matthews (Berkeley and Los Angeles: Univ. of California Press, 1970), pp. xvii–lxvii; Robert Fothergill, *Private Chronicles: A Study of English Diaries* (London: Oxford Univ. Press, 1974); Alain Girard, *Le journal intime* (Paris: Presses Universitaires de France, 1963); Beatrice Didier, *Le journal intime* (Paris: Presses Universitaires de France, 1976); and Peter Boerner, *Tagebuch* (Stutt-gart: J. B. Metzler, 1969).

2. See James Olney's introduction to *Autobiography: Essays Theoretical and Critical* (Princeton: Princeton Univ. Press, 1980) in which he cites the subliterary status of the genre, the demands of formalism, and the autobiographer's own self-reflexivity as explanations for its neglect.

3. I have in mind Louis Althusser's essay, "Ideology and Ideological State Apparatuses" in *Lenin and Philosophy and Other Essays* (New York: Monthly Review Press, 1971), pp. 127–86; Jacques Derrida's *Of Grammatology*, trans. Gayatri Spivack (Baltimore and London: Johns Hopkins Univ. Press, 1976); and Jacques Lacan, *The Language of the Self: The Function of Language in Psychoanalysis*, trans. Anthony Wilden (Baltimore: Johns Hopkins Univ. Press, 1968); and Michel Foucault, *The Order of Things: An Archaeology of the Human Sciences* (1966; New York: Random House, 1970).

4. James Olney suggests that the first "autobiography" was, ironically, a romance by Rev. J. P. Scargill, p. 18.

5. Roy Pascal, *Design and Truth in Autobiography* (Cambridge: Harvard Univ. Press, 1960).

6. John N. Morris, *Versions of the Self: Studies in English Autobiography from John Bunyan to John Stuart Mill* (New York: Basic Books, 1966), p. 96.

7. Among the most recent historical and generic approaches to autobiog-raphy in seventeenth- and eighteenth-century England are Patricia Meyer Spacks, *Imagining A Self: Autobiography and Novel in Eighteenth-Century Eng-land* (Cambridge: Harvard Univ. Press, 1976); William C. Spengemann, *The Forms of Autobiography: Episodes in the History of a Literary Genre* (New Haven: Yale Univ. Press, 1980); Elizabeth Bruss, *Autobigraphical Acts: The Changing Situation of a Literary Genre* (Baltimore: Johns Hopkins Univ. Press,

1976); John O. Lyons, *The Invention of the Self: The Hinge of Consciousness in the Eighteenth Century* (Carbondale: Southern Illinois Univ. Press, 1978); and Karl Weintraub, *The Value of the Individual: Self and Circumstance in Autobiography* (Chicago: Univ. of Chicago Press, 1978). None of these texts considers the historicity of the self.

8. Most scholars have ignored the non-Western tradition of diary. Walter Ong has written, "The personal diary is a very late literary form, in effect unknown until the seventeenth century" [*Orality and Literacy: The Technologizing of the Word*, London: Methuen, 1982); and see also his earlier article, "The Writer's Audience is Always a Fiction," *PMLA* (1977), 53–81.] Similarly, in Arthur Ponsonby's descriptive history of diary, he indicates his belief that diary writing did not arise until the sixteenth century, and did not flourish until the seventeenth century (p. 38). But Earl Miner has pointed to a "continuous tradition of the literary diary" in Japanese from the tenth century until the present including a strong tradition from 935–1350. See Miner's *Japanese Poetic Diaries* (Berkeley, Los Angeles, London: Univ. of California Press, 1969). The Japanese diaries are characterized by the imbedding of poetry and an awareness of time as process, as well as a blurring of the distinction between fiction and truth. To the best of my knowledge, these diaries are not introspective first-person accounts of identity, unlike the late seventeenth-century diaries written by women and Puritans.

9. See Catherine Belsey, *Critical Practice*, New Accents Series, gen. ed. Terence Hawkes (London: Methuen, 1980), p. 7, for a succient summary of "a *humanism* based on an empiricist-idealist interpretation of the world" in which " 'man' is the origin and source of meaning, of action, and of history"—an essential element of eighteenth-century philosophical thought.

10. See "The Rhetoric of Subjectivity," *Poetics Today* 5 (1984), 337–76.

11. Matthews, *British Diaries*, p. x.

12. *A Treatise of Human Nature: Being an Attempt to Introduce the Experimental Method of Reasoning into Moral Subjects* (New York: Doubleday, 1961), p. 173.

13. John Locke, *An Essay Concerning Human Understanding*, ed. P.H. Nidditch (Oxford: Clarendon, 1975), 2.27.9. For a persuasive suggestion that Locke, not Hume, began the debates about the theory of personal identity, see Fox's "Locke and the Scriblerians: The Discussion of Identity in Early Eighteenth Century England," *Eighteenth-Century Studies* 16 (1982), 1–26.

14. Butler, *Of Personal Identity* in *Works*, ed. W. E. Gladstone (Oxford: Clarendon, 1896), I, 259, 392.

15. Hume, II.iv, p. 237.

16. John Morris offers a counterview in *Versions of the Self* when he argues that autobiographical suffering and anxiety are essential to the transformation and crisis that establish identity.

17. Philipe Lejeune contends that the autobiographical contract relies on *public* action (my italics), as well as on the contract between reader and writer, in "The Autobiographical Contract," *French Literary Theory Today: A Reader*,

ed. Tzevtan Todorov, trans. R. Carter (Cambridge: Cambridge Univ. Press, 1982), pp. 192–222.

18. For discussions of the increased desire for privacy, see Lawrence Stone, *The Family, Sex, and Marriage in England 1500–1800* (New York: Harper and Row, 1977).

19. Elizabeth Eisenstein, *The Printing Press as an Agent of Change: Communications and Cultural Transformations in Early-Modern Europe*, I (Cambridge: Cambridge Univ. Press, 1979), pp. 132–33. See Walter Ong, *Orality and Literacy*, especially pp. 26–173, for a description of the transformation from oral to print culture, a shift that includes a turn from exterior to interior, from erasure and revision to greater closure and finish, from a listening public to a reading public, from the achronological to the narrative sequential.

20. *The London Journal 1762–63*, ed. Frederick Pottle (New York: McGraw-Hill, 1950), p. 39.

21. "Confessions and Autobiography," in *Autobiography: Essays Theoretical and Critical*, ed. James Olney, p. 122.

22. Hayden White, "The Value of Narrativity in the Representation of Reality," *Critical Inquiry*, 7 (1980), p. 9. White has written of other forms that lack apparent narrative closure—chronicles and annals—and he remarks that they are not "the imperfect histories they are conventionally conceived to be but rather as particular products of possible conceptions of historical reality, conceptions that are alternative to, rather than failed anticipations of, the fully realized historical discourse that the modern history form is supposed to embody."

23. White, p. 24.

24. I am indebted to Jean Howard's paper on "The New Historicism in Renaissance Studies," forthcoming in *English Literary Renaissance*, in which she speaks of the "arbitrary nature of official constructions of the real" in Renaissance theatricality. I also want to thank my colleague Mas'ud Zavarzadeh, for discussions relating to narratology.

11

The Body, the Book, and "The True Hero of the Tale": De Quincey's 1821 *Confessions* and Romantic Autobiography as Cultural Artifact

Charles J. Rzepka

In the first edition of the *Confessions of an English Opium Eater*, at the conclusion of his brief "Introduction to the Pains of Opium," Thomas de Quincey offers us what he calls "an analysis of happiness" graphically represented by "a picture of one evening" (p. 93)[1] in the life of the anonymous autobiographer, at home in Grasmere Cottage. In this domestic scene—created, we are to assume, by the hand of an imaginary painter—every detail is to be taken as "real" and "actual": "Let the mountains be *real* mountains . . . and the cottage a *real* cottage; let it be *in fact* (for I must abide by the *actual* scene), a white cottage" (p. 93). And yet, as the reiterated *fiats* make clear, the writer himself is wholly in control of this "reality"—"*Let there be* a cottage," "*Let* the mountains be real*," "*let it be*, in fact . . . ,*" "*let it*, however, *not* be spring . . . but winter" (p. 93; italics mine). If these visible things are indeed real, actual, their reality is secured entirely by the narrator's silent word. His is the *logos*, the word which is world, his the disembodied, speaking presence that makes "present" to the minds of his readers these vividly imagined objects, and which is, reciprocally, implied as the agent of their orderly emergence into consciousness.

Of course, the writer's real presence is even further removed from us than that of the objects whose "reality" he bespeaks. At least the mountains and the white cottage can be visualized by means of the words that signify them and that call their images to mind. But the word that is written, not spoken, the word printed on the page, can only signify the absence of its embodied speaker. In his text, the autobiographer has become a spectral, disembodied consciousness containing and, so to speak, "underwriting" the reality of the world invoked on the page. The sole adequate sign of *his* "real" presence, that is, his own proper embodiment, literally remains to be seen.

We enter the cottage. "Paint me, then, a room" (p. 93), the writer continues—his drawing-room and library—into which the painter is to "put as many [books] as [he] can"; "Paint me a good fire, and furniture ... and near the fire, a tea-table"; "place only two cups and saucers on the tea-tray, and paint me an eternal teapot" (p. 95). I will return to the "eternal" teapot, but for now I wish only to note how, preparatory to our introduction to their owners, the focus has narrowed to these particular domestic possessions. Pouring the "eternal" tea is Margaret Simpson, de Quincey's one-time housekeeper and soon-to-be wife, "her arms like Aurora's, and her smile like Hebe's:—but no," the writer hesitates, Margaret is more than her "perishable ... personal beauty" can convey, and the intangible "witchcraft" of her smiles cannot be captured by "any earthly pencil." Unlike objects, persons cannot be fully represented by their material images. There remains the immaterial personality, the mind, soul, heart within.

"Pass, then, my good painter," writes de Quincey, to "the next article" to be "brought forward," which should be "myself—a picture of the Opium-eater, with his 'little golden vial of the pernicious drug' lying beside him on the table" (p. 95). De Quincey has no objection to the opium appearing. It is, after all, as he writes later, "the true hero of the tale" (p. 114). Indeed, he tells his mind-painter, "You may as well paint the real receptacle," and he goes on to describe it in detail. The "real receptacle" of laudanum, "and a book of German metaphysics" beside it, he adds, "will sufficiently attest to my being in the neighborhood."

> but as to myself,—there I demur. I admit that, naturally, I ought to occupy the foreground of the picture; that being the hero of the piece, of (if you choose) the criminal at the bar, my body should be had into court. This seems reasonable: but why should I confess, on this point, to a painter? or why confess at all? If the public (into whose private ear I am confidentially whispering my confessions, and not into any painter's) should chance to have framed some agreeable picture for itself of the Opium-eater's exterior,—should have ascribed to him, romantically, an elegant

person, or a handsome face, why should I barbarously tear from it so pleasing a delusion—pleasing both to the public and to me? No; paint me, if at all, according to your own fancy: and, as a painter's fancy should teem with beautiful creations, I cannot fail, in that way, to be a gainer. (p. 96)

De Quincey's coy nonportrait bears significantly on the transformation of the genre of autobiography during the Romantic period from, primarily, objective memoir, or the record of what the writer did and where he appeared, to, more strictly speaking, subjective remembrance, the attempt to connect, by retrospective reflection, disparate and discontinuous experiences and states of mind into a self conceived almost solely in terms of a maturing consciousness, rather than embodiment. This inner self is to be shared by means of writing, a "speech" that signifies the absence or negation of the embodied self *in propria persona*. In Romantic autobiography, the self of the autobiographer becomes an informed, reflective consciousness and power of evocation that, as writing, is set to work in the mind of the reader without the mediation of embodiment.[2] As for the embodied self, the self as "real" or "actual" thing, it is replaced by a new, self-made object, a cultural artifact—the book at hand, the autobiographical text.

In the "analysis of happiness," the self as an explicit object of consciousness disappears from view, yet persists as an indefinable and elusive presence to which objects—books, tea-tray, teapot, laudanum—can only advert or attest. It is as though this collection of artifacts, of appliances and possessions, had replaced their possessor, and as though De Quincey's reiterated "Paint me"—"Paint me, then, a room," "paint me a tea-table"—were a play on words—"Paint me *as* these things." "Myself," though withheld from view, is even referred to as simply another "article" to be brought forward. But although these things reflect the personality of their owner, they have been shaped by and express the intentions of others, and, to that extent, their owner must be understood to have been shaped by others' intentions as well. These things are a part of the real, actual world of concrete objects and signs— and compendia of signs, "a library," a book—occupying a shared space and time or, to use a broader term, history.

The elision of the embodied self from the heart of De Quincey's objective "analysis" suggests that what we might call the true self of the Romantic autobiographer is, in its essence, withdrawn from history and its impersonal processes of cultural "making"—that is, the making of objects, which is also, always, the making sense of a world of objects, and of ourselves as objects in the world. For the Romantics, the true self is predominantly a mind or consciousness represented in what *it* makes of the world it perceives.[3] De Quincey's *Confessions* as Robert L. Platzner has observed, comprise "a life history that consists entirely of visions, or fugitive images of an increasingly elusive identity," and thus are "not really *history* at all." They lack an "external point of reference, that is, the presumption of historical fact."[4] They are essentially a collection of discontinuous and uneasily amalgamated points of view or states of mind.

But no presumption of the historical facticity of perceived things can be made unless the autobiographer fully accepts his or her physical connectedness to the world "out there," as a part of what Wordsworth calls in the "Intimations" ode, "outward things." To conceive of the self primarily as a perceiving subject, even as the imaginative shaper of its own perceptions, as the Romantics tend to do, is to reduce the world perceived to the status of a mere image in one's mind. At its most extreme, this subjective emphasis can result in an eerie, solipsistic apprehension of outward things. This is why even the waking world of the *Confessions* seems so self-enclosed, why its reality seems a bit hallucinatory and its figures dreamlike. The self, in addition to being, as it was so often taken to be by the Romantics, a mental point of vantage or a lens for apprehending the world in a personally significant way, must also be accepted as one among the world in a personally significant way, must also be accepted as one among the world's many objects that are circumstantially "made"—impinged on and "made sense of"—by a collective cultural and historical process, in the minds of others and by means of a shared system of interpretation.

The embodied self as an object among objects is always, also, a sign among signs, a social self. But in Romantic literature the social self seems vulnerable to the most radical and grotesque reductions. The ghoulish animated corpses of Coleridge's "Rime of the Ancient Mariner," Dr. Frankenstein's "wretch," E. T. A. Hoffman's diabolically life-like automatons, the ghastly, depersonalized figure of the blind London beggar in Book VII of Wordsworth's *Prelude* or of the discharged soldier that Wordsworth meets on a lonely moonlit road in Book IV—all such images reflect a salient fear that the embodied self not only does not represent the self as a mind or a sensibility, but actually negates it. In the eyes of others, the embodied self can be reduced to an opaque object, devoid of consciousness.

For the Romantic writer, the self is taken away from itself in its physical embodiment for others. The social self is always "made something of," and thus victimized by interpretations, categorizations, judgments not its own: "the hero of the piece" (the provisional and apparent hero, we might add, if opium is indeed the "true hero") can in an instant, "if *you* choose," De Quincey tells the reader, become "the criminal at the bar, whose *body* should be had into court." By leaving his own body out of the picture, De Quincey, almost atavistically, denies us possession of his "real" image. Of course, he grants us leave to frame our own (as he hints, flattering) portrait of the "Opium-eater's exterior," but that fancied image will correspond to nothing that he truly is, either within or without. Take the "me," De Quincey seems to be saying, and make of it what you will—it is only a figment of your "fantasy," after all. But the "I" remains elusive; its image cannot be possessed, for it is not merely another thing in the world of things that we can see and hear, which are physically present, and which we call "real" and "actual." The "I" is a mental power of envisioning the world, of "calling" it to mind, by the silent, interiorized speech of writing.

The truest representation of the self as a formative power of consciousness that is negated by its embodied sign is the negation of that sign, its being erased, but in such a way that the erasure draws our attention. For this reason, De Quincey's is a most finely focused absence. But what is implied by making this elusive "I" a mere referent of "real" things, and thus excluding it from the shared world? Do we not suspect that the "true" self, precisely to the extent that it cannot be immediately recognized as a commonly shared object of perception, is not "real"? "My existence for my self depends utterly on [my] self-constitution in the opinion of others," writes Paul Ricoeur. "My Self—if I dare say so—is received from the opinion of others, who consecrate it."[5] To repudiate the embodied self as a thing shaped, in part, by the expectations, interpretations, and intentionality of others is, largely, to repudiate one's own most stable and concrete "reality," the self subject to affirmation and acknowledgment from minds outside its own. It is to disappear from one's continuously identifiable place in history, and thereby to surrender the one undeniable foundation of the continuity of the self as a series of otherwise discontinuous mental states, that is, the inherence of those states in a single, consistently recognizable body.[6]

The *Confessions*, in those parts of it that resemble history, that tell of where De Quincey went, what he did or said, what others thought or expected of him, is a disjointed chronicle of disappearances: from Manchester Grammar School, from his lodging house in Bangor, from a village in Wales, indeed, from the great city of London itself, which he seems to haunt like one of the very ghosts that his young fellow-lodger, who shares an "unoccupied" house with him, says she fears. In each case, the disappearance is precipitated by the real or assumed imposition of expectations or judgments he felt burdensome to the "true" self.[7] The autobiographer, in fact, "occupies" no stable spot in the social scene, establishes practically no real human contacts, not even, it may be plausibly argued, with the starving girl who shares his abandoned house, or with Ann, the tender-hearted prostitute. Both figures, lacking surnames, relatives, friends, or even the sketchiest circle of acquaintances, seem as evanescent and insubstantial a part of the urban scene as the inhabitants of Eliot's "Unreal City."[8]

As a result, De Quincey's tale of his London life becomes the mind-wandering waking-dream of an anonymous outsider, a true Wordsworthian *spectator ab extra*. For him, particularly under the influence of opium, "all the markets, and other parts of London, to which the poor resort on a Saturday night" could be transformed into a large-scale "spectacle" for his own entertainment, while he remained uninvolved, effaced and excluded by his anonymity (p. 80). The scene depicted at the end of "The Pleasures of Opium," where De Quincey yields, under the influence of the drug, to his "natural inclination for a solitary life" and serenely contemplates, in an almost mystical mood, the town of Liverpool from high above, "at a distance, and aloof from the uproar of life," with "its sorrows and graves," typifies not only De Quincey's preference, but that of the Romantics in general, for a physically withdrawn, virtually disembodied envisioning of that social life whose demands they feel to be an insupportable imposition on the embodied self. Throughout the *Confessions*, De Quincey disowns, at every turn, his proper embodiment in the world he observes. Embracing the aloof and atemporal "I" of an ever-changing and thus discontinuous consciousness, he ignores as much as possible the temporally continuous "me," and thus corrodes the historical mortar of memory.

If introspectively, as Hume demonstrated in his *Inquiry*, "I never can catch *myself* at any time without a perception, and never can observe any thing but the perception,"[9] then that is cause for dread. "What is there in thee, man, that can be known?" asks Coleridge in his fragment, "Self-knowledge": "Dark fluxion, all unfixable by thought." In the *Confessions*, scene follows scene as dream follows dream, with little sense of narrative direction. Eventually, these waking dreams give way to nightmares of the abyss within. That De Quincey's "analysis" should elaborate at such length on "real," "actual" objects suggests that the true self, precisely because it is so abstract and evanescent, cannot help but seek anchorage in the things around it.[10] It would seem that, for the Romantic autobiographer, the "true" self, precisely because it is entirely private and not public at all, cannot be "real," and that the "real" self, precisely because it is as much an object of public as of private awareness and interpretation, cannot be "true."

How can autobiographers overcome this dilemma? How can they manifest the abstract and impermanent "true" self as a "real" and permanent part of history without surrendering it to the violence of imposed judgments, expectations, and interpretations over which they have no control, but which they feel are, nonetheless, necessary to confirm its "reality"? The answer lies in the foreground of De Quincey's "painting," and particularly in the two "real" objects closest at hand, nearest the writer's "neighborhood." The book on the table and the vial of opium are emblems of two aspects of textuality—the one an object of sight, the other an agent of visions—sufficient *together* to "attest" his presence.

> Oh! just, subtle, and mighty opium! . . . *eloquent* opium! that with thy *potent rhetoric* stealest away the purposes of wrath . . . that *summonest* to the chancery of dreams, for the triumphs of suffering innocence, false witnesses; and confoundest perjury; and dost *reverse the sentences* of unrighteous judges:— thou . . . 'from the anarchy of dreaming sleep,' *callest* into sunny light the faces of long-buried beauties, and the blessed household countenances. (p. 83, italics mine)

"Eloquent opium," "potent rhetoric," "summonest," "sentences," "callest": opium is the book, and the book (appropriately enough represented by a tome on metaphysics, on things inaccessible to the senses) becomes opium, a summoner of the unseen, the instant the reader reads or "ingests" it. Like opium, the text is a secret or "subtle" power working on, or rather in, the mind of the reader to refute unrighteous sentences and exonerate apparent guilt, and to call forth, by Godlike *fiat*, the "blessed household countenances" within each of us, who will in turn "bless" the accused. If opium is "the true hero of this tale," then the disembodied voice of the autobiographer is its true opiate, working on the reader's imagination without revealing his proper bodily presence.

But De Quincey is also represented by the book as a physical thing,[11] as an opaque object of sight that metonymically "makes real" its creator. The book at hand represents the autobiographer not so much as a spectral witness or ghostly power of evocation working in the mind of the reader, but as a physical agent acting in and leaving his mark on the shared continuum of space and time. For it is not the slippery

internal ordering of past states of mind that will reassure the autobiographer of his continuous reality as a part of the world outside his mind,
but the very act of writing that results in the *grapheme*. As a writer,
a maker of marks, De Quincey has become a "real" and lasting part
of history.

Certainly, the self as "the book," as a cultural artifact, is subject, like
the embodied self, to the interpretations of others. But recognizing the
book as an object of sight necessarily interferes with our "seeing
through" or envisioning it in the act of reading as a text, and vice versa.
To read the text we must, as it were, devour it, internalize it, and thus
give ourselves up, in whole or in part, to its "potent eloquence." Unlike
the body as a passive object of others' interpretations, the book possesses
the "subtle" power to affect those interpretations, to control the flow
of images, to establish the categories by which the embodied self will
be judged, indeed, to withhold the embodied self entirely from view.
Of course, we can "buffer," so to speak, the intoxicating effects of this
rhetorical opiate—stand back and scrutinize, as I have here, patterns
of imagery, tone of voice, diction. But withstanding, overcoming, analyzing the power of the opiate is not the same as denying its intended
effects. Though our scholarly scepticism can defeat it, the aim of the
Romantic autobiographer remains the same: to invade and overcome
the imagination of the reader to whom he would "confess" or reveal
himself.

In the *Confessions*, De Quincey enters history as both "real" object
and "true" potency of consciousness, a cultural artifact. And the self
as artifact will last long after its maker is in the grave. Or, rather, let
us say that the *text* will persist, though *this* book, the one at hand, the
physical object in the library, will perish like all things of this world.
The text will last as a power of evocation constantly renewed, in history,
by the printed and bound volumes that signify its having once entered
history. Whoever the autobiographer "truly" was, whatever the chaos
of sensations, memories, passions, fantasies within him, they are here
given a permanent outward form, in a "real" object that, unlike the
body, can be constantly recreated, reassembled as an object, and yet
which, at the first attempt to understand and interpret it, dissolves into
the "true" self, a power to evoke sensations, memories, passions, fantasies in the mind of the reader. The book makes the disembodied voice
of the true self as real as any perishable thing, but as imperishable as
any impersonal sign. The book is "actual" in one aspect, "eternal" in
another, like that teapot, now a fading word on the page, now an image

to be replicated in innumerable minds for incalculable centuries, from which Margaret, forever, will pour.

Notes

1. All references are to Alathea Hayter's edition, *Confessions of an English Opium Eater* (New York: Penguin Books, 1971).

2. Louis A. Renza, "A Theory of Autobiography," *Autobiography: Essays Theoretical and Critical*, ed. James Olney (Princeton: Princeton Univ. Press, 1980), pp. 268–95, suggests that in its being written rather than spoken, autobiography "would seem to be guilty of a Barthesian mode of 'bad faith,' for is not autobiography an attempt to signify the autobiographer's non-textual identity or 'interiority'?" (p. 276).

3. This, I think it safe to say, has certainly been the central theme of modern Romantic criticism, dating from Robert Langbaum's *The Poetry of Experience* (London: Chatto and Windus, 1957), for example, "The process of experience is for the romanticist a process of . . . a continually expanding discovery of the self through the discovery of its imprint on the external world" (p. 25). The theme has been reformulated with respect to autobiography by critics like James Olney, *Metaphors of the Self: The Meaning of Autobiography* (Princeton: Princeton Univ. Press, 1972). "We become in our creative act," writes Olney, "all the objects we behold, and, more importantly, the order of those objects" (p. 33).

4. Robert L. Platzner, "De Quincey and the Dilemma of Romantic Autobiography," *Dalhousie Review* 61 (1981–82): 614.

5. Paul Ricoeur, *The Conflict of Interpretations*, ed. Don Ihde (Evanston: Northwestern Univ. Press, 1974), p. 112.

6. The necessity of embodiment as the basis for self-continuity has been persuasively argued by, among others, A. J. Ayer, "The Concept of a Person," reprinted in *The Concept of a Person and Other Essays* (New York: St. Martin's Press, 1963), who contends "that personal identity depends upon the identity of the body, and that a person's ownership of states of consciousness consists in their standing in a special relation to the body by which he is identified" (p. 116).

7. For instance, the flight from school seems to be precipitated by no other motive than that his guardians, with his mother's consent, insisted that he enroll there; De Quincey leaves Bangor when his landlady mentions that the local bishop had warned her against taking in roving "swindlers" and the young man, quite without cause and in extreme indignation, assumes that she takes him for one; in a Welsh village, he is befriended by the younger children of the house and becomes their amatory amanuensis—a role he says he commonly played

while wandering the countryside—until the return of their "churlish" (45) parents, unsympathetic representatives of adult authority.

8. V. A. de Luca, *Thomas de Quincey: The Prose of Vision* (Toronto: Univ. of Toronto Press, 1980), observes of De Quincey's kissing a portrait of the school's lovely benefactress goodbye, "De Quincey chooses to launch his narrative therefore with a vision of ideality virtually unencumbered by the compromises imposed by embodiment in the tangible forms of daily life" (p. 15). This sense of ideality suffuses the narrative that follows, particularly with respect to other people. As Platzner notes of Ann, "There is . . . nothing in Ann herself or in her relationship to De Quincey that forces him to acknowledge her *separate* reality; he . . . absorbs her into his private world of reverie" (p. 608).

9. David Hume, *Philosophical Works*, ed. T. H. Green and T. H. Grose (London: Longmans, Green, and Co., 1874), I, 534.

10. Elizabeth Bruss, *Autobiographical Acts: The Changing Situation of a Literary Genre* (Baltimore: Johns Hopkins Univ. Press, 1976), notes in her chapter on De Quincey that "pursued far enough, subjective experience becomes ineffable and identity breaks down in mystery" (p. 95). More generally, Georges Gusdorf, "Conditions and Limits of Autobiography," trans. James Olney, in *Autobiography: Essays Theoretical and Critical*, ed. James Olney (Princeton: Princeton Univ. Press, 1980), pp. 28–48, notes the difficulty of determining the precise object of the autobiographer's "*in*volution of consciousness," in contrast to the clarity of exterior presentation characteristic of biography: "If exterior space—the stage of the world—is a light, clear space where everyone's behavior, movements, and motives are quite plain on first sight, interior space is shadowy in its very essence" (p. 32).

11. Patricia Meyer Spacks, *Imagining a Self: Autobiography and Novel in Eighteenth Century England* (Cambridge: Harvard Univ. Press, 1976), notes the "problem of insubstantiality" that pervades late eighteenth-century literature, and suggests that the "efflorescence of the novel and autobiography as genres may represent a significant response to this problem. Both save individual identity from pure subjectivity by converting human beings into objects: quite literally: pages with words on them: illusions of consistent substantiality' (p. 22).

12

The Objectivity of *The Education of Henry Adams*

Thomas R. Smith

Many readers of *The Education of Henry Adams* (1907) have taken at face value the writer's stated aim in the book's first Preface: "the . . . object, in this volume, is to fit young men, in universities or elsewhere, to be men of the world, equipped for any emergency."[1] One such reader sees the book's goals as experimentally historical and didactic, rather than autobiographical in the conventionally post-Romantic ways we might expect: confessional, apologetic, or expressive.[2] Another has complicated Adams's didactic purpose by seeing his teaching as being so hedged in by the narrator's irony that, for all practical purposes, it is a kind of provocation and baiting of the reader.[3] And another goes even farther to claim that Adams's stated didactic purpose is simply a means to draw readers to his startling conclusions about the uselessness of any education to prepare one for ceaseless change:

> [Adam's] final discovery was that not only his education but all education was pointless, whether it was his own obsolete eighteenth-century one or an up-to-date version. No one could be shown how to cope with an inscrutable, ever-changing world. He did not find a science that could predict the social future accurately and without that no one could really be taught how to adapt. The very idea of an education that prepared young people for success was a delusion. That is his ultimate message. . . .[4]

But even this bleak, utterly ironized version of Adams's goal can be seen as didactic; it ascribes to Adams the desire to impart the wisdom to his readers that the teacher has no wisdom to impart. A Zen master might make understanding such a lesson the end point of a student's struggle to learn.

Opposed to this interpretive line, taken from Adams himself, is an alternate view that minimizes Adams's avowed didactic purpose. One commentator argues that

> The *Education* is not a theoretical work with a specific purpose. . . . Adams does not really address himself to the problems of education. . . . The final irony of the book . . . is that Adams has *no* conscious theory of education. . . . Education, for Adams, represents his complete life experience and is an excuse for talking about himself.[5]

According to this reading of the *Education*, Adams sees his life as a long educative experience, and thus the writing of his book is an attempt to set down what he has learned, primarily for his own benefit. Adams's didactic aim might be explained, from this view, as a displacement onto readers of his reason for writing so that it appears a reason for their reading the book.

If we are to take Adams at something like his own word, however, then the *Education*'s narrator—or behind that construct, Adams himself—should in some way be seen to teach and should treat his reader as a student, more precisely a student of history; furthermore, one might expect that Adams's material would be presented as somehow exemplary, the better to illustrate his points, however we construe them, in didactic fashion.

Adams's Carlylean remarks about the ego in the *Education*'s "Preface" have usually been considered sufficient explanation for his using third-person narration in a book that appears otherwise to be autobiography. There Adams writes that the ego is a "manikin on which the toilet of education is to be draped to show the fit or misfit of the clothes. The object of study is the garment, not the figure" (pp. 721–22).[6] As Adams himself elaborates the metaphor, the older Adams writing is the tailor, and the younger Adams written about is the manikin whose appearance and clothes change according to the needs of the tailor.[7] Adams seems to be giving the reader fair notice that the protagonist of his story is not to be carelessly confused with the flesh-and-blood Henry Adams some readers will have known. In fact, Adams is shrewdly noncommittal about the relationship of his manikin to his past self while at the same time making the puppet's didactic function clear:

> The manikin, therefore, has the same value as any other geometrical figure of three or more dimensions, which is used for the study of relation. For that purpose, it cannot be spared; it is the only measure of motion, of proportion, of human condition; it must have the air of reality, must be

taken for real, must be treated as though it had life. Who knows? Possibly it had! (p. 722)

Some readers link this detachment from his past with Adams's omission of the twenty years of his middle age in which he married, wrote histories, biographies, and novels, and watched his wife's depression over her father's death end in suicide. Taken together, these omissions and Adams's detachment can be seen as evidence for a psycholiterary diagnosis of self-estrangement that leads to an ideological analysis of the *Education*. For instance, Hayden White writes:

> The *Education*'s manifest announcement and demonstration of the end of the ego in the modern age has to be viewed as a message both personal and subjective, on the one side, and social and historical, on the other. Insofar as Adams identifies his own ego with that of his class, the announcement of the dissolution of one is also the announcement of the dissolution of the other.[8]

Adams does invite an identification of ego and class in the book, and there is little reason not to extend one's conclusions about Adams to the upper-crust Bostonians he identifies with, for Adams himself would have done so. Earl Harbert, who affirms Adams's didactive purpose, suggests that the decision to write about himself as if he were another person is one of many instances in Adams's later work of his "expressing [a] deep sense of inner division, the divided personality of Henry Adams acting as author and subject."[9] But when one looks at the *Education* as an autobiography of some perhaps unclassifiable sort, Adams's use of the third person remains an inescapable fact for the reader not fully explained away by psychologizing Adams, however fruitful that might be.

If Adams's choice of third-person narration can also be seen as a strategic choice, then his stance of detachment and objectivity in the *Education* helps him to dramatize his experience as a lack of significant education and a succession of failures and unsatisfying endeavors. Distancing himself from "Henry Adams" the manikin, Adams as narrator can set his puppet in a context of ideas and create a range of concern larger than the autobiographical aims of confession or intellectual and moral development offered by the models of Rousseau or St. Augustine. The *Education* was not for Adams only an opportunity to tell the story of his life. Had it been so, presumably he was capable of telling it much more straightforwardly, even of using the first person. Adams is less interested in revealing his inner life or tracing its growth for its own sake than in using that life and development as evidence in the book's historical argument about the direction of human history toward multiplicity, increasing chaos, and eventually a state of entropic equilibrium. Adams's interests and aims in writing the *Education* are mainly historical and argumentative rather than autobiographical as conventionally conceived. Adams begins his "Preface" by calling Rousseau's *Confessions* "a monument of warning against the *Ego*" and credits Rousseau with part of the blame for the ego's gradual effacement throughout the nineteenth century to the point that "for purposes of model" it has become "the manikin on which the toilet of education is to be draped" (p. 721).

Adams here takes Rousseau's *Confessions* as a counterexample of the kind of autobiographical account he has written. He says "American literature offers scarcely one working model for high education" and names, almost reluctantly, Benjamin Franklin as that one scarce model: "The student must go back, beyond Jean Jacques, to Benjamin Franklin, to find a model even of self-teaching" (p. 721). For Adams, Franklin's *Autobiography* only begins to suffice as a model for the kind of book he has written. Nonetheless, Franklin's shrewd self-editing to create an entertaining, plausible, and determinedly imitable character who gives a matter-of-fact account of his rise to eminence in a democracy may have suggested to Adams how his own life could be presented instructively from the outside in.

Adams's use of the third person is designed to achieve what Jean Starobinski calls a "solidification by objectivity" that renders his life suitable as evidence in the historical argument he wants to make. Without trying to force the *Education* into narrow genre categories, one can consider some of the genres the book draws on to see how Adams's intentions are carried out and to see how both the book's subject, "Henry Adams," labeled a "manikin" by the author, as well as Henry Adams, the producer and controller of meaning, operate in the text.

Third-person autobiographical narrative is oddly biographical rather than autobiographical in tone, and the pseudobiographer or narrator is at once everywhere anonymously present as producer of the text and everywhere visible by name as the text's subject, having shifted his name off the title page onto earlier incarnations of himself in the text. A strange hybrid, third-person autobiographical narrative ought to share features of is parent—third-person narrative in general and first-person autobiography.

Questioning Emile Benveniste's assertion that in French *l'enonciation historique* (historical statement) typically uses the *Passe simple* while *discours* (discourse, statement assuming a speaker trying to influence a listener) uses the *Passe compose*, Jean Starobinski points out that first-person autobiography combines history and discourse: "The traditional form of autobiography occupies a position between two extremes: narrative in the third person and pure monologue."[10]

Having placed autobiography somewhere in the center on a scale registering the felt presence of the narrator, Starobinski then characterizes third-person autobiographical narrative:

> We are very familiar with third-person narrative; it is the form of the *Commentaries* of Caesar or of the second part of the *Memoires* of La Rochefoucauld, namely, narrative that is not distinguished from history by its form. One must learn from external information that the narrator and the hero are one and the same person. In general, such a process is expressly a depiction of a series of important events in which the editor puts himself into the scene as one of the principal actors. The effacing of the narrator (who thereby assumes the impersonal role of historian), the objective presentation of the protagonist in the third person, works to the benefit of the event, and only secondarily reflects back upon the personality of the protagonist the glitter of actions in which he has been involved. Though seemingly a modest form, autobiographical narrative in the third person accumulates and makes compatible events glorifying the hero who refuses to speak his own name. Here the interests of the personality are committed to a "he," thus effecting a solidification by objectivity.[11]

Most of these generalizations hold true for *The Education of Henry Adams*. First, one does learn from external information that the narrator and the hero are one and the same. Ernest Samuels, Adams's biographer and editor, tells us that the subtitle, "An Autobiography," was added in 1918 after Adams's death by the book's first trade publishers, the Massachusetts Historical Society and Houghton Mifflin.[12] Adams himself did not identify his book as an autobiography; it is as if he wanted his readers to approach the book as a biography by Anonymous, even if his identity as the writer were known to them. If it could be read honestly as a biography, however, the *Education* would be seen to claim an exhaustively detailed knowledge of Adams's states of mind and feelings eclipsing the most irresponsible of biographical fantasias. But it is unlikely anyone has gone very far into the *Education* without knowing it was written by Adams himself. Even if one missed the subtitle, the particularity and idiosyncrasy of the details of the child's perceptions at Quincy and Boston in the first two chapters would convince one that only the person who had undergone those experiences early in life could report them so persuasively.

Second, Starobinski claims that the narrator of a third-person narrative is effaced and assumes the role of historian. This is clearly the case in the *Education*, not only because Adams frequently reminds the reader of the historical context in which his protagonist is seeking his education. Adams treats his life as a case study in the results of expecting a child of the well-ordered eighteenth century to deal with the tumultuous nineteenth as it approaches the catastrophic twentieth. And beyond that, as Hayden White has noted, he wants the education outlined in the book to be seen as emblematic of the fate of his society. Adams writes in the first chapter:

> To his life as a while he was consenting, contracting party and partner from the moment he was born to the moment he died. Only with that understanding,—as a consciously assenting member in full partnership with the society of his age,—had his education an interest to himself or to others. (p. 724)

By the time Adams was writing the *Education* in the first five years of this century, the role of historian had long since become familiar to him. He had been president of the American Historical Association; his nine-volume *History of the United States During the Administrations of Jefferson and Madison* was over ten years old, and he had written biographies of Albert Gallatin, Jefferson's Secretary of the Treasury, and of the Virginian John Randolph, a contemporary of his grandfather, John Quincy Adams. Adopting the role of historian to recount his own life would have been easy to do, not only because Adams was experienced at constructing historical narratives, but because as one in the distinguished line of Adamses going back to the Revolution and before, he saw his life and his very identity inextricably connected to American history at large. Furthermore, the *Education* was originally conceived as an "experimental afterpiece" to Adams's earlier highly personal and idiosyncratic historical writing on thirteenth-century art and culture, *Mont Saint Michel and Chartres* (1904). The *Education*'s final chapters are, as Adams wrote to Henry James, a "working out to Q.E.D. of the three concluding chapters" of the earlier book.[13] In addition, at one point in the several revisions of the *Education*, Adams's intended audience was other historians. Around 1908 Adams drafted a letter to them to accompany a reprinting of the book in which he invited them to collaborate with him to reinvigorate American higher education in response to the *Education*. Though Adams quickly gave up the idea, he did publish and distribute in 1910 a short book titled *A Letter to American Teachers of History* that promoted the application of the Second Law of Thermodynamics—the idea that all energy dissipates—to historical study. Clearly, the *Education* was bound up with Adams's sense of his role as a historian and educator.[14]

Starobinski's third point is that third-person, objective narration effaces the narrator and emphasizes the narrative's actions, the "glitter" of which "reflects" onto the "personality of the protagonist." The *Education* confirms this idea as well, though not straightforwardly. The actions of the *Education* are not in any important way the local, national, or world events with which the protagonist is involved as an actor or spectator. The relevant actions in the book are Adams's internal experiences—his thoughts, feelings, impulses, and moods—and the changes these all underwent in time. Such internalized events are in fact highlighted throughout the text. Adams zeroes in on his former perceptions of the world, struggling to discern in them some evidence of a development of his ideas and personality—in short, an education. Notoriously, he usually fails. Though given the protagonist's advantages of birth, position, formal education at Harvard, and proximity as a young man to centers of power in London and Washington, the narrator always expects the protagonist to grow and learn, but instead "Henry Adams" is rarely allowed to assimilate experience to form a new, more coherent vision of things by means of which to act decisively. Moreover, the narrator often belittles the knowledge and experience that the protagonist does gain, stressing years after the fact how illusory was the impression the young man had that he was learning anything substantial. But such failures and such pessimism do not lead the narrator to stop looking for evidence of real education in the protagonist. Thus, the actions in the narrative we are led to think important are not historical events as usually conceived, but the effects of those external events on the protagonist—such effects become incidents in his education, or more often, lack of it. As a result, the paradoxical "glorifying" of "a hero who refuses to speak his own name" is achieved, but cloudily rather than radiantly. Adams's attention is on his own life seen as a history of possible education; his protagonist is the locus of the action and therefore does not receive the reflected "glitter of action" since he is the source and site of it. What does receive the reflection of the narrative's events, if anything, is the narrator himself, as the anonymous controlling intelligence producing the narrative.[15]

As Starobinski suggests is true of all third-person autobiographical writing, the apparent modesty caused by his self-effacing choice of narrative voice allows Adams to aggrandize more and more of his reader's involvement in his neverending effort to be educated. Adams's continual denial that study or experience provided him with any substantial insight into reality drives the reader to hope that such insight will come, to speculate on what will satisfy the narrator as truly capable of educating the protagonist, and to wonder why the narrator refuses to accept almost everything as evidence of any meaningful learning. Hayden White has wondered whether the absent "I" of the *Education* in fact creates egocentricity on the part of the narrator at the expense of the protagonist: "Far from being an 'egoless' text," White suggests, "the *Education* is— in spite of (because of?) the suppression of the authorial "I"—a supremely *egoistic* one."[16] And in fact the book's egoism extends beyond that felt beyond a reader or deduced analytically by a critical method. Adams initially published the book privately in 1907 on wide-margin paper for distribution to friends for their criticisms and comments. In some of the letters Adams sent to the book's recipients, he stresses its purely personal reason for existence: "It served its only purpose by educating *me*."[17] It is fair to say that in these letters Adams self-pityingly bemoans the worthlessness and futility of the book, and here he may be only defensively pointing its usefulness to him if not to others or to posterity. Nevertheless, in the gesture, Adams sets himself up not only as author, narrator, and protagonist, but also as the book's appropriate reader. In so doing, he intensifies what White and others would call the inherent narcissism of the act of writing, in this case already self-absorbed in autobiographical speculation, by ousting his audience in favor of himself.

In characterizing the protagonist of a third-person autobiographical narrative a "hero who refuses to speak his own name," Starobinski refers to the use of the third-person pronouns *he, him, his.* But in the *Education* Adams does little else but speak his own names: "Adams," "Henry Adams," "the private secretary," "the author," and, less individualizingly, "he," and "him." Such names, those others give us, distinguish us from those who use them. The names Adams refuses to speak are the first-person ones that do not individualize us, "I" and "me," names by which all of us customarily name ourselves and, perhaps, know ourselves from within. These names do not distinguish us from each other, as Starobinski points out when he invites us to consider Beckett's work "to discover how the continually repeated 'first person' comes to be the equivalent of a 'nonperson.' "[18] Adams's reversal of usual autobiographical practice helps to consolidate the protagonist's identity as the narrator's puppet; correspondingly, it blurs the narrator's identity and invites readers to focus their attention on the manikin. Adams's viewing his past as a historian or biographer would—from the outside in—encourage his readers also to see him that way. So what would otherwise be the indisputable hero of the book, the active "I" telling its own story, is reduced by the overwhelming power of the analytical narrator to a pawn, Adams's "manikin," a figure created to illustrate the narrator's ideas and to be the exemplary figure in whose life story readers will find a negative kind of edification.

Since all readers know the *Education* to be autobiographical rather than biographical, the distancing and detachment Adams strives for cannot be entirely successful. Eventually all the third-person formulations Adams uses come to function as the text's substitutions for first-person forms. To reverse Starobinski's formulation about Beckett, in the *Education* the continually repeated third person comes to be the equivalent of the first person. But such a substitution is merely mechanical and results from a forced effort difficult to maintain. The reader's being forced to provide the absent "I" because of the text's refusal to do so paradoxically makes more visible the activity of the older Adams, the unnamed, putatively anonymous narrator, creating the younger Adams over the course of the narration. Such attention by the reader to the narrator is important for Adams to maintain the historian's role. We must believe in the authority of the narrating voice if we are to accept the claims it makes about the protagonist, for, as the narrator never tires of hinting, "Henry Adams" would be an extremely unreliable narrator of the book dedicated to showing his inadequacies in the modern world. As with *Ulysses's* Leopold Bloom, "Henry Adams" would not be able to tell his own story, let alone understand it. But in the case of the *Education,* despite the narrator's assertions to the contrary, that is precisely what happened, of course.

Try as one might to get around it, Adams's third-person narration of the *Education* is an integral aspect of the book's style, complicating any response to the story being told. As readers, we are always trying to discern the difference between the narrator's *ex post facto* responses to the events he narrates, on the one hand, and the protagonist's responses reported to have been felt at the time, on the other. Such a readerly effort goes on in all autobiography, but in the *Education* such distinctions are made more difficult to perceive by the almost shieldlike carapace of supposed objectivity that Adams's third-person narration creates. This defensive purpose of Adams's narration was deliberate: he wrote to Henry James that he thought the book "a mere shield of protection in the grave."[19] Because Adams's effort to preempt his biographers succeeds so well, Starobinski's "glitter of action"—the silent movements of change and growth within Adams that led to the narrator's telling the very different story recorded in the book—is obscured by the glare of the narrator's searchlight gaze bouncing off his manikin.

Notes

1. Henry Adams, *The Education of Henry Adams*, eds. Ernest Samuels and Jayne N. Samuels (New York: Library of America, 1983), p. 722. Subsequent quotations are from this edition.

2. For example, Earl Harbert sees the *Education* as "less a disguising of self-revelation as impersonal art than a disguising of impersonal and experimental art as self-revelation." Earl Harbert, *"The Education of Henry Adams*: The Confessional Mode as Heuristic Experiment," *The Journal of Narrative Technique* 4 (1974), 3; rpt. in *Critical Essays on Henry Adams*, ed. Earl N. Harbert (Boston: G. K. Hall, 1981), pp. 220–35.

3. Howard Munford sees in Adams's encouraging young men to "diminish friction [and] invigorate the energy" at work around them a "double-edged . . . prescription" since "the forces he has been reporting are multiplying at a rate which threatens catastrophe." For Munford, Adams knew that if the young men among his readers "get in line with these forces and contribute to their movement, they are hastening that very catastophe" that will ruin them and everything else. Adams, according to this view, can only encourage those who want to learn from the failures of his own life to do a better job of aligning themselves with the mechanical and scientific forces rapidly changing the world in the early twentieth century; paradoxically, by following such advice, Munford claims, Adams knows his more ambitious students will abet the destructiveness those forces entail. He explains this ironic didacticism by harking back to Adams's teaching days at Harvard, where "he had in his history seminars engaged in the method of outrageous statement to court opposition and stimulate discussion"; Munford suggests that Adams is trying the same method "in this book [the *Education*] designed to be a handbook for the young men of the new society." Howard M. Munford, "Henry Adams: The Limitations of Science," *The Southern Review* 4 (Winter 1968), 63.

4. Judith N. Shklar, *"The Education of Henry Adams* by Henry Adams," *Daedalus* 103 (Winter 1973), 60. Henry B. Rule associates the *Education* with *Don Quixote, Candide*, and *Gulliver's Travels* as a satire on the "feebleness of the human intellect." Rule's argument about the book's genre is not convincing, and his invention of the "Double Technique" whereby the narrator distinguishes himself from "facets" or "doubles" of his personality is not significantly different from self-directed irony to justify his new term. Nonetheless, Rule's analysis hits on the effect of Adams's use of the third person: "By turning aspects of life and personality into 'character,' [Adams] was able to gain the objectivity, the aesthetic distance, that satire and irony require." Henry B. Rule, "Henry

Adams' Satire on Human Intelligence: Its Method and Purpose," *The Centennial Review*, 15 (Fall 1971), 431–32.

5. Ross Lincoln Miller, "Henry Adams: Making It Over Again," *The Centennial Review*, 18 (1974), 288–90. And William Dusinberre, in line with his view of the *Education* as Adams's "purposeful travesty of the meaning of [his] life," judges as Adams's "pretense" the idea that his "sole object was didactic rather than autobiographical." Dusinberre points to Adams's "obvious pleasure in telling of his own life" and rates the first section of the book highly as autobiography: it "rings with intelligence and shrewd observation." William Dusinberre, *Henry Adams: The Myth of Failure* (Charlottesville: Univ. Press of Virginia, 1980), pp. 1, 206.

6. An instance of a critic following Adams's own interpretation of his book is Charles R. Anderson, who by substituting "persona" for Adams's term "garment," develops Adams's analogy by analyzing the *Education*'s scheme of narration as the presentation of a series of personae by various narrative voices. Charles R. Anderson, "Henry Adams" in *Critical Essays*, ed. Harbert, pp. 119–21.

7. Robert F. Sayre also follows Adams by explaining that the manikin grows into the tailor by donning and doffing "the clothes of successive educations." Sayre argues that Adams's choice of the third person helps him to oppose the past to the future and to avoid egotism and sentimentality. Robert F. Sayre, *The Examined Self: Benjamin Franklin, Henry Adams, and Henry James* (Princeton: Princeton Univ. Press, 1964), pp. 96–109.

8. Hayden White, "Method and Ideology in Intellectual History: The Case of Henry Adams," in *Modern European Intellectual History: Reappraisals and New Perspectives*, ed. Dominick La Capra and Steven L. Kaplan (Ithaca: Cornell Univ. Press, 1982), p. 304.

9. Earl N. Harbert, *The Force So Much Closer Home: Henry Adams and the Adams Family* (New York: New York Univ. Press, 1977), p. 145.

10. Jean Starobinski, "The Style of Autobiography," in *Autobiography: Essays Theoretical and Critical*, ed. James Olney (Princeton: Princeton Univ. Press, 1980), p. 76. Starobinski accepts Benveniste's characterization of third-person narration as personless: "In the narrative, if the narrator doesn't intervene, the third person is not opposed to any other, it is truly an absence of person" (p. 76n).

11. Ibid., pp. 76–77.

12. Henry Adams, *The Education of Henry Adams*, ed. Ernest Samuels with Jayne N. Samuels (Boston: Houghton Mifflin, 1974), p. xvii.

13. Ibid., p. 513.

14. Ibid., pp. xvi–xvii, 515–18.

15. In discussing Starobinski's essay in connection with the *Education*, James Goodwin sees the "event" emphasized by Adams's third-person narration as "the extinction of individuality." Goodwin argues that Adams is a "non-person in his own autobiography," offers "necrospective" as a description of Adams's

point of view, and describes Adams's writing the book as an "exercise in . . . killing himself." One might easily say that all autobiography is to varying degrees "necrospective" in that in order to write it, one must "stand outside" one's life, or adopt a "posthumous" view toward one's previous experience. Goodwin's anxiousness to make Adams's self-destructiveness explain the peculiarities of his book blinds him somewhat to the workings of its rhetoric. What I call the "anonymous controlling intelligence producing the narrative" is individualized, in fact. Could one mistake this narrator for another? The mental and verbal activity evident on each page of the *Education* is idiosyncratic and easily distinguishable from that of other writers. In his function as generator of the discourse, Adams simply chooses not to name himself. Anonymity is not necessarily a lack of individuality, even though choosing it enacts a desire for self-effacement. James Goodwin, "The Education of Henry Adams: A Non-Person in History," *Biography* 6, 2 (Spring 1983), 117–35.

16. Hayden White, p. 304.

17. *Education*, ed. Samuels, p. 515; see also pp. 509–11.

18. Starobinski, p. 77.

19. *Education*, ed. Samuels, p. 512.

13

On Writing Autobiography

Wallace Fowlie

It is a privilege for me to discuss informally and briefly, in a post-prandium style, a kind of writing I have been trying to do these past three or four years: journal-writing, or memoir-writing, or simply autobiography.

A first volume came out in 1978 that was largely concerned with my relationship with France: my early study of French, my first visit to Paris at the age of nineteen, and then later visits for work on my doctoral thesis. If there is any coherence in that book, it is the role of France in the life of an American French teacher.

When I received the first copies of that book, I sent one to a good friend and mentor who had been my chairman at Yale at the beginning of my career. He wrote a letter of approval and encouragement, but in the second part of the letter, he proposed a blueprint for the next book. He said:

> You should write a second volume and in it treat three subjects in particular. 1. Since you have been teaching more than half a century (that was a shock to read although it was accurate), tell us frankly what you think about American education, based on your own experience. 2. Rather than telling us more about authors you have met and observed, tell us about your parents, especially your father. 3. Tell us what it means to be a believer today. Is your religious belief as real for you now as it was in earlier years?

I took to heart those three topics and tried to develop them in the second volume, recently published. Those topics and others too. That second book is primarily about teaching.

This chapter appeared in *The Southern Review*, 22, no. 2 (1986): 273–79. Copyright © 1986 by Wallace Fowlie. Reprinted by permission of the author.

At this moment when I am engaged in work on a third volume of recollections or memoirs, I am becoming quite familiar with an emotion that seems to take over when I begin the writing of an episode in my life, or a portrait of an eminent person I may have encountered, or the portrait of an obscure person whom I know and like.

The most exact word I can find to describe the emotion is *panic*. Easy synonyms would be fear or dread. But the word panic comes first to my mind. Recently, I began wondering about the origin, the etymology of the word, and discovered that it may well come from the god Pan of Greek mythology. In my sketchy memory I had always thought of Pan as being a rollicking deity, associated with woods and fields and fertility. A semi-god perhaps, part animal, with horns and hoofs, and the ears of a goat. A musician also who played reeds or pipes named after him: *pan pipes*.

There my memory stopped and I was not close to understanding why panic comes from Pan. A bit of research helped. It would seem to spring from the fear of travellers at night who believed they heard the sound of his pipes in the wilderness, an eerie menacing noise. This fear is related, I presume, to the ugliness of Pan which caused the nymphs wooed in great numbers to reject him.

So, the emotion of panic and the shadow of Pan presided over many of the pages I have written and am trying to write now. In this life of a chronicler, of a man tracking down the past, wooing the past in order to exploit it, I have felt myself turning into a predatory animal-personality, not too far removed from Pan himself. In my own case at least, the tension is always there in the need to write a work that will be at once confessional and reticent. If I expressed the meaning of these two words, I might call this need, this vocation, the desire to write about what may seem significant and even universal in any man's life, and to refrain from speaking of the trivial and the trite, of the infertile. Pan led a shoddy life in his lechery and was at the same time a skilled musician.

In these efforts to recollect the past and to recreate it, to record particulars that may stir the imagination of a reader, I start quite deliberately on this third round with the word *sites*, that is, with places, with ambiences that retain for me very special atmospheres not always easy for me to describe.

Once Apollo beat Pan in a musical contest. Apollo had a seven-stringed lyre whereas Pan had fashioned his pipes from uneven reeds he had found growing out of marsh water. He had been chasing a nymph and she had been magically metamorphosed into the reeds. So, in a way, the playing on the pipes was a substitute for love-making, a means of grasping what a man has lived or has not lived. And "panic" is a mental state induced by god Pan whenever I begin a search, not with musical notes, but with words, for some clearer vision of the past.

Every life is mysterious. No one can really see anyone else's life unless perhaps it is written about. But when it is being written about and then possibly read later, it turns into allegory, into some form of figurative plausibility. It is not quite fiction, but it is not very far from it.

A simple sentence in Yeats's *Autobiography* says more to me than most learned disquisitions on the art of autobiography. "It is myself that I remake." A few years ago an autobiographer might easily have called his work a reconstruction of his life, the writer's self-picturing. Today a more exact term, taken from the new criticism, would be "deconstruction." This word, as used by the critics, would seem to mean that the true self of a man is always displaced in language.

We might contrast in terms of length Marcel Proust's very long autobiographical novel, *A la recherche du temps perdu,* with Jean-Paul Sartre's brief autobiography, *Les Mots,* and yet find in each, in the elaborately conceived and written fiction of Proust, and in the few pages of the philosopher, the same goal, the same conclusions: the account of how a man, in writing about his life, becomes a stranger to himself. Writing is indeed a process of self-alteration. Living belongs to the past. Writing is the present.

Each new autobiographer, in joining a long succession of others, sees the foolishness of what he or she is doing: this curious escape from life into words, this leap from an intention (to depict this episode and that incident) to the expression of the intention. Because of this sense of foolishness, most are only part-time autobiographers. Saint Augustine was, after all, primarily a theologian, Cellini a goldsmith and sculptor, Rousseau a *philosophe*, Gide a novelist, O'Casey a playwright, Thomas Merton, the author of mystical writings. In most cases, the autobiography is the book standing apart from the principal books, an adjunct book, an exercise book in the somewhat shameful art of confession.

Throughout my life I have been attached deeply to very few people. But I have been interested in and attracted to many because of whom and through whom I have tried to understand my own feelings, hopes, and motivations. In my meetings with famous people, or almost famous people, I have learned very little. I have learned a great deal from their work—but that is something else. In their role of human beings they tend to be (and perhaps have to be) masks. Obscure and humble people are far richer in their simplicity than famous people in their visible masks.

The character of a fellow pumping gasoline into my car, or the character of a waitress serving me my soup and sandwich for lunch, or my twenty-year-old student reading Proust for the first time, is far more exciting to me than the character of a United States senator or president. The gift of speech in senators and presidents does not often accompany the power of thought.

As the events in an autobiography form a pattern, it may appear to be prose fiction. At least it uses all the devices a novel does: characters and the chronicle of a family, maxims and lyric passages, confessions and narrative. In trying to trace its history, critics claim that Saint Augustine invented the form and Rousseau made it into a modern type of literary expression. But one might move back earlier in history, to Petronius and his *Satyricon*, and today, to the protean form of autobiography, add Fellini's films, such as *Amarcord*. And why not, to the selfportraits of Rembrandt, add those of Van Gogh and Chagall and Giacometti? In the spring of 1984 the Martha Graham Dance Company revived several of her dances created in the 1950s and 1960s. I remembered one especially, *Deaths and Entrances*, based, as we learned from a program note, on the three Brontë sisters. But in 1984, we knew that it was also based on Martha Graham and her two sisters. An autobiographical dance.

The use of memory, indispensable to autobiography, is a recycling of memories, both conscious and subconscious aspects of living, by means of which a life story may be transformed into a personal myth. Images persistently return in this recycling, and typical scenes or episodes return. These images and patterns reveal the identity of the writer, to himself first, and then to a reader.

As an example of these somewhat abstract points, I would like to speak of a very early childhood experience I am trying to write about at this time and which contains elements I barely understood until I set myself the exercise of putting them on paper.

Popham Beach, Maine. It is among the earliest of my memories, rich in memories of smells, sights, of food, and, above all, of a way of living that was totally exotic for me in my ninth, tenth, and eleventh years when I spent two weeks there each August. To say these two words, Popham Beach, is to conjure up a vision of wonderment and delight, of a first experience of living away from home in a world different from Brookline, Massachusetts.

Those three summer vacations I owed to an aunt who spent the entire month at Popham every August through all my childhood and adolescence.

There were four major points of interest about which I was enthusiastic: Fort Popham, to the left on leaving the hotel; the Coast Guard Station, to the right, at the end of the long boardwalk; South Beach beyond that; and best of all for me: the Riverside Hotel itself.

Almost no one went swimming because of the strong undertow and the extreme cold of the water. I dipped into the water each day but stayed close to the shore and enjoyed being vigorously towelled after a few minutes of pretending to swim. Since my skin burned easily, I cut short my visits to the beach and made off for more shady spots.

The nearest was the Coast Guard Station where the two men in charge allowed me to examine the large rowboats and the rescue equipment they maintained in good condition. Popham had a long history of shipwrecks. Navigation into the mouth of the Kennebec River was hazardous. It was sixteen miles upriver to Bath, and there was often danger from wind, fog, and tide.

The two coast guards were friendly to me those three summers when I paid them very regular visits. They knew the history of the place and enjoyed rehearsing it. Each year they used me in one of their more impressive exercises. I was placed in a basket—I weighed very little at that time—and shot out by means of a cable to a ship they pretended was caught on a sand bank or wrecked on a reef. Thus, I became one of their assistants, and so learned about Popham. A riverside-seaside village they called it, with its three miles of perfect beach.

They taught me how to look for sandpipers skittering along the beach at the water line, and how to watch sea gulls and especially the friendly seals bobbing up and down close to shore. They told me about foghorns and I often watched them repair bellbuoys. I tried to enjoy, as they did, the smell of sweet grass, and the mixed smell of salt air and pine. One early morning, before my hotel breakfast, they took me clamming at low tide in the bay.

Best of all, after South Beach, after the Life Guard Station, after Fort Popham, was my return to the Riverside Hotel, to my small room at the end of the long hallway on the second floor, and to all the other parts that were open to me: the lobby and the front desk, the parlor, the dining room and the piazza with its line of rocking chairs. There I encountered a variety of people young and old. It marked the beginning of my social life, and many years later when I read the second volume of Proust's novel, *A l'ombre des jeunes filles en fleurs*, I knew that

Popham was my Balbec, and the old Riverside Hotel was le grand hôtel de Balbec.

They were worlds apart, my Popham and young Marcel's Balbec, continents and social classes apart. The elaborate summertime life at a Normandy beach resort bore little resemblance to the rigid simplicity of Maine where no Mme de Villeparisis took me on carriage drives. Only "flivers" dared tackle the roads around Popham at that time. There was no Mlle Stermaria in the hotel, and no Albertine on the beach, but I was much younger than Marcel. Only the two coast guards were firm friends. The hotel guests were passing figures. I have forgotten their names and their faces. But I have not forgotten the excitement I felt in having them about me in the hotel, and in greeting them as my aunt and I made our way to our table in the dining room.

I will leave Maine now and return to thoughts about this kind of writing that continue to obsess me.

There have been countless efforts to define autobiography, but no one seems accurate or even satisfactory. Anthony Trollope once wrote: "In our lives we are always weaving novels." This thought has been said in many varying ways. Thomas Wolfe, closer to us in time than Trollope, has observed: "All serious work in fiction is autobiographical."

"Myself am the groundwork of my book." It is John Florio's translation in 1603 of Montaigne's sentence: *Je suis moi-même la matière de mon livre.* I find it a remarkable translation.

Ernest Renan, in his *Souvenirs d'enfance et de jeunesse*, writes: "What one says of oneself is always poetry." (*Ce qu'on dit de soi est toujours poésie.*) Of all the statements of this nature that I have come across, the most awesome, the most definitive, is by Oscar Wilde: "All artistic creation is absolutely subjective."

Now, these sentences contradict what I was taught by the first group of "new critics" when I was in college in the 1930s and 1940s. They taught us to trust the tale rather than the teller of the tale. They taught us to look on a story or a poem as an object, an artifact that has little to do with the place where it was written, or the time when it was written, or indeed the personality of the man who wrote it. I am not convinced. The desire for self-portraiture is in evidence everywhere. Self-portraiture for me now is a synonym of self-knowledge. And that admonition to know oneself comes to us from the Greek philosophers. The loftiest interpretation given to this advice is in Cardinal Newman, in the "apology" he wrote for his life (*Apologia pro vita sua*), where he says: "self-knowledge is the source of man's knowledge of God."

In our secular world of the twentieth century, the word *self* has replaced the word *soul*. Most theorists today would say that memory is the core of selfhood. The pronoun "I" is really what "I" has remembered. Saint Augustine has often been called *the* philosopher of memory. He describes it as "an inner chamber, vast and unbounded." Then several centuries later Rousseau secularized Saint Augustine's Christian introspection by emphasizing his childhood and adolescence.

The life of a man is always larger than the book he writes about his life. From the opening lines he writes, the autobiographer knows that all is approximate. And the reason for this is the language he has to use. Language is opaque.

Thoreau died at the age of forty-four. In his *Walden*, he wrote a book that is still read today, and especially by youngsters, by young people who are thrilled by that life in the woods, by that hut close to the pond, by that independence of a man living close to nature and calling himself "inspector of snow-storms and rain-storms." When Thoreau is released from jail, adolescent boys reading that passage today are captivated by such a sentence as: "I returned to the woods in season to get my dinner of huckleberries on Fair Haven Hill." *Walden* is our Yankee substitute for *Robinson Crusoe*.

The source of that panic that often takes over an autobiographer's feelings is possible in the conflict between the two lives he is trying to narrate and join: the life that others saw him live and the life known only to himself. They are related, those two lives, and it is the art of the writer that relates them.

The audience of a writer—and I believe this is especially true for biography and autobiography—is composed in part of voyeurs, thieves, parasites. They read—and that means they walk off with whatever they feel is worth taking. This is an ancient habit belonging to the world of literature, as well as to other art worlds: painting, dance, architecture. In some versions of mythology, Apollo himself is made to look like an unimaginative bully and bore. In fact, in some tales, he stole from Pan, the god or the goat who got there first.

There is today a polite term, an erudite term, designating such thefts. Intertextuality. But since the writer (be he poet or autobiographer) is the instrument of culture, such thefts are forgiven, and, like Pan, he is free to remain the rebel, the singer who shocks his community and even terrifies, through occasional excesses, those who hear him. At first the community will tend to exclude him from the tribal dance. In modern times they have done that with Osip Mandelstam in Russia, with Federico Lorca in Spain, with Arthur Rimbaud in France, with Walt Whitman and Henry Miller in America—and with other Pan-like figures.

14

Autogynography

Germaine Brée

My title needs some explanation. In the overall planning for the Baton Rouge symposium on autobiography, the section which I was to introduce was entitled "Women's Autobiography." I was somewhat puzzled by the implications of the title. We were not, in any other section, invited to discuss "men's autobiography." The plural in "women" itself was disconcerting in relation to the singular "autobiography." Beyond that difficulty did the title imply that autobiographies written by women constituted a subgenre? Or a different genre—in which latter case perhaps they should acquire a different label? Leaving aside such questions of terminology, I borrowed my title—in response to my uncertainties—from Domna Stanton's recent article entitled "Autogynography: Is the Subject Different?" It is the last article in the 1984 issue of the *New York Literary Forum* (v. 12–13), *The Female Autograph*, which Stanton edited. "Autogynography": that is to say, writing by women about themselves. At the outset the article raises questions which go beyond the realm of literary definition and theory, although it proposes a new generic label.

Stanton's essay is cast in a witty imitation of that section of Virginia Woolf's *A Room of One's Own* in which the "I," the persona standing in for the author, surveys some library bookshelves in frustrated search of female signatures. Stanton, similarly, surveying the abundant array of critical literature on autobiography, finds, like Woolf, a "parsimonious" number of works focusing on women's writing. For scholars, critics, and meta-critics—men and women—she notes, the autobiographer is "he"; and the works described are overwhelmingly written by men.

This chapter appeared in *The Southern Review*, 22, no. 2 (1986): 223–30. Copyright ©1986 by Germaine Brée. Reprinted by permission of the author.

To a certain extent, of course, this reflects a linguistic convention and constraint. But it sustains a more or less unconscious assumption, pervasive in our culture, that what is "important" is coextensive with what is masculine, "human." Stanton describes her approach to literature as "textual, non-referential." As a critic she is not then concerned with "real" persons "out there" but with the self as it unfolds in the text. The persona is constituted in a discourse through the specific strategies, perspectives that that discourse adopts. When confronted by the paucity of texts on autobiographies by women, Stanton set herself a precise problem. "What heuristic claims could be made *at this moment* for the difference of autogynography, for the status and significance of the female signature?" She finds first that among male critics whose theoretical definitions of autobiography present themselves as "gender-blind," there is no consensus of opinion as to what formally characterizes the autobiographical work. As James Olney put it: "There is no way to bring autobiography to heel as a literary genre with its own proper form, terminology, and observances." Women scholars here are no exception, tending when they do not overlook the gender issue merely to reverse the criteria in use: if male autobiographical writing is seen as teleological and linear, female is described as fragmented and circular; if male is defined as using a rhetoric of assertion, female is defined as using a rhetoric of seduction, and so on. We all know how easily those categories migrate from male to female in the ever-growing corpus of writings at present loosely grouped under the label autobiographical.

To her question, "What heuristic claims could be made for the difference of autogynography?," her very honest answer is "none." But she promptly qualifies it—"at this point in time." Our current approach she feels may be deficient. Even qualified, her conclusion makes her uneasy. In relation to her *feeling* that the gender of the "subject" *does* make a difference, she must register her illogical belief that the gender of the author did make a difference at the discursive "point in time." So she opens wide the door to the problematic area of "l'écriture féminine," turning her attention and ours to the speaking subject as locus of emission of the text. She scrutinizes her position as historically situated, raising the question of the relation of the "I" of the critic's text to the autobiographical "I's"; of her own relation to the world and those others in it. All the elements of uncertainty that accompany our contemporary theoretical discourse are realized as she sets forth the dilemma of definition versus feeling.

Let us turn to another critic, Susan Friedman of the University of

Wisconsin, who addresses the question from a different angle. With characteristic generosity she allowed me to consult a soon-to-be-published essay entitled "Women's Autobiographical Selves, Theory and Practice." Friedman scrutinizes the predominant generic models of autobiography in relation to a corpus of autobiographical writings by women—quite a vast corpus though recently constituted: Anaïs Nin, Gilman, H.D. Her conclusion, like Stanton's, is simple: the generic models proffered do not apply to women's autobiographical writings. Her critical approach is historically based. She examines the "seminal" essay by Georges Gusdorf of the University of Strasbourg which established a basic definition of autobiography as narrative, of life as story. In Gusdorf's view, the autobiographical impulse in its modern form emerged at a certain moment in Western culture with the Industrial Revolution. A new image of the individual was in the making as old economic and social structures crumbled. The individual then "disencumbered" could look within himself as an isolated self-directed unit who could assume command of his life. Though the goals were different, the concept merged with the topic of pervasive "spiritual autobiographies" of Christian inspiration. Thence the form taken by the autobiographical act, a retrospective reconstruction through language of a developing sense of self—Rousseau after St. Augustine.

Let me open a parenthesis here. Today we generally consider the concept of the isolated self, what Sande Michael calls the "unencumbered" self, as a historically conditioned myth. In *The Public and Its Problems* (1920) John Dewey demystified the concept with blunt irony:

> The theory of the individual, possessed of desires and claims surfaced at just the time (the mutation of western society) when the individual was counting for far less, a time when the mechanical forces and vast impersonal organizations were determining the frame of things.

This view does not invalidate the model Gusdorf purposes. For the myth of the independent individual dominated our culture for some 150 years from the Romantic to the "authentic" existentialist self. But it does undermine the claim for its ontological universality corroborating Friedman's thesis. Friedman points out that it even affects theoretical systems that challenge its validity. Both Freud and Lacan, she notes, though differently, think of the process of individuation as story. For them self-realization takes place within an internalized nexus of family relations developing in *stages* and in terms of conflict, power, separation, dominance. Friedman argues that these structures of the developing self are "male" and not applicable to women's autobiographical writings. Thence the absence of these from the critical corpus, an absence noted by Stanton.

Gusdorf in his article had defined the preconditions without which, according to him, modern autobiography is *impossible*. Friedman reverses his enumeration: women's autobiography is *possible* when the individual does *not* feel herself to exist outside of others but feels she is included in an independent existence that asserts its rhythms everywhere in the community. The important unit is never for her the isolated human being but the presence and recognition of another consciousness. Since women on the whole did not "go" anywhere, the sense of life for them is not teleological. Thence the exclusion of their autobiographical works from the accepted canon.

Friedman here makes another significant suggestion: the formal characteristics of the autobiographic text are inseparable from the concepts of self held by the writer. And these are in turn determined by the circumstances of women's and men's lives. Their significance and the forms they take cannot be understood apart from their socio-historical context: "Women's autobiographies come alive as a literary tradition of self-creation when we approach these texts from a perspective based on the lives of women," she concludes. In consequence, as those lives change—and they are fast changing—the forms in which they choose to "inscribe" their sense of self may change. Like Stanton, Friedman is aware of the historical conjuncture that is putting its mark on the feminine sense of self at "this point in time."

Rather than referring to Freud or Lacan, Friedman relies on recent research in this area by psychologists and sociologists. Sheila Rowbotham and Nancy Chodorow corroborate her analyses. Predominant in women they find is the consciousness of a collective identity; thence of a "dual consciousness, 'self' represented in the hall of mirrors" of a culture, as well as in their own sensibility; a sense of the importance of interpersonal relations in the formation of a sense of self. Not least among these is the "mother-daughter" relationship which has been so thoroughly obscured by the Freudian emphasis on "father-figure," the Oedipal construct, the phallic cult; the emblematic virgin and man-child model. In conclusion and within the perspectives established by my two theorists, I should like to take a brief look at three recent autobiographic texts by women—short texts. The longer biographies become, it seems, the shorter autobiographies. Before I do so, I note that, in the last years, many men's autobiographies have broken with the paradigmatic Gusdorf pattern: one need only quote from a long list, such examples as, in

France, *Roland Barthes par roland barthes* or the four-volume work of Michel Leiris. From a speculative point of view I should like to quote from an essay by J. F. Lyotard, one of the contemporary French thinkers who cause so much irritation, perhaps because of their abstruse language, in our academic circles. The essay is entitled "One of the Things at Stake in Women's Struggles": "The decision constituting the discourse of knowledge, constructing a constituting order, appears as a fact of power and a power of fact."

The attempt to construct a constituting order is what we as critics have all been engaged in here. Lyotard continues, "It follows that men in all *their claims to construct meaning, to speak the truth, are themselves only a patchwork where it becomes impossible to establish or validly determine any major order."* Why not then return to the multiplicity of the lived? If I may make my own leap into speculation, it might well be that at this time of spectacular change in our sense of the macrocosm we inhabit—women, because until now they have had little occasion, therefore little inclination, to "construct meaning" on a grand scale, are in a better position to see beyond the constraints of our conceptual representations, beyond our dichotomies and abstractions (not the least of which is the male-female dichotomy) and to look to the "multiplicity of the real." The dismantling of the concept of the "unencumbered" self disrupted the conventional patterns of autobiography. The growing awareness of the presence of the "other" also caused further perturbation in the oriented narrative of self-realization. Michel Leiris in the conclusion of *Biffures* humorously stated the case:

> It is decidedly fitting that I should leave you here and however mortifying it is to end a book *without having reached a point of arrival* (that is some truth which didn't exist at the outset) it is fitting that I stop like a locomotive which finds the tracks are blocked and stops in the middle of the fields after a series of blasts.

Two of the three recent autobiographical texts I have in mind, *L'Enfance* (*Childhood*) and *L'Amant* (*The Lover*), have been best-sellers in France, written by two well-known fiction writers, Nathalie Sarraute and Marguerite Duras. The third, "My Memory's Hyperbole," by the psychoanalyst and linguist Julia Kristeva was published in *The Female Autograph*, for which it was written. All three are concerned with the working of memory. We have been so obsessed by the problem of the persona or self in the text that we have bypassed the question of memory and its complex layerings; so obsessed with life as story that we have tended to overlook the question of the world, the space we inhabit.

The best introduction to *Childhood* and *The Lover* is, I think, Cartier-Bresson's preface to his 1952 photographic album, *The Decisive Moment*. "Space in the present," he writes, "strikes us with greater or lesser intensity and then leaves us an image *visually to be closed in our memory and to modify itself there*. We photographers deal in things that are constantly vanishing and when they have vanished there is no contrivance on earth which can make them come to life. We cannot develop and print a memory." But can a writer do so? And how would a "modification of memory" differ from fiction? The photographer's art is, according to Cartier-Bresson, the art of catching the "decisive moment," when emotions become concrete and communicable. Its dangers are in the temptation of the "blow-up" which may suggest what is not there. These are suggestive metaphors that can be applied to the autobiographer's project.

Sarraute's *Childhood* opens with a discussion of how a writer "develops" "unassuming memories." A series of fragmentary recollections are framed by a dialogue between two personae who address each other in the intimate "tu" form as they engage in an ironic argument: "So you're really going to do it . . . to 'evoke your childhood memories.' How those words bother you; you don't like them. . . . " "Yes; I can't help it, I'm tempted by it, I don't know why." We, the readers are cast in the role of internal observers at the inception of the autobiographical act wherein the writer-critic (who, incidentally, is not genderized as feminine) struggles against the writer's (a feminine persona) desire to reach back to something that *is there;* and to "develop" the vague "vanished" things, as yet untouched by words. The "don't do it" of the conscious critical self, its "No you won't do it" acts as a kind of god that starts the process of emergence of the image. The word "no" literally "reanimates" another "no" in another visually recaptured scene. A young woman is seated in an armchair, sewing; in front of her is a large pair of scissors. A child—five or six years old—grabs the scissors and announces her intention. She will rip the blue silk cover of the couch. "No, you won't do it," says the governess; the child promptly does. A short episode. But the connection is striking. The gesture of violence that tears apart the smooth silk cover of the sofa is the gesture of violence that, through the agency of words, tears apart the smooth surface of the present.

From vignette to vignette, a story is uncovered. The vignettes are fragmentary, situated more or less chronologically though not teleologically. They set up a fragile chain of "signifiers," images that refer to a singular identity: a Russian child, whose parents divorce, who moves between Moscow and Paris, who has stored and forgotten scenes, felt, not expressed, with their seasons and setting. Concomitantly the writer's effort, akin to the photographer's, is to restitute them in words, for what they are, "being there" of childhood in some global, ultimate sense. All are connected with words—heard, said, exchanged—that activate the process of textual translation.

Marguerite Duras' *The Lover* begins with two quasiphotographic images: stark image in a mirror, a ravaged face, the face of the writer. Secondly, the vague outline of another "shot" one might call it: a fifteen-and-a-half-year-old girl, on a ferry, crossing the Mekong River on the way to Saigon, a black limousine drawn up alongside the bus on the ferry. From the initial scene, she slowly reevokes the whole, the wild love story of a poor "little white girl" in Saigon and the son of a wealthy Chinese banker. This is not the beginning of an organized autobiographical "story" retrospectively narrated: "The story of my life does not exist," the writer warns, "It does not exist. There was never any center, no road, no line. There are vast spaces in which one could pretend there was someone. It's not true there was nobody." *The Lover* is a complex book. What Duras seeks to explore with unusual intensity, even for her, are the ambiguous unformulated relationships of love and hatred that link to one another her beleaguered white family group in a pre-World War II Cambodia. Central is the strange figure of the mother: "We loved her beyond love." The "I" and her love affair are decentered; and the writing develops in sequences forever circling back to the vanished figures, all dead (mother, brothers) according to its own internal principles. The time frame is wide, the experience many layered and chaotic as it is fragmentarily "re-visualized." A microcosm builds up beyond the crisscrossing of patterns of domination and control that define the colonial world: white, Chinese; Paris, Saigon; poor, rich; male, female; sane, mad. It is not identity that emerges, so much as the confused outline of merging worlds—a new sense perhaps of the bounds of our geographic, social, psychological representations. The first scene, the adolescent girl "crossing the Mekong," seems quasi-symbolic.

In her short text, Kristeva presents an intellectual odyssey, the recognizable odyssey of a "group," the avant-garde group, the "we" in whose work she participated from the time of her arrival in Paris and the founding of the review "Tel Quel"—through 1963 and its aftermath. "I" is there but it is that of the narrator; the "significant odyssey" is that of a "we," of a group. And the significant setting is the "universalist" "cosmopolitan" academic setting of a post-World War II Paris. One may smile a little at the importance attributed to this group as modifiers of a traditional culture and heralds of new cultural vistas, but the text invites us to "read" the changing perspective of Kristeva's work in terms of a particular philosophy of the autobiographical subject. The sense of self, as understood by Kristeva, may at the outset be contingent on the possibilities provided by a specific culture. She sees that culture as an entity in motion; the self then is the "perpetually de-centered, socially constituted subject of a mutual discourse" forever called on to reassess the mental structures it inhabits in the articulation of a future about which it has no omniscience. Whether it is guiding or following the forces of change in action it cannot know. The text does not attempt to examine other more intimate layers of experience and so, rather like a documentary, seems almost comically flimsy. The disproportion between the "group" (young "intellectuals" in Paris; Paris "intellectuals" in China on a guided tour, the USA seen from the precincts of a campus) and the world scene surveyed, makes the narrative seem perfunctory. But the attempt to mesh the intellectual saga of a barely articulated group with its "collective" experience, rooted of course in Marxist theory, opens new vistas for the autobiographer. "Isn't any autobiography," queries Kristeva, "even if it doesn't involve 'us,' a desire to make a collective public image exist, for you, for us?" St. Augustine would not, probably, have disagreed. Like Domna Stanton's reinstatement of the "writing-speaking subject" as locus of emission of the text, Kristeva's attribution of a shared collective motivation for the autobiographical genre as such seems to mesh with the kind of contextual approach proposed by Friedman.

To conclude, theories, like perceptions, eventually fade and vanish. It is not astonishing, given human "narcissism" and the human urge to order, understand, and communicate, that new forms of autobiography not necessarily literary will, inevitably, appear. They are here already: interviews, recorded, filmed, or taped; photographic records of lives, from cradle to grave. If a sense of self is in fact closely linked to cultural phenomena, we can envisage the possibility that our male-female polarization cannot even now furnish the proper frame of reference for "understanding the relation of self to the world" as Merleau-Ponty put it. But though the autobiographical *persona* may appear to us today as something of a joke, it may well also be the joker; that is, as the dictionary defines it, the prankster or "wild card" from which anything might be expected. It might be tempting to conclude—and it has been suggested—that somewhere along in our mid-century years the "moije" inherited from the Romantics waned and moved away from the center stage carrying with it the autobiographical narrative. As we have seen, new forms of autobiography, women's predominantly among them, may be pointing to new, viable, less theoretical forms of the autobiographical narrative.

15

Shadowed Presence: Modern Women Writers' Autobiographies and the Other

Julia Watson

One of several essays that distinguishes James Olney's anthology *Autobiography: Essays Theoretical and Critical* is Mary G. Mason's contribution, "The Other Voice: Autobiographies of Women Writers."[1] In this essay Mason argues for women's autobiography as a separable genre of life-writing on the basis of criteria that are internal to the work, that is, criteria for how the woman's writing voice discovers and presents itself as an Other in discourse. Indeed, in the four models of women's autobiography that she discusses extensively, Julian of Norwich, Margery Kempe, Margaret Cavendish, and Anne Bradstreet, the journey toward literary selfhood is charted in the writing; but the "I" enunciated in no case manifests the self-dramatizing egoism and obsessive self-reference of the Rousseauean autobiography, understood by most critics as prototypical for the genre. The "I" may be transformed within mystic union, as in the case of Julian of Norwich; or distinguished by its struggle to differentiate itself from the religious collective, as in Margery of Kempe; or alluded to via a chronicle of family and daily life, as in the case of Margaret Cavendish; or defined within the norm of collective experience, as in the Puritan Anne Bradstreet's writing. Professor Mason points out that these models are exemplary, not exhaustive, of modes of otherness in women's life-writing. In each the "I" is mediated by the agency of a significant other(s) and originates as an Other to itself.[2]

Historical gender differences in the roles, classes, social positions, and life models of women and men also contribute to women's discovery of their designation as cultural Other. For each woman writing, her own gender status and her female models (mother, grandmother, mentor, friend) contribute to a concept of self and a quality of writing voice that are distinctively of women. Our problem remains, however, to *describe* the interplay of others that constructs the Other of the emerging subject's attempts to vocalize an "I," to claim a history. Mason observes, "The history of autobiography is largely a history of the Western obsession with self and at the same time the felt desire to somehow escape that obsession. Our four models . . . record and dramatize self-realization and self-transcendence through the recognition of another" (p. 235). Mason argues for otherness in women's autobiographies not as the mirror reverse of the Rousseauean drama of the self, but as a different valuation of the several voices of a protean self, discoverable to some extent in all autobiography, including Rousseau's. These voices are, however, frequently mistrusted and deflected—into fantasy, confession, eroticization, or suppression of the Other—in many male autobiographies that strive toward the unitary ego as an empowered self within the dominant ideology. Importantly, the Other who is recognized in women's autobiographies may be multiple or serial, according to Mason; it is incorporated as a self-concept while maintaining an external referent in that origin.

Mary Mason is by no means the only theorist of women's autobiography to argue for the importance of a concept of the Other in distinguishing the genre's separable boundaries, and thereby redefining the concept of autobiography itself. The strategy of the Other has helpfully been defined and developed psychoanalytically with respect to Lillian Hellman's memoirs by Marcus Billson and Sidonie Smith.[3] They argue for the proliferation and importance of real others in Hellman's writing as models and mirrors in front of which she tries to create a reality that permits exploration of the self as a history rather than an ego and as a drama enacted over the duration and against the lapses of memory; repossession and renewal form a dialectic in the articulation of the Other, itself ultimately a figure of the reader's silent other.

In an effort to redefine the theory of autobiography through the female text, Nancy K. Miller has argued, on the basis of women's autobiography in France, that the (male) autobiographer's tactic of performing a masculine reading à la the Rousseauean model of self-dramatizing and erotic frankness has displaced the real center of women's autobiographical texts: namely, in a dialogue with received notions of femininity and the advocacy of a freer concept of text and of gender identity.[4] Women's autobiography, Miller argues, calls for a gender-bound reading, one that "would recognize . . . the reading subject named by gender and committed in a dialectics of identification to deciphering the inscription of a *female* subject" (p. 267). That is, the reader's task is in part to discover what Phillipe Lejeune has termed "the autobiographical pact," here situated in a female difference that asks to be decoded.

While I am indebted to Miller's helpful insights about the limitations of a "masculine reading" à la Lejeune, the concept of women's auto-biography in which identity is exclusively bio-logical or bio-graphical seems restrictive. I would argue less for a "feminine" reading than for a reconsideration of the metaphysical imposition by which autobiography is restricted to the history of the lived life rather than that internal history of the subject's writing. If we decenter the *bios*-bias in auto-biography, we begin to observe the accretion of moments of self-apprehension and display *as* the auto-graph. For those writers, not all of the female gender, to whom the present acts as a pressure to displace the self from center-stage into the shadow of a real or typical other, self-disclosure is a process continually in the making. Its text retains something of the fragmentary, mosaical quality of the "I" in dialogue with powerful others. The contours of the anti-metaphysical autograph may lack the firm and finished voice of self-justification we find in empowered autobiography of "masculine," that is, metaphysical, assertion.[5]

I will propose a sketch of some representations of the Other in Western women's autobiographies in the nineteenth and twentieth centuries. Not surprisingly, both the modes of otherness and the strategies for discovering and mediating the voices of the self multiply and modulate as we approach the present, when gender stratifications are becoming less rigid and the concept of identity less fixedly encoded in a masculine/feminine bipolarity. At the same time I want to "worry" the concept of otherness by displacing it from a cognitive mode (as Mason presents it) to a rhetorical strategy grounded in recognition and displacement of the empowered male voice. The metonymy implicit in women auto-biographers' strategy of otherness—presenting the "I" through the models of others—is in fact less a *sub*stitution, more a *con*stitution, of the autobiographical "I" in texts where an external other seems to loom largest as the apparent subject of life-writing. That is, several women's autobiographies masquerade as the life of another in which the writing "I" is presented as only a kind of connective tissue. Yet the reader's experience of an autonomous voice narrating a life may be strongest where the self is apparently suppressed, suggesting that *for the woman writer*, the tactic of writing in the shadow of an Other can be an act of liberation from the constraints of conventional accounts of female lives.

The veiled autobiographies I have in mind are Gertrude Stein's *The Autobiography of Alice B. Toklas*, Lillian Hellman's "Julia" in *Pentimento*, and the contemporary East German writer Christa Wolf's *The Quest for Christa T.*[6] I will situate these "shadowed" autobiographies within the more conventional otherness of models in the autobiography of George Sand and Mary McCarthy's *Memories of a Catholic Girlhood*, two prototypes of modern women's autobiography.

The voluminous autobiography of George Sand (Aurore Dupin Dudévant) uses several modes of literary fiction to present her life as a fable for instructing and educating the reader, much as a *bildungsroman* might. A long section of the autobiography is set before Sand's birth, in a correspondence between her father and grandmother. She recounts several anecdotes of early childhood that are clearly a pastiche of oral history and the historic record of the Napoleonic wars; indeed her parents are cast melodramatically as the Romantic, aristocratic dandy and the passionate plebeian mistress. Sand is almost consistently a character within a story complete with dialogue, setting, and other characters. Thus, she gives the lie to the stuff of the autobiographical act—the faultiness of memory and the intertwining of past and present in an act of recollection.[7] Sand is consummately the narrator in the present of herself as a girl in the panorama of the past, which is dominated at different moments by different Others, notably her mother and her grandmother as alternative models of a female selfhood dominated by passion or by reason.

Germaine Brée has argued convincingly that the family romance, the "matrix of fabulation" that forms the central triangle of Sand's childhood and is replayed in permutations throughout her life, is constituted through her two "mothers," her own plebeian mother and her aristocratic paternal grandmother.[8] Sand's autobiography, according to Brée, employs the forms of popular romance to dramatize her quest for identity through the conflicts of her "good" and "bad" mothers. The Other stands in the places of the mothers and witnesses the drama of assertion, appeal, humiliation, and ultimate self-vindication that Sand plays out to her readership.

In constituting two opposed maternal Others as powerful figures, Sand inscribes her own role as the mediator who can ultimately integrate and internalize their oppositions. Otherness is a strategy of self-understanding which, constituted as maternal power, permits her escape from the social powerlessness of nineteenth-century French women. In this account of how engaging the maternal others structures the fictions of Sand's autobiography and creates its "I," Brée offers a crucial component for defining what distinguishes women's autobiography as a genre. Nonetheless, in *Histoire de ma vie*, the life of the autobiographer itself remains in some crucial ways concealed and in the shadow of those maternal voices it has dramatized. Sand's autobiography is vexing for its suppressions. We would like to know more of her mad early passion or of the internal suffering in her problematic marriage; but Sand is explicitly silent about the feelings of the private self.[9] To that extent otherness supplants the quest for her own voice, rather than supporting it. Within the fictional framework we see several Others who highlight aspects of the emerging Aurore's selfhood; but an absolute narrative distance between narrator and persona suggests that this otherness eludes an authentic autobiographical confrontation. The complexity of Sand's notion of the female self may be manifested more in her novels, as several critics have suggested, than in her life-writing. Certainly the public and serial way in which her autobiography was published, as well as her own reticence, act as injunctions to silence, making the otherness of her discourse engrossing, but in some ways resistant to the reader's desire for dialogue with the confessed private "I."

In Mary McCarthy's *Memories of a Catholic Girlhood* one finds a similar presentation of the emerging self via a series of significant others on whom she models, and against whom she defines, herself. While it is impossible briefly to do justice to the complexity of the book's triple narrative and the richness of its snapshot metaphor, I would suggest that McCarthy emphasizes the importance of self-discovery through scrutiny of, desire for, and appropriation of the Other in the act of role-playing, itself both act and metaphor in her development. Otherness implies trying on roles that her family and friends then respond to as images of the hidden self, and which she modulates and eventually casts off in the act of becoming that Mary McCarthy who is the writer in the present. That writer is defined by her distance from the postures of the girl-self dramatized in roles—the suffering victim, the rebel, the convert, the hedonist, the classicist—that she then discarded as old skins which would constrict the self she has become, locatable not as an entity but by its distance from the earlier actress. For McCarthy, otherness is a mode of self-understanding that explains her past through stories that question their own status as explanatory fictions. She is *of* those others; yet she is neither them nor the earlier self that narrated them, but a third voice found in each chapter's epilogue. The incidents recalled by a "present" narrator are undercut by a more "present" questioner in a text constructed as a mosaic of temporal "snapshots." In that difference reside the successive layers of a self that escapes its others by the complexity of its self-reference.

Sand's and McCarthy's autobiographies are models of the genre in their careful and extensive tracing of female development toward authorship. But their reliance on others as foils to highlight the shadowy self may at times, particularly in Sand, permit autobiography's tension between past and present to slacken. In three memoirs that *claim* to be anti-autobiographies, the story of someone else, the woman autobiographer's voice may emerge more fully for standing more deliberately in another's shadow.

To consider this paradox, let us turn first to Gertrude Stein's *The Autobiography of Alice B. Toklas*. All of Stein's works have an autobiographical dimension locatable in her remaking of the written word as communal speech. *Everybody's Autobiography* and *The Autobiography of Rose* are such because they claim to be. But *The Autobiography of Alice B. Toklas* occupies a special place. It is the autobiography of Stein's significant and *real* Other, and has a historical particularity and density that convince us this work is retrieval and creation in roughly equal measure. Too, it is a work of voices. One has only to read the first page to discover the cadences of Alice's voice—the sentences either clipped or in rolling periods, the syntax precisely relational, the definiteness of naming—to realize that *The Autobiography of Alice B. Toklas* has to be a work of otherness; that is, no one could write of herself with such consciousness of her own unself-consciousness. At the same time, the strategy of writing *as* Alice permits Stein to escape from inhibiting self-consciousness into the world of speech, which, as utterance, is "the rhythm of the visible world." Taking Alice as the means of charting her own life permits Stein to escape the solitude and the danger of solipsism that threaten the autobiographer.

But if *The Autobiography of Alice B. Toklas* is an interplay of private voices situated in an historical moment, what makes it autobiographical for Stein rather than simply a memoir of Alice? First, the autograph of Stein is always there in the interstices, not only as the person Alice addresses, but more important as the Other about whom Alice's own life is modeled. "Alice" starts by saying that "a bell rang" for her when she met Gertrude Stein and that her life began on that day.[10] The tracing of Alice's life is the act of alluding to an unspeaking Other, Gertrude, who is determinant for her; in Stein's portrayal of Alice's discovery of Gertrude in Paris, we obliquely locate Stein. Further, Stein's own life story is a narration embedded within Alice's story, so that an Other comes to tell her autobiography, an empirically impossible but rhetorically persuasive gesture: Stein authors Alice's narration of Gertrude's emergence into voice. Alice can attribute a facticity to the life of Gertrude that Stein could not do prior to becoming her "self."

In *The Autobiography of Alice B. Toklas*, it is clear that another narrator is organizing Alice's story in terms of metaphors of composition and voice. For example, Cubist painting is a model and metaphor of the texture of prewar life in Paris. The disarranged fragments evoke a mosaic of lived complexity that would be inadequately represented by chronological syntax and sequence. Stein approaches the authenticity of an autobiographical act by her strategy of otherness; fragmented and discontinuous voices evoke the cadences of a real speech community. Stein's displacements of self prove her a writer for whom coming into voice is the making of a life; external fictions about her history are in a sense irrelevant. Every page of *The Autobiography of Alice B. Toklas* is an autograph of the apparent nonself, at once the shape, model, and privileged audience for whom Stein obliquely constructs her "speaking" self-portrait. Stein's concept of self is neither static nor unitary because it is postulated through sketching the Other; the act of writing is a spur to discovering, in that privileged voice, the echo of her own which thereby constitutes her in speaking. Monologue has become a dialogue in which the authorial persona is the addressee of an Other that, by her sympathetic impersonation of the autobiographer, can authorize her.

Similarly, in Lillian Hellman's story "Julia," within *Pentimento*, the strategy of selecting another as focus of a memoir brings the writer's own life into relief more effectively than would making herself the central character in an autobiographical story. Hellman offers us the metaphor of *pentimento* to elucidate how life-writing is a temporal accretion of multiple, fragmentary instances. *Pentimento* implies the traces of earlier paintings sometimes visible in a later work such that fragments of images from different times can be seen simultaneously; *pentimento* is about their differences rather than one resolved image. Most fully in the memoir entitled "Julia," Hellman uses the problem of discovering her subject to create a complex narrative of different and discontinuous times. Though the story is in one sense a progress from their shared childhood toward discovering Julia's political activities, her eventual death, and its aftermath, posing her as the Other permits Hellman to take a measure of her own growth in political awareness and to interrogate the person that she glimpses as herself in the years preceding and during World War II. Julia is, in a sense, an overlay permitting traces of Hellman's self-image to emerge as she sketches the Other. She is all that Hellman was not and could not become, but also a loved and loving second self; and she remains elusive, incomprehensible, an Other to be interrogated. The complexity of this knowledge of another is continuously modulated through Hellman's own flawed ability, at various times, to understand and to act. The narrative breaks down in the wordlessness of love, grief, and passion, and at those points reveals, in its silences, the shadow of Hellman's own emotions. Verbal fragments attest to moments of herself caught in the act of listening and retrieving. In "Julia," as in *Alice B. Toklas*, the resistance of an Other to being appropriated becomes a *literary* discovery as it occasions revelation of, and reflection on, an authorial self in a process of recapturing in writing what it could not seize and hold by an act of conscious will.

The preeminence of the Other and the quality of sympathy and lack of competitiveness in the intersubjective relationship are characteristics that distinguish women's autobiographies. They transcend the boundaries of the self in recognizing the real existence—as *different*, not as mirror-image—of the Other to the extent that the self, that which says "I," is what must be recuperated; the Other is a firm identity even in its absence or idealization. In women's autobiographies, as a result, voice is generated in dialogue that noncensoriously includes the reader, unlike rejection of the public and the injunctions on how to be read that we find in Rousseau.

The creation of a speaking voice as identity in the autobiography of otherness is difficult to describe, as our critical language remains within the constructs of metaphysical autobiography. To evoke a sense of both voice and critical problems, I turn to a text that offers a language for representing the peculiar quality of autobiographical reflection and the subjective perception of time's passage, Christa Wolf's *The Quest for Christa T.*

Wolf, a contemporary German Democratic Republic writer, began by writing narrative fiction that became increasingly autobiographical. *The Quest for Christa T.* straddles the boundary between novel and biography in being a first-person narrator's problematic recollection, in Nazi and postwar Socialist Germany, of a girlhood friend who died at thirty-two of leukemia. But in fact the book is about the difficulty of retrieving memory and the radical separateness of moments of apprehension, themselves different from "memory" because they must be linguistic. There can be no reflection on Christa T. that does not include the narrator's own subjectivity. Much of the book is directed to Christa T. as an absent addressee in a dialogue that will never find completion. The unnamed narrator moves back and forth between being author and character for Christa T.'s story, often within a sentence. From chapter to chapter of a roughly chronological narrative there are shifts and discrepancies in her voice that suggest different distances between the writer's present and herself in the past. I consider *The Quest for Christa T.* a veiled autobiography, in that Christa T., while significantly the book's "subject," is primarily an occasion for acts of meditation in which the narrator is thrown back on herself as the questor in a necessarily incomplete intersubjective discourse with the Other.

In *The Quest for Christa T.* Wolf offers us a language for self-apprehension and presentation via the Other. Several citations from it form a coda to my study.

> On the narrator's purpose in writing the life of Christa T.: "Just for once, for this once, I want to discover how it is and to tell it like it is: the unexemplary life, a life that can't be used as a model" (pp. 44–45).
> On the relation of other and self in memory: "Certain questions I wanted to ask her I can just as well, or better, ask myself. . . . Moreover, all questions lose their edge in time; and language allows the evasive use of 'we' in place of 'I,' nearly always" (p. 50).
> On the relationship of image to voice in the present moment: "Every thing points to transience. Nothing stays as it is. The signs we make are provisional; if one knows it, well and good. . . . Images lose now their firm outlines. We're approaching the vague territory of the present. Perhaps one can hear what one doesn't see" (pp. 142–43).
> On the self-referentiality in her selection of another as model and subject: "Writing means making things large. Pulling ourselves together, let's see her writ large. One's wishes are only what one is capable of. Thus her deep and persistent wish guarantees the secret existence of her work: this *long and neverending journey toward oneself.*
> The difficulty of saying 'I'" (pp. 174).

Notes

1. This essay is a refining and expansion of her introduction to *Journeys: Autobiographical Writings by Women*, ed. Mary Grimley Mason and Carol Hurd Green (Boston: G. K. Hall, 1979).

2. I capitalize Other to designate a psychoanalytically oriented use of the concept, as Simone de Beauvoir employs it in *The Second Sex*. While this essay does not explore that concept, my intent is to refer to both the separable other—God, community, husband, etc.—that Mason examines, and to conflate that with the Other as a category of self-relationship, so that "others" serve as mirrors, echoes, or respondents in an internal dialogue.

3. Marcus K. Billson and Sidonie A. Smith, "Lillian Hellman and the Strategy of the 'Other,' " *Women's Autobiography*, ed. Estelle Jelinek (Bloomington: Indiana Univ. Press, 1980), pp. 163–79. My own discussion of Hellman in this essay is indebted to their conceptualization, although I formulated it before discovering their argument.

4. Nancy K. Miller, "Women's Autobiography in France: For a Dialectics of Identification," *Women and Language in Literature and Society*, ed. Mc-Connell-Ginet et al. (Ithaca, N.Y.: Cornell Univ. Press, 1980), pp. 258–73.

5. The prototype here is probably the anti-metaphysical "autograph" of Montaigne in which the types of the self are oddly privileged others: nobody, the liar, and the spontaneous voice of the "natural." In an unpublished monograph, *The Strategy of Self-Presentation in Montaigne's Essais*, I explore these.

6. *Nachdenken Über Christa T.* (Halle: Mitteldeutscher Verlag, 1968). Translated by Christopher Middleton as *The Quest for Christa T.* (New York: Farrar, Strauss and Giroux, 1970).

7. See especially Louis Renza, "The Veto of the Imagination: A Theory of Autobiography," *New Literary History*, Autumn 1977, pp. 1–26, for a subtle and complex definition of autobiography as a genre defined by its temporal shifts, its lapses, and the changing point of retrospection.

8. Germaine Brée, "George Sand: The Fictions of Autobiography," *Nineteenth-Century French Studies* 4, 1976, pp. 438–49. Also, "Le mythe des origines et l' autoportrait chez George Sand et Colette," *Symbolism and Modern Literature*, ed. Marcel Tetel (Durham, N.C.: Duke University Press, 1978).

9. "During the years whose principal agitations I have just sketched, I locked within my breast other, more poignant sorrows, whose revelation would serve no purpose in such a book as this. I have said all that I wanted to say or should have said. . . . As for those mortal sorrows which other natures caused to weigh upon me, they are the story of the secret martyrdom to which we all submit, either in public or in private, and which we must suffer in silence." George Sand, *My Life*, translated by Dan Hofstadter (New York: Harper & Row, 1979), p. 240.

10. "I may say that only three times in my life have I met a genius and each time a bell within me rang and I was not mistaken, and I may say in each case it was before there was any general recognition of the quality of genius in them. The three geniuses of whom I wish to speak are Gertrude Stein, Pablo Picasso and Alfred Whitehead. I have met many important people, I have met several great people but I have only known three first class geniuses and in each case on sight within me something rang. In no one of the three cases have I been mistaken. In this way my new full life began." Gertrude Stein, *The Autobiography of Alice B. Toklas* (New York: Random House, 1955), p. 5.

16

Midwestern Diaries and Journals: What Women Were (Not) Saying in the Late 1800s

Suzanne L. Bunkers

For Rachel Susanna

The late 1800s found Americans reading not only such works as George Washington Cable's *The Grandissimes*, Henry James's *The Portrait of a Lady*, and William Dean Howells's *A Modern Instance* but also Sarah Orne Jewett's *A Country Doctor* and Mary Murfree's *The Prophet of the Great Smoky Mountains*. Critics and readers alike were awakening to the literature of American women writers whose works contributed to the growing effort to portray American life realistically. In actuality, however, the majority of fiction published in the United States during these decades offered a realistic assessment of the lives of only a small percentage of Americans. To understand better what women's lives were like during the late 1800s, we must examine their autobiographical texts, for it was in diaries, journals, letters, and memoirs that many women expressed their attitudes, opinions, and beliefs concerning their lives in late nineteenth-century America.

Such was the case particularly in the Midwestern United States, where most women writing in the 1800s were not famous literary or historical figures but unknown women writing privately about the events of their everyday lives. Thanks to the recent work of women's historians, we no longer view these women in terms of stereotypes such as the "saint in the sunbonnet" or the "little woman," patient and long-suffering, who followed her man west into the wilderness.[1] Instead, we are beginning to explore the diversity of women's lives and experiences as presented to us in their autobiographical writings.

Women's diaries and journals chart unmapped territory in such an exploration because they challenge the reader to formulate a more inclusive definition of autobiography than has traditionally been used to delineate the boundaries of the genre.[2] Unlike a traditional autobiography, a diary or journal is written day by day, often with no editor but the writer herself, with brief (if any) statements about purpose or intended audience, and with few preconceptions about the form the finished text might take.[3] A diary or journal is not written as a retrospective narration and interpretation of a life already lived but as a commentary on life as it *is* lived, that is, on life as process rather than as product.[4] It might well be argued that the diary or journal can rightly be considered the most authentic form of autobiography because it is least subject to outside editing and censorship and because it most fully represents life as process.[5]

My examination of this form of autobiography is based on my study over the past five years of the unpublished diaries and journals of approximately fifty women who lived and worked in Minnesota, Iowa, and Wisconsin from approximately 1840 to 1900.[6] Among these unpublished writings are several texts that shed useful light on what some American women were thinking, feeling, saying, and doing during this period of time.

My interest in this research has grown out of my own autobiographical writing. I began keeping a diary in 1960 as a ten-year-old girl in rural Iowa. Faithfully, I recorded in this diary the daily events of my life, not realizing at the time how fascinating my entries would prove to be twenty years later, when I would rediscover the diary while rummaging through a box of memorabilia in my mother's attic. The many hours I spent puzzling over what I had meant by such cryptic entries as "I wish I could tell this secret to somebody" led me to wonder whether nineteenth-century Midwestern American girls and women had written similar entries in their diaries and journals. Thus, I began my search for the unpublished autobiographical texts that I eventually found in historical society archives.[7] My work has led me to concur with other scholars of women's history that the central strategy of the women who wrote these diaries and journals was the selective use of speech and silence. What remained unsaid was every bit as important as—and, in some cases, more important than—what was said.[8]

To examine this issue, it is important to locate these diaries and journals within their cultural and historical milieu. By the late 1800s in Minnesota, Iowa, and Wisconsin, the American Indian population, while still substantial, was for the most part confined to reservations, and the small black American population was centered primarily in larger Midwestern cities. In these three Upper Midwestern states, immigrants from Norway, Sweden, Germany, Luxembourg, Holland, and Ireland predominated, having established cities, towns, villages, and homesteads among the lakes, rolling hills, and prairie farmlands.

Not surprisingly, most of the diaries and journals I examined have been those of Caucasian women of the middle to upper-middle class, many with access to at least some education, particularly if they lived in larger towns or cities. In many rural areas, education was much harder to obtain, especially for the daughters of immigrant women. Some of these daughters were able to attend "country school" for a few years; most could speak English but not read or write it well.[9]

The form and content of Midwestern women's private writings were shaped by the writers' experiences of four interwoven contexts: the geographical, the cultural, and socioeconomic, and the situational. A few words follow concerning each of these contexts. Women in Minnesota, Iowa, and Wisconsin lived in more varied geographical settings than might initially be assumed. Women in northern Minnesota or Wisconsin, for instance, dwelled in small lumber towns and mining villages, in woodland, lakeland, and farming areas, and in larger cities. Women in the southern parts of these states as well as in most of Iowa lived in ethnically segregated farming villages, on homesteads ranging from acreages to farms of several hundred acres, or in towns like Mankato, Minnesota; Fort Dodge, Iowa; and Janesville, Wisconsin. Women in urban centers such as Milwaukee, Des Moines, and Minneapolis-St. Paul might have been members of the founding families, but they could just as easily have been schoolteachers, seamstresses, or homemakers. Wherever these women lived, however, their lives were affected by extremes of Midwestern weather as well as by the region's topography. Thus, the diversity of living conditions experienced by women in the Upper Midwest during this era was an important factor in their writing in a variety of autobiographical forms such as calendar inscriptions, three-line daily reports, lengthy introspective journal entries, and carefully structured retrospective memoirs.

As I have noted, in the predominant Midwestern culture of the times, women of color were a silenced and nearly invisible presence, particularly as reflected in historical accounts and in autobiographical records extant in historical societies today.[10] A Caucasian, second- or third-generation, Euro-American woman was far more likely than a woman of color to have kept a diary or journal; and her socioeconomic status had a major influence on whether she did any autobiographical writing at all.[11]

Simply stated, the more economic resources available to a woman, the greater her opportunity for education. The greater her opportunity for education, the greater her ease with writing, her familiarity with texts that might serve as models, her free time for writing, and her money for writing materials. Predictably, a good number of the diaries and journals I have studied have been those written by young women from financially secure families whose descendants donated family papers, among them these diaries and journals, to state, county, and local historical societies during the early to mid 1900s. A Midwestern woman's class played a central role in determining not only whether she wrote diaries and journals but also whether her autobiographical writings were considered worth saving and donating to historical society archives.[12]

Finally, we cannot examine these diaries and journals without recognizing that a specific situational context existed for each entry. The form of a woman's autobiographical writings was shaped both by her purpose and by her perception of her intended audience. A homesteading woman might have recorded her daily observations on the weather so that she and her husband could keep track of weather patterns that would yield information on crop development. A first-year teacher in a small-town elementary school might have described her interactions with students both to reassure herself of her capabilities and to create a record of activities for her superiors. An older woman might have referred to her diary as her friend or confidante not as a literary convention but as a means of making herself more comfortable with expressing her thoughts and feelings in what she hoped would be a safe place. Certainly, the situational context surrounding a woman's writings, while one of the most difficult aspects for a researcher to reconstruct, is one of the most fascinating areas for examination because it yields a sense of the writer's character and personality as she shapes her self-image through her writing.

Given these considerations how have I constructed a framework for my research? Two ethical issues in particular have concerned me. First, I have needed to develop a respect for the personality of each writer as revealed through her diary or journal. Doing so has meant attempting to develop a nonjudgmental attitude toward the writer, regardless of whether I agree or disagree with beliefs expressed or implied in her work. Sometimes I have found it hard to keep from thinking, *All she wrote about was what she did. This isn't a very good diary.* Part of my ongoing process has been learning to withhold judgment about the relative value of one individual's life as compared to another's.[13] I do not study these texts in a vacuum. I examine them from my own perspective, which is based on my own beliefs and experiences and is not value-free. My research requires that I do my best to scrutinize the ways in which my own predispositions, biases, and experiences shape my responses to what a woman writes in a given diary or journal. Such self-scrutiny does not ensure that I can then approach my research from an objective point of view; to the contrary, it ensures that I am well aware of the subjectivity inherent in the research process and that I incorporate this awareness into the work that I do.[14]

At the same time as I have tried to refrain from judging the quality of a diarist's life or experiences as reflected in her text, I have needed to compare and contrast the techniques of diary and journal writing used by several of the women whose works I have studied. At this point a second ethical issue has come into play: respect for and sensitivity toward the writer's use of self-editing and self-censoring as a means of encoding messages and maintaining a perceived sense of self in her text. Encoding, as I am using the term, means the transmission of the writer's message in an oblique rather than in a direct manner. For a woman writing in a diary or journal, encoding can take a variety of syntactic or semantic forms, including indirection, contradiction, deviation, and silences.[15] A woman might speak indirectly by deleting the pronoun "I" or by using qualifiers such as *possibly* or *I think that*.... She might contradict herself by stating that she is dissatisfied and then asserting that she is nonetheless content. She might deviate from standard American English sentence structure or orthography by using sentence fragments, ellipses, neologisms, or even a sophisticated code of visual symbols. She might employ silences in choosing not to write about such taboo subjects as sexuality, labor and childbirth, and menstruation. She might be circumspect about such events as the death of a child, the leave-taking of a beloved friend, or the failure of a hoped-for dream to materialize.

Such techniques of encoding, of course, are not unique to Midwestern American women's writing or even to women's writing in general. Scholars have recognized, however, that such encoding tends to be more evident in a writer's work when it is necessary to suppress one's ideas or when one's right to speak has been denied.[16] The writer's use of encoding in her diary or journal, then, becomes her way of breaking silences, that is, of finding avenues in which to speak, either directly or indirectly, about what has previously remained unspoken.[17] The importance of encoding cannot be overestimated, for it enables a writer to use speech and silence selectively (whether consciously or unconsciously) to address a variety of issues in her diary or journal. For many Midwestern American women writing in the late 1800s, diaries or journals became the vehicles through which they could break silences about their own lives as well as about their interactions with others. The sheer number of extant diaries and journals by women in Minnesota, Iowa, and Wisconsin provides strong evidence for the assertion that this form of autobiography functioned as an essential means of personal expression for women in the Upper Midwest during the latter 1800s.

Four primary themes emerge in these autobiographical texts. First, each writer expressed a need to view the use of her time and energies as worthwhile. It might, of course, be argued that simply by recording her activities, any writer asserts the belief that what one does is important, yet the tone of many of these diaries and journals reveals that their writers felt the need to explain their activities in detail, not so much as a means of filling pages but as a way of justifying to themselves that they were using their time well and that their activities were appreciated by others. The activities recorded in a diary or journal function as the individual writer's attempt to validate her work and, by extension, her sense of self. The October 16, 1883, journal entry of Abbie T. Griffin, a Minneapolis seamstress, is representative of such attempts:

> This day I am thirty-two years old and a quiet day it has been. This morning I did up my work, bought eight bushels of Beauty of Hebron potatoes and this afternoon bought 2 1/2 tons of nut coal & 1/2 ton of Ill. Lump of N.W. Fuel Co. Went over to Nellie's and she cut me a velvet vest for my black broadcloth jacket. It is a cold stormy windy night.

The writer's comment here might appear self-deprecatory in its passing reference to her birthday amidst the recitation of chores completed. The fact that she noted the date at all, however, indicates that her birthday was important to her, even though she spent the day working rather than celebrating.

Abbie T. Griffin's diary, which she kept from January 1882 until May 1885, is structured around her daily reports on her work as a seamstress and as a nurse for her ailing mother.[18] Specific entries recount her sewing projects, her attempts to find work, the weather, visits to and from friends, and her mother's worsening condition. On June 11, 1882, Abbie wrote of meeting Clint Dike, who visited her home with a mutual friend. Abbie and Clint's courtship apparently began soon afterwards, although Abbie generally wrote sparingly, if at all, about her suitor in subsequent diary entries, such as this one from August 7, 1882: "Hot until noon and then a shower cooled the air. Went to the store early and worked hard at the dress all day, began at four o'clock this morning. Mr. Dike saw me safely home. He goes with Ettie in the morning to Dodge county Minn."

Abbie's reference to "Ettie" in this entry concerns Clint Dike's young daughter Etta Dike, who came to Minneapolis to board with Abbie later in 1882, after living for some time with her father's brother and sister-in-law, Morrel and Jemima Dike, and their three children near Big Lake, Minnesota. Clint Dike had apparently been widowed sometime after 1872, when Etta was born, and before 1880, when the state census listed Etta as part of her uncle and aunt's household in Sherburne County. By 1882, he had arranged for his nine-year-old daughter to live with Abbie, whose growing affection for the girl is reflected in diary entries such as that made on November 4, 1882: "Sat up late and worked on Ettie's dress, but did not finish it but made her a pair of flannel panties, very pretty ones of red with a little frill embroidered with black."

While specific entries describe Abbie's relationship with Etta, her work, and social activities, the diarist said little about her relationship with Clint until an entry made in early 1885. On January 26, after not writing in her diary for three months, Abbie matter-of-factly described her wedding to Mr. Dike:

> I have determined to write a Journal once more & record many trans-actions. Last Tuesday night at 11:50 P.M. we had a very interesting cer-emony here. For two weeks mother had been very low and on that night we gave up all hope of her and feeling her end was approaching she felt as if she would like to see us married. Clint went directly to get cousin Ed and they went together to get a licence came back hunted a minister and were ready. I had only a common dress and it was a dark grey trimmed with pipings of crimson, just a full skirt and slashed basque. The Rev. Archibald Hadden transformed me from Miss G. to Mrs. S. C. Dike. Mother has been very low and is so still. Last night was the first night for eighteen nights that I could sleep all night. Mrs. Hull came & watched with mother. Nettie Sullivan wrote us a letter today and I received one from Poughkeepsie.

The wedding, which occurred shortly before the death of Abbie's mother on February 5, 1885, was recorded by the diarist in much the same way as she had reported on her daily work and activities. Because the entry reflects Abbie's preoccupation with her mother's decline and says little about her new husband, it is difficult to infer how Abbie felt about marrying Clint. The writer's selective use of speech and silence in encoding her message is evident here, not so much in what she has said as in what she has not said.

Abbie's two final entries, one from February 10, 1885, and the other from May 25, 1885, tell of her collapse from arthritis and exhaustion following her mother's death and of her attempts to recover her physical and emotional health. Ironically, the last sentence in Abbie's diary reads: "I hope to write more now." But Abbie T. Griffin wrote nothing more about her daily activities, her husband and stepdaughter, or her health. We can only speculate about what direction her life took after May 1885, yet we can view her diary as representative of many kept by Midwestern women during the 1880s in its emphasis on sense of self as defined by the recording of the writer's daily work and activities.

Like Abbie T. Griffin, fifty-eight-year-old Maria Merrill wrote often in her journal about her work, first on a farm near Sechlersville, Wisconsin, and later in Winona, Minnesota, where she moved with her son so that he could attend the State Normal School to become a teacher.[19] Maria's journal entry on October 31, 1890, is representative of her many commentaries on her life as a widow raising her children on a small Wisconsin farm:

> We threshed the 21st and 22nd of August. We had 128 bushels of wheat and 542 bushels of oats and about 50 bushels of potatoes which were very poor. Our corn is good and yields well. We have not got it all husked yet. It is not very dry this year. Waldo had to build a new crib to hold all the corn. We have sold all the hogs, except four little pigs, and we bought a sow for breeding purposes. . . . Clara has been husking corn a long time and I have done the housework.

It is evident from what Maria wrote here that she played an integral role in the operation of the farm and that her work contributed to her sense of worth as a person. Witness this journal entry made shortly after Maria and her son Waldo had rented out the farm and moved to Winona in late 1894:

> It was a great sacrifice to me to break up my home where I had lived so long and go among strangers in my feeble old age but I thought that perhaps I ought to give [Waldo] all the chance I could for an education. . . . I can't say that I have enjoyed life much since I have been here. It seems as if it would be all that I would ask in this life if we could all be back on the farm again and have everything as it used to be but since it cannot be I try very hard to bear it patiently.

Maria Merrill, like Abbie T. Griffin, used speech and silence selectively to encode her feelings into her journal entries. She tried to mitigate her sense of personal unhappiness with an admonition to herself to be patient and accept her lot, but the undercurrent in the entry above is one of dissatisfaction and great sadness at having lost her identity as a farm woman. Regardless of differences in age and environment, Abbie T. Griffin and Maria Merrill displayed in their writing one notable similarity: the need to validate their lives and develop some sense of self through the recording of their daily work and activities.

While Midwestern diarists and journalers of the late 1800s clearly needed to view themselves and their work as important, a second major thematic focus in their writing is the need for connection with other human beings. For these women, the diary or journal became a place to write about relationships with others, thereby validating themselves as members of communities. In her diary, kept during the first several months of 1888, Ida M. Bliss, a fourteen-year-old schoolgirl from Janesville, Wisconsin, wrote often about her activities with family and friends.[20] Typical entries reported on Ida's lessons at school; and some entries, like the two that follow, offer hints about how she was feeling:

> *January 3, 1888.* School commenced today. I went, of course. Miss Green is our teacher she is the same one we had last term. It has been very cold all day. Our Holiday vacation is gone and I don't know whether to be glad or sorry.

> *January 11, 1888.* I went to school and did nothing else worth speaking of. It is as cold as ever and no signs as yet of moderation. I am reading hospital sketches by Miss Alcott.

These entries do more than simply report on the weather and on Ida's ambivalence toward school. They also let us know that, although she was reading Alcott's work, Ida viewed her reading and her other daily activities as "nothing else worth speaking of." Again, as in Abbie T. Griffin's birthday entry, a self-deprecatory tone appears, a tone that might reflect only an offhand remark, or which might function as a purposeful strategy for encoding a pattern into a text.[21] Whether or not this was the case with Ida M. Bliss's diary, the writer's repetition of daily activities, broken only by references to friends' visits, provides evidence that much of Ida's self-concept as an adolescent was formed as the result of her interactions with others. Her diary is important because it reflects the day-by-day process by which that self-concept was formed.

Ida's diary entries stopped abruptly on April 3, 1888, and the diary's pages remained blank until June 20, 1888, when the writer penned this cryptic entry:

> I begin my diary again on the 20 day of June; after skipping about two months. It has been one of the most wreatched days in the short fourteen years of my life.
>
> Continued in Memoran.

The implications of this brief entry become even more fascinating when one turns to the back of Ida's diary to the pages labeled "Memorandum" and finds that the page on which she had continued this entry had been torn out. Evidently, Ida's encoding of her message by writing it in the "Memorandum" pages proved insufficient for her or whoever else removed this page from her diary. Whatever was written there must have been so private or so taboo that it had to be expurgated. Such an act offers perhaps the clearest indication thus far of how speech and silence could be used selectively in a diary or journal by a young woman writing during the late 1800s.

A third theme emerging in women's diaries and journals of this era is the writer's need for an outlet for emotions such as intense grief and anger, which her culture did not deem appropriate for public expression by a woman. In many circumstances, the diary or journal functioned as a friend or confidante whom the writer could trust with her innermost feelings and secrets. Such is the case with Martha Smith Brewster of Mankato, Minnesota, who began keeping a diary in 1876, shortly after the death of her young son, Georgie, and who continued writing in it until early 1880.[22] In several entries, such as this one from March 14, 1876, Martha spoke of the difficulties she faced in dealing with her sorrow over her son's death: "Somehow I feel sad & lonely this evening. I can't write nor work guess had better to go to bed."

Martha's references to her grief were more often oblique than direct, yet throughout the diary she made a consistent effort to come to terms with her emotions while at the same time not say too much. It is as if she did not want to give herself away, not even to herself. Specifically, the first entry in Martha's diary made careful use of encoding to express grief in a culturally acceptable manner. Martha began by writing a prayer to "Our Blessed Master," but she soon changed direction, writing, "Four weeks ago on Sabbath night my little boy...." She went no further, however. She carefully crossed out those words before continuing: "What a comfort this assurance of the saviour is to us when we are called upon to part from our little ones." The writer's use of a prayer to begin her diary entry might seem appropriate, given the circumstances, but it is significant that she chose to delete any personal reference to the loss of her son and instead to encode her grief in the formal, stylized language of prayer.

Few entries in Martha Smith Brewster's diary speak directly of her grief, yet the pervasive tone of sadness in the diary cannot be overlooked. This is a form of autobiography that records how a woman worked through the grieving process over a period of several years. Even in Martha's final diary entry, almost four years after Georgie's death, there is a muted expression of that same grief:

> *October 20, 1879.* Georgie's 6th birthday. It is a beautiful summer day so warm. This year I have had a dollar for Missions for Georgie's birthday gift again. Dear child how distinctly I can remember him both from voice & expression of features.

This diary is characteristic of many nineteenth-century diaries and journals by both women and men that recount the writer's loss of a loved one, either by death or by separation, and which fulfill the writer's intense need for an outlet for the expression of grief. As twentieth-century theorists have observed, several stages comprise the grieving process.[23] For women such as Martha Smith Brewster, who lived in an environment where the infant mortality rate was high but where most survivors had little time or opportunity to express their grief, the diary or journal became an indispensable tool for a partial or complete working through of the grieving process.

In addition to the three themes discussed thus far, Midwestern women's diaries and journals of the late 1800s embody a fourth: the writer's need for a forum for commentary on such subjects as marriage, religion, politics, and world events. Contrary to popular myth, Midwestern women were not isolated and unaware of what was going on in the world. In fact, many of these women used their diaries and journals as places for expression of their opinions on social issues. Abbie T. Griffin, for example, wrote this terse journal entry, which expressed her shock at an event that had outraged her community:

> *Friday April 28, 1882.* A terrible thing happened here on Fourth Ave. S yesterday a man Frank McManus decoyed off a little daughter of Jason Spear & outraged her & at night a group of vigilantes took him out of jail & hung him up.

Another diarist, Emily Hawley Gillespie, who lived in rural Iowa and whose ten-volume journal spanned the period from 1858 to 1888, regularly recorded details of life on the family farm near Manchester.[24] In one entry dated July 29, 1877, Emily wrote this in response to receiving the news that a neighbor woman had been committed to an asylum:

> I only wonder that more women do not have to be taken to that asylum, especially farmers' wives. No society except hired men to eat their meals. Hard work from the beginning to the end of the year. Their only happiness lies in their children with the fond hope that *they* may rise higher.

Emily's journal entries functioned not only as a measure of her awareness of the potential isolation of farm women but also as an indictment of her culture's failure to treat such women with more understanding and compassion.

As the years passed, Emily Hawley Gillespie used her journal as a place to record her activities in the temperance movement, her interests in writing and phrenology, and her attendance at agricultural association meetings. Certain entries made from 1880 to 1885, however, concerned her deteriorating relationship with her husband of twenty years, James Gillespie. At one point during 1883, Emily commented, "When a man lays his hands hold of his wife & children I think tis time something was done." Her use of the third-person rather than the first-person forms in this entry functioned as an encoding strategy by which Emily could break the silence about her husband's violence and at the same time distance herself from it.

By 1885, Emily's comments on her domestic situation had become more direct. On April 26, 1885, she wrote:

> I only hope that [Sarah] may not see the trouble I have. Ah, *marriage is a lottery*. how full of deceit do they come with their false tongues and *"there is no one as dear as thee"* until one is married then *"you are mine now we have something else to do besides silly kissing."*

What makes entries such as this even more interesting is the fact that, due to Emily's worsening dropsy (edema), her daughter Sarah took over writing some journal entries for her mother in 1886 and thus had the opportunity to read earlier entries as well as those she recorded for Emily. How much of Emily's journal was written with the purpose of providing a record of her life for her daughter is an intriguing, if unanswerable, question. Emily Hawley Gillespie's journal ended with her death in 1888. Today it remains one of the most comprehensive longitudinal documents on the life of a nineteenth-century Midwestern American woman.

Much remains to be said about the diaries and journals of women writing during the late 1800s, and more work needs to be done in unearthing these forgotten but nonetheless significant source materials. As a form of autobiography, these texts serve an important function: They enable us to alter our field of vision and enlarge our perspective on the expanding boundaries of the genre. Through an analysis of the writers' selective use of speech and silence to encode messages into their texts, we can see how these women shaped their autobiographical writings to record a sense of a changing, growing self. Texts like these require that we reexamine traditional assumptions about what women's lives were like in nineteenth-century America. They encourage new approaches to studying the lives of women who were not well known and whose diaries and journals were in many cases the only autobiographical statements they left behind.

Diaries and journals such as those by Abbie T. Griffin, Maria Merrill, Ida M. Bliss, Martha Smith Brewster, and Emily Hawley Gillespie are indeed worth reading as one form of autobiography written by nineteenth-century women, not only because they provide an accurate accounting of women's lives during that era but also because they point the way toward Virginia Woolf's *A Writer's Diary*, Joanna Field's *A Life of One's Own*, Anne Frank's *The Diary of a Young Girl*, and countless other diaries and journals being written by women today.

Notes

Funding for this research has been provided by the National Endowment for the Humanities, the American Council of Learned Societies, and by Mankato State University. I wish to thank the Center for Advanced Feminist Studies at the University of Minnesota-Minneapolis and the Women's Studies Research Center at the University of Wisconsin-Madison for awarding me affiliated scholar status and providing valuable nonmonetary support for my research. Finally, I wish to thank James Olney, to whom I am deeply indebted for encouraging me in my work. In a National Endowment for the Humanities Summer Seminar entitled "The Forms of Autobiography," conducted by James Olney at the University of North Carolina, Chapel Hill, in 1983, I first began to explore many of the issues I discuss in this essay.

1. The works of such historians as Gerda Lerner, Annette Kolodny, Elizabeth Hampsten, Lillian Schlissel, and Glenda Riley analyze the ways in which such images came into existence and expose the limitations that such stereotypes impose on our understanding of nineteenth-century American women's lives. Glenda Riley in particular cites the need to test such stereotypical images of

women against the primary documents left behind by women—not only diaries, journals, letters, and memoirs, but also artifacts of material culture (p. vii).

2. This study presupposes a more inclusive definition of autobiography than that offered by Roy Pascal, which is based on the idea that an autobiography must render a "coherent shaping of the past," something Pascal says a diary or journal cannot do (p. 5). Although in her most recent work Estelle Jelinek states that she does not consider diaries and journals autobiographies (*Tradition*, p. xii), in her earlier work she called for a broader definition of autobiography, one that would include a variety of works by women as well as by men (*Women's Autobiography*, pp. 19–20). Like Margo Culley, Carolyn Heilbrun, Patricia K. Addis, and other scholars, I call for an expanded definition of autobiography that would take into consideration the diary, journal, letter, and memoir—all forms commonly used by women.

3. I use the terms *diary* and *journal* interchangeably because I have discovered few texts that can be clearly labeled a diary *or* a journal. Most incorporate characteristics of the diary (e.g., brief descriptive entries, daily reports on events) as well as of the journal (e.g., lengthy introspective entries, narratives, commentary).

4. This is not to say that a diary or journal never reflects its writer's attempts to look back over his or her experiences and place them in context. Many diaries and journals do, in fact, include reflective and analytical passages as well as descriptive and narrative passages. Cynthia Huff (*British Women's Diaries*) and Joanne E. Cooper, among others, address this issue in their work on women's diaries and journals.

5. I have also explored this question in recent articles appearing in *Women's Studies International Forum* and *A/B: Auto/Biography Studies*, as well as in papers presented at several conferences. I am grateful to Susan Armitage, Susan Arpad, Virginia Walcott Beauchamp, Lynn Z. Bloom, Margo Culley, Robert Fothergill, Penelope Franklin, Joanna Bowen Gillespie, Dure Jo Gillikin, Elizabeth Hampsten, Rebecca Hogan, Gloria T. Hull, Cynthia Huff, Estelle Jelinek, Suzanne Juhasz, Carol F. Karlsen and Laurie Crumpacker, Janet Lecompte, Thomas Mallon, Mary Jane Moffat and Charlotte Painter, Paul C. Rosenblatt, Marlene Springer, and Haskell Springer—all of whose scholarly works have sparked my thinking about the diary or journal as a form of autobiography.

6. The primary repositories for these manuscript and typescript diaries and journals are the Minnesota Historical Society in St. Paul, the State Historical Society of Iowa in Iowa City, and the State Historical Society of Wisconsin in Madison. I have also studied primary source materials in many county and local historical society archives in the three-state area.

I have chosen this time period for my study because during these sixty years the greatest influx of Euro-American immigrants into the Upper Midwestern United States occurred.

7. I am indebted to the many archivists who have helped me locate source materials. The following written resource guides have also proven useful. Dan-

ky's *Women's History Resources* has been helpful in my search for source materials at the State Historical Society of Wisconsin. An unpublished bibliography, "Women: Diaries and Letters," made available to me by Ruth Bauer of the Minnesota Historical Society, has aided me to locate source materials there. An unpublished "Diary Bibliography," sent to me by Kathy McLaughlin of the State Historical Society of Iowa's Manuscripts Department, has given me valuable information on women's diaries and journals in the Iowa archives. Finally, Hinding et al.'s *Women's History Sources* has been a highly useful reference work for my research.

8. Elizabeth Hampsten's work is particularly insightful on the issue of women's selective use of speech and silence in diaries and letters. Hampsten writes: "private writings of women ask of us, if we wish to read them knowlingly, a special inventive patience. We must interpret what is not written as well as what is, and, rather than dismiss repetitions, value them especially. 'Nothing happened' asks that we wonder what, in the context of a particular woman's stream of days, she means by something happening" (*Read This Only*, p. 4).

My unpublished article, "Reflections of Gender Identity in Nineteenth-Century Midwestern Women's Diaries," also addresses this issue. In this article, I discuss the ways in which several women's diaries use specific semantic and syntactic strategies to encode perceptions of oneself as a woman within nineteenth-century American culture. I have drawn on Susan Sniader Lanser's excellent work in my analysis of encoding strategies.

9. Take, for instance, my great-grandmother, Elizabeth Simon Klein. She came to the United States from Germany in 1880, entered into an arranged marriage, moved to a farm in northwest Iowa in 1883, and had fifteen children. According to family sources, Elizabeth could neither read nor write English. Her four daughters received a minimal education at a "country school" a mile from the family farm. Her granddaughter, Verna Klein Bunkers, who is my mother, received an eighth-grade education at the same "country school" during the 1930s. The educational experiences of these several generations of women in the Klein family are not unlike those of women in many other Midwestern families.

10. Hine, Bidelman, and Ford describe the recently started Black Women in the Middle West Project (BWMWP), funded by the National Endowment for the Humanities. The purpose of the BWMWP is to collect and index records that reflect the lives of black women in Indiana, Illinois, and Michigan. The eventual goal is to publish a much-needed comprehensive resource guide to collections of materials on Midwestern black women in libraries and archives.

11. I do not assert that no diaries or journals by nineteenth-century American women of color exist, only that my sample is comprised primarily of texts by Caucasian women. Elizabeth Hampsten's, Trudelle Thomas's, Gloria T. Hull's, and Dorothy Sterling's analyses have been especially useful to me in examining issues of race and class in American women's diaries and journals.

12. A good number of these women's texts are housed in collections of family

papers, many times catalogued under the name of a man in the family. I would also suggest that a woman's experience of class was often dynamic rather than static. That is, a woman born into an upper-middle-class family might have, as an adult, found herself on a lower socioeconomic level, particularly if she was unmarried or divorced and responsible for her own financial support. Such circumstances, more so than those into which such a woman had been born, would influence whether she kept a diary or journal and whether her texts were preserved in archival collections.

13. Paul C. Rosenblatt's comments on ethical issues in the study of diaries have greatly helped me in formulating ethical frameworks for my research.

14. I comment in more depth on issues of subjectivity and reflexivity in my research in an unpublished paper, "Issues in the Study of Nineteenth-Century Women's 'Private' Writings," presented at the National Women's Studies Association Conference, 24–28 June 1987, Atlanta, Georgia. I am indebted to Jay Ruby and Barbara Myerhoff's analysis of reflexivity in the research process. They define *reflexive* as "the capacity of any system of signification to turn back upon itself, to make itself its own object by referring to itself: subject and object fuse" (p. 2).

15. As noted above, Susan Sniader Lanser's work in this area presents a superb analysis of the ways in which women use encoding in their writing. I am grateful to Lanser for her explanation of the terms *indirection, contradiction, deviation,* and *silences*, which I have adapted for the purposes of my study.

16. Susan Sniader Lanser argues this point most convincingly in her study of surface text and subtext in women's writing.

17. Tillie Olsen writes poignantly about the necessity of women's breaking silences. She asks us not to forget the silencing of our foremothers and their/ our struggles to break those silences: "How many of us who are writers have mothers, grandmothers, of limited education; awkward, not at home, with the written word, however eloquent they may be with the spoken one? Born a generation or two before, we might have been they" (p. 184).

18. This hardbound 7 1/2″ × 9 1/2″ manuscript diary of 77 pages is housed in the Abbie T. Griffin Papers at the Minnesota Historical Society in St. Paul. Abbie's name appears regularly in Minneapolis city directories from 1876 until 1885. Various directory listings give her occupation as clerk, nurse, and art worker. She apparently lived with her mother, Mrs. V. R. Griffin, a widow, at the western edge of Minneapolis. After 1885, the year of Abbie's marriage to S. Clint Dike, Abbie's name disappears from city directory and census records. I continue to search for information about Abbie after that date.

19. The typescript of Maria Merrill's journal, comprising 36 double-spaced pages, is housed in the Maria M. Merrill Papers at the Area Research Center, University of Wisconsin-La Crosse. According to Mrs. Merrill's grandson, Horace S. Merrill, who donated the journal to the archives, the original manuscript journal burned along with the family home in 1940.

Maria Merrill was born in Monson, Maine, in 1832. After completing her elementary school education, she worked in the textile mills in Biddeford, Maine. Later, she continued her education and eventually taught Latin, French, and German at the Gainesville Female Seminary, south of Buffalo, New York. In 1859 she went to Jackson County, Wisconsin, to care for her sick sister, Augusta Morton Merrill, wife of Chauncey Merrill. After Augusta's death, Maria married Chauncey. She raised her three nieces, Eva, Gertrude, and Clara, along with her and Chauncey's son, Waldo. After her husband's death in 1882, Maria Merrill continued to run the family farm near Sechlersville.

According to Horace S. and Marion Galbraith Merrill, who graciously provided me with detailed biographical information about Maria Merrill, she "suffered from ill health, a severe cough, and periods of depression" throughout the late 1880s and the 1890s, the period during which she kept her journal. In 1904 Maria Merrill died from "what the family believed to be an overdose of medication that her doctor had given her for the pain of neuralgia," as Horace and Marion Merrill explained in their biographical information on Horace's grandmother.

20. Ida M. Bliss's diary is a tiny (approximately 3 1/2″ × 5 1/2″) bound volume with handwritten entries of several lines each. It is housed in the M. N. Bliss Family Papers at the State Historical Society of Wisconsin in Madison, along with several similar diaries kept by Ida's mother, Martha Bell Rundlett Bliss, and one by her father, M. N. (Newt) Bliss. The Bliss family lived in Baraboo, Wisconsin, during the time Ida was keeping her diary. I continue to search for further information about Ida M. Bliss subsequent to 1888.

21. Elizabeth Hampsten notes that the "spare" style used by many women is characterized by "repetition and sameness—all strategies for controlling disturbances and asserting normality" ("Tell Me All You Know," p. 57).

22. The handwritten diary of Martha Smith Brewster is housed in the George H. Brewster Family Papers at the Blue Earth County Historical Society in Mankato, Minnesota. The diary is a small (4″ × 5″) bound volume, with 15 to 20 pages of pencilled entries, many blank pages, and some pages torn out. Biblical quotations and notes for Sunday School lessons are written in the back pages of Martha's diary. Also included is a recipe for codfish balls.

Martha, born in 1839 in Newport, Pennsylvania, moved to Mankato with George H. Brewster after their marriage in 1869. The couple had three children, Carrie and Grace, who lived to adulthood, and George Sheldon, who died as a young child. Her diary was donated to the Historical Society by Carrie, who was a schoolteacher in Mankato, and Grace, who lived with her mother and cared for her until Martha's death in 1925.

I am grateful to Audrey Burmeister-Hicks and Denise Hudson of the Blue Earth County Historical Society for bringing this diary to my attention.

23. Elisabeth Kubler-Ross has outlined these stages as denial, anger, bargaining, depression, and acceptance. Paul C. Rosenblatt has analyzed 56 diaries and journals to determine how their writers used them to face up to the pain

of loss and to work through the grieving process. His intriguing analysis is based on Kubler-Ross's theories.

24. The journals of Emily Hawley Gillespie are housed in the Sarah Gillespie Huftalen Papers at the State Historical Society of Iowa in Iowa City. The journals in the archives were recopied from the originals by Emily H. Gillespie and her daughter Sarah G. Huftalen. They were donated to the State Historical Society in 1951 by Sarah G. Huftalen.

Judy Nolte Lensink, Christine M. Kirkham, and Karen Pauba Witzke's article provides a detailed analysis of Emily's thirty-year account of her life in rural Iowa. The authors describe Emily as having had "a youth full of promise and hope fading into middle and declining years of lost dreams and eventual tragedy" (p. 289). I am appreciative of this thoughtful and well-written article, which has given me added insights into Emily's experiences.

Emily Hawley began keeping a journal in 1858 at the age of nineteen, while still living in the family home in Morenci, Michigan. In it she recorded social activities, teaching experiences, and national events. In 1861 she traveled to Manchester, Iowa, to care for the daughter of her widowed uncle. There she met James Gillespie, whom she married on September 18, 1862. The couple farmed near Manchester, and their son Henry was born in 1863. In 1865, Emily gave birth to twins, a daughter Sarah and a stillborn son.

Throughout the years, Emily wrote in her journal about her family, her daily work, her social and political activities, and her feelings. As Judy Lensink et al. point out, her journal became a "therapeutic 'confidante' " for Emily (p. 305). In Emily's final years, Sarah began to record journal entries dictated by her mother. This fact makes Emily's journal all the more fascinating as a text that is both public and private and that can be viewed as having specific purposes and an intended audience. (In "Issues in the Study of Nineteenth-Century Women's 'Private' Writings," I discuss at greater length the false dichotomy of public and private vis à vis women's diaries and journals.)

Emily Hawley Gillespie died on March 24, 1888. Her estranged husband James Gillespie died in 1909. Both are buried in the Manchester, Iowa, cemetery.

Sources Consulted

Addis, Patricia K. *Through a Woman's I: An Annotated Bibliography of American Women's Autobiographical Writings, 1946–1976.* Metuchen, N.J.: The Scarecrow Press, Inc., 1983.

Armitage, Susan. "Aunt Amelia's Diary: The Record of a Reluctant Pioneer." In Hoffmann, Leonore, and Deborah Rosenfelt, eds., *Teaching Women's Literature from a Regional Perspective.* New York: Modern Language Association, 1982, 69–73.

Arpad, Susan, ed. *Sam Curd's Diary: The Diary of a True Woman.* Athens: Ohio Univ. Press, 1984.

Beauchamp, Virginia Walcott. *A Private War: Letters and Diaries of Madge Preston, 1862–1867.* New Brunswick, N.J.: Rutgers Univ. Press, 1987.

Bliss, Ida M. Unpublished Diary Munuscript, 1888. In M. N. Bliss Family Papers. Madison: State Historical Society of Wisconsin.

Bloom, Lynn Z. "The Diary as Popular History," *Journal of Popular Culture*, 9.4 (Spring 1976):794–807.

Brewster, Martha Smith. Unpublished Diary Manuscript, 1876–1880. In George H. Brewster Family Papers. Mankato, Minnesota: Blue Earth County Historical Society.

Bunkers, Suzanne L. " 'Faithful Friend': Nineteenth-Century Midwestern Women's Unpublished Diaries," *Women's Studies International Forum*, 10.1 (1987): 7–17.

———. "Issues in the Study of Nineteenth-Century Women's 'Private' Writings." Unpublished Paper Presented at the National Women's Studies Association Conference, 1987.

———"Reading and Interpreting Unpublished Diaries by Nineteenth-Century Women," *A/B: Auto/Biography Studies*, 2.2 (Summer 1986): 15–17.

———"Reflections of Gender Identity in Nineteenth-Century Midwestern Women's Diaries." Unpublished Article Based on Paper Presented at the Midwest Modern Language Association Convention, 1986.

Cooper, Joanne E. "Shaped Meaning: Women's Diaries, Journals, and Letters—the Old and the New," *Women's Studies International Forum*, 10.1 (1987): 95–99.

Culley, Margo, ed. "Introduction," *A Day at a Time: The Diary Literature of American Women from 1764 to the Present.* New York: The Feminist Press, 1985, 3–26.

Danky, James P., et al. *Women's History Resources at the State Historical Society of Wisconsin*, 4th edition. Madison: State Historical Society of Wisconsin, 1982.

"Diary Bibliography." Unpublished Bibliography. Iowa City: State Historical Society of Iowa Manuscripts Department.

Fothergill, Robert. *Private Chronicles: A Study of English Diaries.* London: Oxford Univ. Press, 1974.

Franklin, Penelope, ed. "Introduction." *Private Pages: Diaries of American Women, 1830's–1970's.* New York: Ballantine Books, 1986, xiii–xxvii.

Gillespie, Emily Hawley. Unpublished Diary Manuscript, 1858–1888. In Sarah Gillespie Huftalen Papers. Iowa City: State Historical Society of Iowa.

Gillespie, Joanna Bowen. "Martha Laurens Ramsay: Her Diary as Autobiography," *Women's Diaries*, 4.4 (Winter 1986): 1, 3–6, 10.

Gillikin, Dure Jo. "A Lost Diary Found: The Art of the Everyday." In Hoffman, Leonore, and Margo Culley, eds., *Women's Personal Narratives: Essays in Criticism and Pedagogy.* New York: Modern Language Association, 1985, 124–38.

Griffin, Abbie T. Unpublished Diary Manuscript, 1882–1885. In Abbie T. Griffin Papers. St. Paul: Minnesota Historical Society.

Hampsten, Elizabeth. *Read This Only to Yourself: The Private Writings of Midwestern Women, 1880–1910*. Bloomington: Indiana Univ. Press, 1982.

———. " 'Tell Me All You Know': Reading Letters and Diaries of Rural Women." In Hoffmann, Leonore, and Deborah Rosenfelt, eds., *Teaching Women's Literature From a Regional Perspective*. New York: Modern Language Association, 1982, 55–63.

Heilbrun, Carolyn. "Women's Autobiographical Writings: New Forms," *Prose Studies*, 8.2 (September 1985): 14–28.

Hinding, Andrea, et al., eds. *Women's History Sources: A Guide to Archives and Manuscript Collections in the United States*. New York and London: R. R. Bowker, 1979.

Hine, Darlene Clark, Patrick Kay Bidelman, and Bridgie Alexis Ford. "The Invisible Woman: Midwestern Black Women's History," *History News*, 39.2 (February 1984): 6–11.

Hogan, Rebecca. "Diarists on Diaries," *A/B: Auto/Biography Studies*, 2.2 (Summer 1986): 9–15.

Huff, Cynthia. *British Women's Diaries: A Descriptive Bibliography of Selected Nineteenth-Century Women's Manuscript Diaries*. New York: AMS Press, Inc., 1985.

———. "From Faceless Chronicler to Self-Creator: The Diary of Louisa Galton, 1830–1896," *Biography*, 10.2 (Spring 1987): 95–106.

Hull, Gloria T., ed. *Give Us This Day: The Diary of Alice Dunbar-Nelson*. New York: W. W. Norton, 1984.

Jelinek, Estelle. *The Tradition of Women's Autobiography: From Antiquity to the Present*. Boston: G. K. Hall/Twayne Publishers, 1986.

Jelinek, Estelle, ed. "Introduction: Women's Autobiography and the Male Tradition." In *Women's Autobiography: Essays in Criticism*. Bloomington: Indiana Univ. Press, 1980, 1–20.

Juhasz, Suzanne, "The Journal as Source and Model for Feminist Art: The Example of Kathleen Fraser," *Frontiers*, 8.1 (1984): 16–20.

Karlsen, Carol F., and Laurie Crumpacker, eds. *The Journal of Esther Edwards Burr, 1754–1757*. New Haven: Yale University Press, 1984.

Kolodny, Annette. *The Land Before Her: Fantasy and Experience of the American Frontiers, 1630–1860*. Chapel Hill: The Univ. of North Carolina Press, 1984.

Kubler-Ross, Elisabeth. *On Death and Dying*. New York: Macmillan, 1969.

Lanser, Susan Sniader. "Feminism (Suppressed/Expressed) and Literary Form." Unpublished Paper Presented at the Midwest Modern Language Association Convention, 1980.

Lecompte, Janet, ed. *Emily: The Diary of a Hard-Worked Woman*. Lincoln: University of Nebraska Press, 1987.

Lensink, Judy Nolte, Christine M. Kirkham, and Karen Pauba Witzke. " 'My

Only Confidante'—The Life and Diary of Emily Hawley Gillespie," *The Annals of Iowa*, 45.4 (Spring 1980): 288–312.

Lerner, Gerda. *Black Women in White America: A Documentary History*. New York: Pantheon, 1972.

———. *The Female Experience: An American Documentary*. Indianapolis: Bobbs-Merrill, 1977.

Mallon, Thomas. *A Book of One's Own: People and Their Diaries*. New York: Ticknor and Fields, 1984.

Mason, Mary G. "The Other Voice: Autobiographies of Women Writers." In *Autobiography: Essays Theoretical and Critical*, ed. James Olney. Princeton, N.J.: Princeton Univ. Press, 1980, 207–35.

Merrill, Maria Morton. Unpublished Diary Typescript, 1890–1899. In Maria M. Merrill Papers. La Crosse: University of Wisconsin Area Research Center.

Moffat, Mary Jane, and Charlotte Painter, eds. *Revelations: Diaries of Women*. New York: Random House, Inc., 1974.

Myerhoff, Barbara, and Jay Ruby. "Introduction." In Ruby, Jay, ed., *A Crack in the Mirror: Reflexive Perspectives in Anthropology*. Philadelphia: Univ. of Pennsylvania Press, 1982, 1–35.

Olney, James, ed. "Autobiography and the Cultural Moment: A Thematic, Historical, and Bibliographical Introduction." In *Autobiography: Essays Theoretical and Critical*. Princeton, N.J.: Princeton Univ. Press, 1980, 3–27.

Olsen, Tillie. *Silences*. New York: Delacorte Press, 1978.

Pascal, Roy. *Design and Truth in Autobiography*. Cambridge: Harvard University Press, 1960.

Riley, Glenda. *Frontierswomen: The Iowa Experience*. Ames: Iowa State Univ. Press, 1981.

Rosenblatt, Paul C. *Bitter, Bitter Tears: Nineteenth-Century Diarists and Twentieth-Century Grief Theories*. Minneapolis: Univ. of Minnesota Press, 1983.

Schlissel, Lillian. *Women's Diaries of the Westward Journey*. New York: Schocken Books, 1982.

Springer, Marilyn, and Haskell Springer, eds. *Plains Woman: The Diary of Martha Farnsworth, 1882–1922*. Bloomington: Indiana Univ. Press, 1986.

Sterling, Dorothy, ed. *We Are Your Sisters: Black Women in the Nineteenth Century*. New York: W. W. Norton, 1984.

Thomas, Trudelle H. "Women's Diaries of the Westward Movement: A Methodological Study," *Forum: A Women's Studies Quarterly*, 10.3 (1984): 7–11.

"Women: Diaries and Letters." An Unpublished Bibliography. St. Paul: Minnesota Historical Society.

17

Gender and Autobiographical Form: The Case of the Spiritual Autobiography

Linda H. Peterson

In the index to William Matthews's *Annotated Bibliography of British Autobiographies*, under the heading "spiritual autobiography," there lies hidden a curious problem of gender and autobiographical form. Let me formulate the problem both statistically and descriptively. For the seventeenth century, Matthews lists twenty-one examples of the spiritual autobiography, nearly a third composed by women. For the nineteenth century, however, a period that generally saw an increase in women writers, Matthews lists only five such accounts by women, little more than one-sixth of the total.[1] Why should the number of spiritual autobiographies by women have decreased when the number of women writers in other literary genres was increasing?

The problem becomes more curious if we consider descriptively the differences between the seventeenth- and nineteenth-century autobiographies included in Matthews's list. For the seventeenth century, all six accounts written by women are genuine examples of the spiritual autobiography—that is, they are accounts of waywardness or spiritual malaise, conviction of sin, and eventual redemption—and they represent women as diverse as Elizabeth West, an Edinburgh servant girl; Jane Turner, a sea captain's wife; and Mary Rich, the fourth Countess of Warwick.[2] A Quaker account, Alice Hayes's *Legacy, or Widow's Mite*, is, moreover, a classic of the genre—thoroughly retrospective in approach, every bit as biblical in self-interpretation as Bunyan's *Grace Abounding*, and far more engaging than George Fox's *Journal*.

For the nineteenth century, however, none of the accounts written by a woman is, in fact, a true spiritual autobiography: one is a memorial for the minor poet Francis Ridley Havergal, assembled from biographical and autobiographical documents by her sister Maria; two others are diaries of spiritual meditation, written during periods of illness and doubt and later rearranged by a friend; the fourth begins with an account of conversion, which an anonymous editor amplifies with personal letters but that soon becomes a daily record of "spiritual blessings" (including such benefits as a present of "dried buffins" from "dear brother S—" and "a plum pudding and sausage rolls" from "my dearest B—"); the fifth recounts a conversion to Catholicism, but one written in 1926 and thus mistakenly listed as a nineteenth-century spiritual autobiography.[3] I describe these examples not to suggest the inadequacy of Matthews's bibliography, which few of us could do without, but rather to note an absence of spiritual autobiographies written by nineteenth-century women and thus to raise questions about the genre of autobiography as it developed in Britain and about the problems that women faced when they attempted to write the form.[4]

The facts suggest that, by the nineteenth century, women avoided the form of the spiritual autobiography—or perhaps, to use the passive in an appropriate context, that women were avoided by the form. In general, they did not compose retrospective accounts of spiritual or psychological progress, they did not use principles derived from biblical hermeneutics to interpret their lives, and they did not attempt to substitute another system of interpretation to create a secular variant of the form. They did not, in other words, compose what we usually call the spiritual or "developmental" autobiography, the primary tradition of autobiographical writing in Britain from the seventeenth through the nineteenth centuries.[5]

There is, of course, no reason why anyone, man or woman, should feel compelled to write a spiritual autobiography: One might with good reason adopt Ruskin's view that the genre is "morbid" and "dangerous," encouraging its writer to dwell "painfully and exclusively on the relations of the deity to his own little self" and proving the case that religion is "nothing more than a particular phase of indigestion, coupled with a good imagination and a bad conscience."[6] Nevertheless, the finest examples of nineteenth-century English autobiography exemplify this form: Carlyle's Book Second of *Sartor Resartus*, Mill's *Autobiography*, Newman's *Apologia*, Gosse's *Father and Son*. And the nineteenth-century women who contemplated the possibility of autobiography were conscious of their exclusion from the mainstream—and conscious as well of their diversion to other forms of self-expression: to the diary, the

family memoir, and that oddity of Victorian literature, the autobiography of the clergyman's wife.[7]
The usual explanations for this dispersion of women's forms of self-writing are cultural and vaguely positive in their formulation. Women, it is said, are taught to be selfless and self-effacing and hence turn readily to the memoir form in which they can write as mother, wife, or daughter; women are interested in the "circumstantial, complex, and contextual" and hence prefer the diary for the detail it allows; women see their lives in "repetitive, cumulative, and cyclical structures" and hence choose generic forms that allow patterns different from the chronological, linear, and developmental style of the traditional male autobiography.[8]
While these explanations may be true, it is also the case that Victorian women did not view the matter as one of generic choice—as, say, the felicitous decision to write a diary or the desirable stance of the memoir writer. Those who contemplated the matter felt themselves prohibited from writing autobiographies of spiritual or psychological progress for specific generic reasons.
These reasons involve, I believe, the hermeneutic origin (or basis) of the genre. The English autobiography derives from a Protestant tradition of religious introspection, one that is insistently hermeneutic. By "hermeneutic" I mean first that the autobiography from Bunyan to Gosse has placed in the foreground the act of self-interpretation: the autobiographers's interpretation of himself and his experience. Second, I mean that English autobiographers have traditionally appropriated their patterns and principles of interpretation from biblical hermeneutics (originally from biblical typology) and that they have done so self-consciously. One might even call autobiography a "hermeneutic" genre.
Both instances of hermeneutics are prominent in Bunyan's *Grace Abounding,* a work that helped to establish the formal patterns of the English autobiographical tradition. In the Preface to *Grace Abounding,* Bunyan uses Moses and other biblical types of justify the publication of his account, treating the wanderings of the Israelites as prefigurative of his own experiences and Moses's act of recording their wanderings as prefigurative also:

> Moses (Numb. 33. I, 2) writ of the Journeyings of the children of Israel, from Egypt to the Land of Canaan; . . . Wherefore this I have endeavoured to do; and not only so, but to publish it also; that, if God will, others may be put in remembrance of what he hath done for their Souls, by reading his work upon me.[9]

Bunyan's choice of scriptural texts was necessary for his own autobiographical act; as Sacvan Bercovitch has observed for early American writers, without such biblical models autobiography would have been impossible, its goal being not to proclaim the self but, as for Bunyan, to efface it, to "dissolve [it] into some timeless pattern of spiritual biography."[10] But Bunyan's choice of the Exodus also profoundly affected the subsequent tradition of spiritual autobiography. As history made literary classics of *Grace Abounding* and *The Pilgrim's Progress*, autobiographers came to follow the narrative patterns and hermeneutic system that Bunyan had introduced.

For a short time, both men and women autobiographers imitated this model. A generation after Bunyan, the Quaker convert Alice Hayes recounted her spiritual history with the same hermeneutic intensity that Bunyan exhibits and with the same typological patterns: "I had surely fell in the vast howling Wilderness," Hayes writes, except "I came to read in the Mistery, in the Gospel Dispensation, what *Israel* of old passed through, while in *Egypt's* Land, and by the Red Sea; and their Travels through the Deeps, with their coming up on the Banks of Deliverance." When Hayes describes her conviction of sin, it is "the Day of Jacob's trouble" witnessed on her. When she receives no assurance of salvation, she "roars" "like David" in Psalm 22: ["I was ready to say, my Bones were all out of Joynt; and in the Depth of Distress, the Enemy was very strong with his Temptations."] She argues with her husband and priest, who oppose her attendance at Quaker meetings, by quoting the scriptures; she defies opponents like her father-in-law, who threatens to chain her to a tree and starve her into submission, by taking to heart the account of "what *Israel* of old passed through while in *Egypt's* Land, and by the Red Sea."[11] Hayes is thoroughly intent on interpreting her experience in terms of scriptural patterns, and she articulates the typological basis of her interpretation as clearly as any male spiritual autobiographer:

> We have all these great Benefits which do accrew to both Soul and Body, in learning of Him who was the Pattern in every Age: *Moses* in the Mount, did his Work according to the Pattern, by the Wisdom of our God, and *David* His Servant, gave Orders unto his Son *Solomon* and the Elders, how to carry on, and build that great house which was in its Time. But now how much more Glorious is this Dispensation of Light and Grace, which shines from the *Son Himself, the express Image of the Father, into our Hearts*, whereby we may now see our Way, and follow the Pattern, and need not to stumble where Thousands have fallen.[12]

Her biblical precedents are the same as those Bunyan cites, and like him, she draws on the same hermeneutic tradition.

A century later, however, when evangelicals like John Newton, William Cowper, and Thomas Scott were continuing to write within and revitalize the tradition, women like Alice Hayes had ceased to write spiritual autobiographies. And when major Victorian autobiographers began to experiment with variations on the form, both spiritual and secular, women had been effectively prevented from attempting the genre. For, by the end of the eighteenth century, when hermeneutics was entering the English consciousness as a special activity and its domain within biblical studies was being carefully defined, the relationship of women to hermeneutics was also being defined.

Generally speaking, women were discouraged from sustained attempts at interpretation because of assumptions about the female intellect. Elaine Showalter has detailed these assumptions in *A Literature of Their Own*, but let me offer as specific evidence about women and hermeneutics a passage from the most popular treatise on female education of the early nineteenth century: Hannah More's *Strictures on the Modern System of Female Education* (1799). In her advice to young ladies with literary aspirations, More theorizes about the limitations of the female mind:

> In summing up the evidence . . . of the different capacities of the sexes, one may venture, perhaps, to assert, that women have equal *parts*, but are inferior in *wholeness* of mind, in the integral understanding: that though a superior woman may possess single faculties in equal perfection, yet there is commonly a juster proportion in the mind of a superior man: that if women have in equal degree the faculty of fancy which creates images and the faculty of memory which collects and stores ideas, they seem not to possess in equal measure the faculty of comparing, combining, analysing, and separating these ideas; that deep and patient thinking which goes to the bottom of a subject; nor that power of arrangement which knows how to link a thousand connected ideas in one dependant train, without losing sight of the original idea out of which the rest grow, and on which they all hang.[13]

What this statement implies for the composition of autobiography is devastating. While More allows women a measure of fancy "which creates images," she denies them the power to arrange the images into a coherent, casual sequence; while she admits that women possess the faculty of memory "which collects and stores ideas," she denies them both the patience for "deep thinking" and the analytic capacity to compare or combine their ideas. It is scarcely possible to imagine an autobiographer who could not arrange memories into a coherent sequence or who could not combine a series of experiences to delineate a pattern of growth or who could not compare ideas at two points in life to chart that growth. If More is correct, women are generically unfit to write autobiography: The form demands precisely the qualities that the female mind lacks.[14]

Beyond general strictures that denied women the capacity for sustained interpretation, nineteenth-century women faced specific prohibitions against engaging in biblical hermeneutics, whether in theology or autobiography. By Pauline injunction, they had been admonished to "learn in silence with all subjection." "I suffer not a woman to teach," St. Paul had written, "nor to usurp authority over the man" (I Tim. 2:11–12). By ecclesiastical decree, women were denied ordination in the Church of England, prohibited from interpreting the Scriptures to a congregation in most Dissenting sects, and banned from Methodist pulpits by the Convention of 1803.[15] John Wesley's comments to Sarah Crosby, a woman who felt the call to preach, are instructive:

> Even in public you may properly enough intermix short *exhortations* with prayer; but keep as far from what is called preaching as you can; therefore never take a text; never speak in continued discourse without some break, about four or five minutes.[16]

For Wesley the crucial issue is not public speaking but taking a biblical text—and, worse yet, expounding on the text in "continued discourse." His comment is not as nasty as Samuel Johnson's, which compares "a woman's preaching" to "a dog's walking on its hind legs."[17] But Wesley's comment is the more inhibiting for the woman who would write spiritual autobiography, for it removes the source from which self-interpretation proceeds. Moreover, Wesley represents the stance that became increasingly common during the eighteenth and nineteenth centuries as biblical hermeneutics became a privileged endeavor, one that required a knowledge of the original biblical languages and a systematic use of interpretive principles and procedures.[18]

Women were not denied, of course, the right to use the lessons or models of the biblical text privately; indeed, from the pulpits that denied women the right to expound the text publicly, they were encouraged to apply it to their personal lives. But such encouragement implied that women could handle the biblical text only after a priest or a man (the Pauline text gave husbands a priestly authority over wives) had interpreted it first. They were themselves unfit to deal critically with the text—that is, to expound or interpret its meaning independently.

Such hermeneutic prohibitions provide a key to the absence of spiritual autobiographies by nineteenth-century women (if, indeed, I may call "absence" a key). As substantiating (and more "substantial") evidence, I would cite Charlotte Brontë's *Jane Eyre*, taking it as a fictional case that illustrates the general problem. Brontë did not, of course, write her own autobiography, a fact significant in itself. She explored through autobiographical narratives, however, the effects of hermeneutic prohibitions against women as self-interpreters.

Jane Eyre is an experiment in the autobiographical mode: Brontë subtitles the novel "An Autobiography," presents it as a work edited by another (as women's accounts usually were), and makes her narrator's primary concern that of interpretation—interpretation for self-understanding and self-direction.[19] In the first third of the novel, Brontë allows her protagonist only to *narrate* her experience. For these chapters, Jane's experience at the entrance to Lowood School becomes the emblem of her difficulty as autobiographer. She can see the name of the institution and read the biblical inscription below it: "Let your light so shine before men that they may see your good works, and glorify your Father which is in heaven." Jane cannot, however, make interpretive connections between what her eyes read and what the biblical text says: "I read these words over and over again: I felt that an explanation belonged to them, and was unable fully to penetrate their import" (p. 42). The hermeneutic impulse is present (Jane feels the need for "explanation" and ponders the "signification" of the words), but as yet, the biblical text provides Jane no means of self-interpretation.

It is only when Jane falls in love with Rochester, discovers his mad wife in the attic, and flees Thornfield to avoid what she fears might become a moral bondage, that the biblical types begin to apply. Then the traditional hermeneutics of the spiritual autobiography gives meaning to her experience, and she attempts to interpret her narrative. On the morning she leaves Thornfield, she reads in her experience a repetition of the tenth plague of Moses:

> My hopes were all dead—struck with a subtle doom, such as in one night, fell on all the first-born in the land of Egypt. I looked on my cherished wishes, yesterday so blooming and glowing: they lay stark, chill, livid corpses that could never revive. (p. 260)

She recognizes this plague as a spiritual warning: she has made Rochester "an idol," "almost my hope of heaven," and has substituted an earthly Canaan for a spiritual one, in her dreams imagining beyond the "wild waters" of an "unquiet sea" "a shore, sweet as the hills of Beulah" (p. 133). As she flees her Egypt and wanders (literally) in a wilderness, she continues the interpretation: "I could not turn, nor retrace one step. God must have led me on" (p. 283). Moreover, as she views her life some months later, she retrospectively recognizes a providential exodus: "Yes; I feel now that I was right when I adhered to principle and law, and scorned and crushed the insane promptings of a frenzied moment. God directed me to a correct choice: I thank his providence for the guidance" (p. 316).

If Brontë allows a female autobiographer to interpret her experience within traditional autobiographical patterns, she at the same time makes us understand that Jane's act of self-interpretation is subversive: it violates hermeneutic rules. First, the male characters also use types to interpret Jane's character: Rochester calls her a vexatious Delilah over whom he "long[s] to exert a fraction of Samson's strength" (p. 266), and St. John Rivers says he suspects in her "the vacillating fears of Lot's wife" which "incline [her] to look back" (p. 318). As these men would have it, the types appropriate to delineate Jane's character are only those of Old Testament women—the lovers, wives, and mothers of the Bible who offer limited autobiographical models. Jane's attempt to apply the types universally (i.e., without reference to gender) is seen by these men as subversive of cultural codes.

More important, when Jane tries to turn her interpretation into action, she meets imperious resistance from St. John, who thinks he offers a more authoritative interpretation for her life. St. John, too, foresees an exodus, but the destiny he envisions is India, not Thornfield or Canaan. His text for Jane is the Revelation of St. John, "the vision of the new heaven and the new earth" (p. 367), and when Jane refuses to apply his text to her life, he decrees that she has refused "the Christian's cross and the angel's crown" (p. 370). Of St. John, Jane observes, "As a man, he would have wished to coerce me into obedience" (p. 360), and, as a clergyman, St. John had the authority to expect obedience. Through Jane's comment Brontë recognizes the limits placed on the woman who attempts to become an autobiographer, and at the same time she articulates her heroine's need to exercise hermeneutic freedom, to interpret her life for herself.

If a woman is to write autobiography, she must be allowed to use the language and conventions of the autobiographer, and Jane Eyre does finally shape her own autobiography, using the traditional language and interpretive patterns. Brontë even allows her another sort of hermeneutic victory. At the end of the novel, when Jane returns to Thornfield, Rochester no longer thinks of her in gender-linked types. He has learned the universal intention of the biblical models: instead of Delilah, she is now David to his Saul (p. 386). But in the world outside the novel, Brontë assumes no such enlightenment. Jane Eyre's autobiography makes its way into the world through the offices of a man, Currer Bell, who appears on the title page as the editor and who, according to Victorian convention, selects and arranges what a woman has to say about her life.

This convention of publication, testifies to the difficulty of women writers who wished to work within the primary tradition of English autobiography. Unlike their seventeenth-century counterparts, who had recounted their lives to gain membership in a spiritual community, nineteenth-century women were restricted from publishing their autobiographies and thus from gaining membership in a literary community. The restrictions were inherent in the generic form. The primary question for women writers then became What should we do? Should women attempt to revise the dominant (male) forms of autobiography, substituting other hermeneutic systems for biblical typology, or should women create their own autobiographical tradition, their own forms of self-expression?

Let me add, as a coda to this essay, that nineteenth-century women writers came to no agreement on this question. On the one hand, writers like Harriet Martineau attempted to write autobiography within the main (male) tradition. In place of biblical types and language, Martineau substitutes in her *Autobiography* a gender-free system of interpretation, introducing the terminology of Comtian positivism and its "great fundamental law": that all human beings and humankind itself must pass through three stages of development—"the theological, or fictitious; the metaphysical, or abstract; and the scientific, or positive."[20] On the other hand, many women—like Charlotte Brontë herself—imagined specifically female forms of self-interpretation. In *Shirley*, Brontë's heroine chooses to ignore the traditional biblical types and the injunctions against women as hermeneuticists, and instead creates her own feminine myth. Outside in the evening air, away from the parish church, she envisions an archetypal woman, whom she alternatively calls "Eve," "Eva," and "a woman-titan," and whom she imagines "bore Prometheus," from whose breast was "yielded the daring which could contend with Omnipotence: the strength which could bear a thousand years of bondage,— the vitality which could feed that vulture death through uncounted ages,—the unexhausted life and uncorrupted excellence, sisters to immortality, which, after millenni[ia] of crimes, struggles, and woes, could conceive and bring forth a Messiah."[21] Shirley's vision recreates mythical and biblical history; while the parallel phrases seem logically to describe the hero Prometheus and hence masculine achievements, they culminate in feminine acts of conception and birth and hence, in effect, describe "Eva," the woman who becomes the focal point of history and who nourishes, imaginatively at least, Brontë's young would-be autobiographer.

Brontë never completes the female myth in *Shirley*, but we can guess the possibilities she imagined for women's forms of self-interpretation. Like Martineau, she agreed that women must abandon the traditional hermeneutics of the spiritual autobiography. But she disagreed about what should replace that system. This difference represents the legacy that nineteenth-century women writers left for their successors to resolve.

Notes

1. See the index to *British Autobiography: An Annotated Bibliography of British Autobiographies Published or Written Before 1951* (Berkeley and Los Angeles: Univ. of California Press, 1955).

2. *Memoirs, or Spiritual Exercises of Elisabeth West: Written by Her Own Hand* (Glasgow: John Bryce, 1766); Jane Turner, *Choice Experiences of the Kind Dealings of God, Before, in, and After Conversion* (London: H. Hils, 1653); and *Autobiography of Mary Rich, Countess of Warwick*, ed. T. C. Croker (London: Percy Society, 1842). I have been unable to locate the fourth autobiography under the title that Matthews lists, *An Account of Anne Jackson*.

3. *Memorials of Francis Ridley Havergal*, ed. M[aria] V. G. H[avergal] (London: James Nisbet, [1880]); *Memoir of Mary Ann Gilpin of Bristol, Consisting Chiefly of Extracts from Her Diary and Letters*, 2nd ed. (London: Edmund Fry, 1841); Eliza Edward, *Diary of a Quiet Life* (n.p.: n.p., 1887); *Memoir of Sarah Elizabeth Stacy* (Norwich: Josiah Fletcher, 1849); Anonymous, *Experiences* (London: J. M. Watkins, 1926).

4. Matthews's bibliography may not achieve full accuracy or "completeness," but it attempts "comprehensiveness"; see p. x.

5. The term developmental autobiography derives from Wayne Shumaker's *English Autobiography: Its Emergence, Materials, and Form* (Berkeley and Los Angeles: Univ. of California Press, 1954), but the generic connection between the spiritual autobiographies of the seventeenth and eighteenth centuries and the secular developmental autobiographies of later centuries is discussed most thoroughly by John N. Morris in *Versions of the Self: Studies in English Autobiography from John Bunyan to John Stuart Mill* (New York: Basic Books, 1966). According to Morris, self is the modern word for soul: "the experiences recorded in 19th-century autobiography are ... secular counterparts of the religious melancholy and conversions set down in the autobiographies of earlier heroes of religion," pp. 5–6. See also my "Biblical Typology and the Self-Portrait of the Poet in Robert Browning," in *Approaches to Victorian Autobiography* (Athens: Ohio Univ. Press, 1979), pp. 235–43, for the hermeneutic transition from spiritual to secular autobiography.

6. See Ruskin's letter to his mother, 20 April 1845, in *Works*, ed. E. T. Cook and Alexander Wedderburn (London: George Allen, 1903–1912), IV, 349. Ruskin made the comments specifically about Bunyan's *Grace Abounding*.

7. Matthews's index includes a special subcategory of spiritual autobiography, which he labels "Clergymen's Wives." In fact, these accounts are all ecclesiastical versions of the family memoir, not examples of the introspective spiritual autobiography. It is telling that these tales of the religious deeds of a husband or father substitute for a woman's own personal account of her inner life.

8. See, for example, Suzanne Juhasz, "Towards a Theory of Form in Feminist Autobiography: Kate Millett's *Flying* and *Sita*, and Maxine Hong Kingston's *The Woman Warrior*," in *Women's Autobiography*, ed. Jelinek, pp. 221–37, as well as Jelinek's introduction to the collection.

9. *Grace Abounding to the Chief of Sinners*, ed. Roger Sharrock (Oxford: Clarendon Press, 1962), p. 2.

10. See *The Puritan Origins of the Self* (New Haven: Yale Univ. Press, 1975), p. 15.

11. *A Legacy, or Widow's Mite, Left by Alice Hayes, To Her Children and Others* (London: J. Sowle, 1723), pp. 15, 28, 30, 47.

12. Hayes, pp. 68–69.

13. *The Works of Hannah More* (New York: Harper & Brothers, 1854), I, 367; cf. other comments in ch. XIV, "The practical use of female knowledge, with a sketch of the female character, and a comparative view of the sexes." Such comments seem to derive from a popular application of David Hartley's associationist theory, *Observations on Man, His Frame, His Duty, and His Expectations* (1749), for although Hartley's work itself contains no discussion of gender and intellectual capacity, it could easily have been used to draw such conclusions by anyone who assumed the physiological inferiority of women.

14. More's influence was immense. Considered "advanced" for their day, the *Strictures* were reprinted in thirteen editions of 19,000 copies and dominated attitudes toward female education well into the nineteenth century. Even as discerning a young woman as Harriet Martineau treated More as an authority, praising in an 1822 essay on female writers More's "perspicuity and accuracy" and signing herself "Discipulus." See Martineau's "Female Writers of Practical Divinity, No. II, Mrs. More and Mrs. Barbauld," *Monthly Repository*, 17 (1822), 747.

15. The notable exception is the Quaker sect, which allowed women to "divide the word" in its meetings and which, not coincidentally, also encouraged women to publish the Quaker form of spiritual autobiography, modeled on the journal of George Fox. Indeed, Quaker journals provide the few examples of women's spiritual autobiography that survive in the nineteenth century.

16. Quoted by Frank Baker in "John Wesley and Sarah Crosby," *Proceedings of the Wesley Historical Society*, 27 (1949), 79. Wesley later changed his mind about some women preachers.

17. Johnson continued to remark, "It is not well done; but you are surprised to find it done at all." Quoted by James Boswell, in his *Life of Samuel Johnson* (New York: Everyman, 1763), I. 287.

18. This sense of hermeneutics as a special, restricted domain is evident even in the first recorded English use of the term: Waterland (1737) is concerned about interpreters "taking such liberties with sacred Writ, as are by no means allowable upon any known rules of just and sober hermeneuticks." See *OED*, s.v., hermeneutics.

19. *Jane Eyre*, ed. Richard J. Dunn (New York: Norton, 1971). All citations will be to this edition.

20. See her *Autobiography, with Memorials by Maria Weston Chapman*, 3 vols. (London: Smith, Elder, 1877). This version of Comte's "great fundamental law" appears in Martineau's translation of *The Positive Philosophy of Auguste Comte*, 2 vols. (London: John Chapman, 1853), pp. 1–2. Martineau completed the first English translation of Comte's *Cours de Philosophie Positive*, a work that Comte himself approved and that remains today the standard translation.

21. Charlotte Brontë, *Shirley* (Oxford: Clarendon Press, 1979), chap. xviii.

Index